The Astaires

Fred and Adele Astaire photographed by Cecil Beaton in Condé Nast's
apartment, 1929.
Cecil Beaton Studio Archive, Sotheby's

The Astaires

Fred & Adele

KATHLEEN RILEY

OXFORD
UNIVERSITY PRESS

OXFORD
UNIVERSITY PRESS

Oxford University Press is a department of the University of Oxford.
It furthers the University's objective of excellence in research, scholarship,
and education by publishing worldwide.

Oxford   New York
Auckland   Cape Town   Dar es Salaam   Hong Kong   Karachi
Kuala Lumpur   Madrid   Melbourne   Mexico City   Nairobi
New Delhi   Shanghai   Taipei   Toronto

With offices in
Argentina   Austria   Brazil   Chile   Czech Republic   France   Greece
Guatemala   Hungary   Italy   Japan   Poland   Portugal   Singapore
South Korea   Switzerland   Thailand   Turkey   Ukraine   Vietnam

Oxford is a registered trade mark of Oxford University Press
in the UK and certain other countries.

Published in the United States of America by
Oxford University Press
198 Madison Avenue, New York, NY 10016

© Oxford University Press 2012

First issued as an Oxford University Press paperback, 2014.

Library of Congress Cataloging-in-Publication Data
    Riley, Kathleen, 1974-
    The Astaires : Fred & Adele / Kathleen Riley.
        p. cm.
    Includes bibliographical references and index.
    ISBN 978-0-19-973841-0 (hardcover : alk. paper); 978-0-19-935894-6 (paperback : alk. paper)
    1. Astaire, Fred. 2. Astaire, Adele. 3. Dancers—United States—Biography. 4. Actors—United States—
Biography. 5. Actresses—United States—Biography. I. Title.
    GV1785.A64R55   2012
    792.802'80922—dc22   2011018462
[B]

9 8 7 6 5 4 3 2 1

Printed in the United States of America
on acid-free paper

As always, for my beloved parents
Jean and Frank Riley

And in memory of my aunt
Joy Levins
(1926–2010)

On with the dance! let joy be unconfined;
No sleep till morn, when Youth and Pleasure meet
To chase the glowing Hours with flying feet.
—Byron, *Childe Harold's Pilgrimage*

CONTENTS

Chronologies   192

LIST OF ILLUSTRATIONS

FOREWORD

I have often—very often—wondered what Fred and Adele Astaire could possibly have been doing onstage to inspire what is quite likely the most spectacularly extravagant critical praise in history: "Nothing like them since the Flood." It certainly surpasses the more conventional "taking the world by storm" by many watery leagues.

Straining for an orderly and reasonable explanation, I have mused that perhaps the writer was simply trying to one-up earlier critics like the one who had compared the discovery of the performing duo to the one experienced by Columbus some years after the Flood or like the one who had compared their cavortings to those that are presumed to have taken place in and around the Garden of Eden some time earlier.

But could it be possible that the critic essentially had it right? Indeed, perhaps in a moment of comparative restraint the flabbergasted writer had actually decided a comparison to the Creation would be verging distastefully on the sacrilegious and downsized the praise, settling instead on a comparison merely with the Almighty's second most cosmic recorded undertaking.

In this wonderful book Kathleen Riley gives us the first fully developed discussion not only of what inspired such immoderate, even intemperate, praise, but also of the deeply affectionate and mutually dependent relationship of the Astaires. Especially valuable, she supplies for the first time a fully developed portrait of Adele Astaire, one of the most important and fascinating characters in theatrical history not only for the way she mesmerized audiences, but for the way she captivated just about everybody offstage as well. The world has been waiting much too long for the story of this high-spirited, mercurial, petty, profane, acerbic, charming, possessive, witty, exasperating, unpredictable, loving, and, I suspect, deeply vulnerable woman.

The book relies on Kathleen's discerning insights as well as on her skilful and systematic use of a treasure of written and recorded material—letters, diaries, interviews—that have never been fully exploited, or even known very much, before. In the process, she has deftly placed the Astaires in their theatrical and social milieux, and she has come up with some startling new revelations about the many fascinating people—famous, unfamous, and infamous—who surrounded them.

We are all the beneficiaries of her dedicated work. I'd like to come up with an appropriately exuberant metaphor to convey my enthusiasm for the book, but, as it happens, the ones I might find most apt have already been used up.

John Mueller
15 November, 2010

ACKNOWLEDGMENTS

My research for this book began when I was ten years old and received a biography of Fred Astaire as a birthday gift from my grandmother, Lillian Dobler, who, along with my niece Rebecca, shared and indulged my early fascination with all things Fred. To both of them I record my loving gratitude.

I would like to express my sincere thanks to the Tara Old Girls Association for awarding me the Joan Waugh Scholarship and to the Society for Theatre Research for a research award. Together these grants assisted considerably in funding my research and travel expenses.

Among the libraries and collections I have consulted in the course of my research, particular thanks must go to the staff of the V&A Theatre Collections Study Room in London; to Maryann Chach at the Shubert Archive in New York; and to Maria Morelli, formerly of the Howard Gotlieb Archival Research Center at Boston University's Mugar Memorial Library. I would also like to acknowledge the research efforts of Adele's unpublished biographer, the late Helen Rayburn, and especially the unique interviews she recorded on audio cassette, which are now housed in the Mugar Library.

I owe a special debt to Fred's daughter, Ava, and her husband, Richard McKenzie, for donating a sizable portion of the Adele and Fred Astaire Collections to the Howard Gotlieb Archival Research Center, where researchers like myself can relive the Astaire history in a very tangible and comprehensive way. I also thank them, more generally, for their positive efforts to share the Astaire legacy with new generations in a gracious, undemonstrative manner befitting the Astaire name.

I am extremely grateful to John Mueller, not only for his generous foreword but also for his proactive support for this project, his sage advice, and the provision of certain unpublished material housed in the United States.

My dear friend Edward Petherbridge inspired the book's preface with his poem "F's for First Night" (an excerpt from his epic "Theatrical ABC"), which I am honored to reproduce with his kind permission. His creative camaraderie and daily encouragement and solicitude are greatly cherished. To borrow a Stoppardian tribute, "Admiration jostles gratitude."

Among other friends and colleagues whose interest and encouragement have helped sustain me in the writing of this book, I would like to single out for thanks Chris Bamberger (my codirector of the Astaire Conference in Oxford), David Benson, Trevor Bentham, Sallyann Halstead, Fiona Macintosh, Gillian Mann, Helen Mileshkin, and Laurie Rokke.

I am deeply grateful to Norm Hirschy at Oxford University Press for his enthusiastic advocacy of, and unfailing faith in, this project and for guiding it, with care and efficiency, through the review and production processes.

As ever, my greatest debt is to my mother and father, whose moral and material support, unconditional love and belief in me have made this book, and all my endeavors, possible.

F's for First Night

F's for First Night, inescapable vice
Have *you* ever thought it'd be rather nice
To choose out of history one famous night
That's tickled your fancy and then take a flight
In a time machine to find yourself there
Amongst the first audience, privileged to stare
At Burbage's Hamlet, a boy as the Queen
The first time Kean's Shylock crept onto the scene
Something of Siddons, go as far back as Thespis
And when the show starts hold tight unless this
Actual presence in what was a dream
So completely confounds any possible scheme
Built up from old fragments of writings and pictures
Bursts bloody, alive, writhing out of those strictures
Or—and this could be possibly more disturbing—
Unfolds only quaintly, tamely, curbing
Your wild expectations of moment and pith.
Can this pallid cast substantiate myth?
How would you return so unsatisfied
Reporting history must have lied
Or, worse, with a suddenly desperate inkling
You'd failed, not up to the task of winkling
Out of a distant convention contending
The art in the artifice, truth in pretending? . . .
To make it more fun, here's what you can do
Sit next in the theatre to somebody who
Historically probably could have been there
Ben Jonson, first night of *Bartholomew Fair*
I know for example Jane Austen once saw
Edmund Kean playing Shylock; would I be for
Using my ticket for that, or finding
Myself at the Globe next to any old groundling
While Shakespeare played Adam or Hamlet's Ghost
You can't say that that isn't making the most . . .
Unless that you think it would thrill and please
To be seeing the *Bacchae* with Euripides
Or something quite utterly utterly other:
First night of *The Vortex* with Noël Coward's mother.
—Edward Petherbridge

PREFACE

Ever since I can remember, I have dreamt of just such a flight in a time machine, penetrating the mysterious fabric of the space-time continuum, to glimpse a page in the annals of theatre history freshly unfolding, to breathe for a moment the selfsame air as the actors and audience on a famous first night, as they settle to the serious, primordial business of making imaginary puissance. The choice of a single first night would be the ultimate embarrassment of riches, and the journey back would entail a perilous leap of faith as one bore one's own and history's accumulated weight of expectation. But high on my list of choices—as high as a first performance at the Great Dionysia or by the Lord Chamberlain's Men on Bankside—would be the London debut of Fred and Adele Astaire, the opening night of *Stop Flirting* at the Shaftesbury Theatre, 30 May 1923. The reason is its giddy combination of time, place, and personality—a city I love deeply, a period I have great affinity for, and a pair of performers who have held a powerful fascination over my imagination from childhood.

In some very real sense I have made that flight through time, without transgressing the laws of physics. My fellow classicist, Edith Hall, has said that the performance historian is essentially a time-traveler with access to a unique conduit of human history: "Watched in physical company with many other spectators, performance offers privileged access to mass ideology and collective taste and prejudice. . . . But it simultaneously permits access to the private imaginative worlds of the individual members of previous generations."[1] The story of the Astaires conjures up a vanished world. Born at the close of the nineteenth century, they, in effect, grew up together with the new century. Manifestly children of their time, they glamorously embodied the interwar style they had partly invented. At the same time, their appeal as performers, particularly in London, was based largely on their apparent defiance of the darker aspects of the interwar psyche, their modernism free of modernist angst. This book, then, seeks to recapture something of "the first fine careless rapture" of the Astaire phenomenon, and something, too, of the essence of that vanished "Long Weekend" between the wars.

In researching the lives of the Astaires I have had access to a wealth of primary source material, much of it housed in Boston University's Mugar Library. There is something singularly moving about seeing a letter written decades ago in a person's own hand, as opposed to a transcript. It makes history more immediate, sensory, human. As I pored over letters Fred and Adele wrote from London during their first visit, the scrapbooks diligently and lovingly kept by their mother, Ann, diaries, ships' menus, Christmas cards, and costumes they wore as child vaudevillians (including Fred's first tailcoat and a small, solitary sock), history came to life in my hands and before my eyes. I also spent hours listening to Adele's voice on audio cassette, unpublished interviews recorded in the last two to three years of her life, as she recounted tales of her childhood and career with Fred, a narrative filled with sharply remembered, and sometimes the oddest, detail and interspersed with snatches of songs she had sung long ago onstage, the voice little altered from the tremulous, strangely beguiling, and piquant soprano squeak preserved in recordings of the 1920s.

In the midst of my research, and my postdoctoral fellowship in classics at Oxford, I had the idea of staging the first international conference on Fred Astaire—a leap of faith in itself but one, in the end, curiously blessed by *esprit de corps*. This was held at Oriel College and the Holywell Music Room (once graced by Haydn and Mozart) in the summer of 2008 and attracted scholars, performers, and enthusiasts from around the world (including the cultural attaché for Gunnedah, NSW!) and ranging in age from fifteen to eighty-five. Joining us as special guests were two of the last and closest living links to Fred and Adele—Fred's daughter, Ava, and her husband, Richard McKenzie. They were an incomparable double act, who, within this celebration of Astaire's professional legacy, provided invaluable insights into the more private personae of Fred and Adele.

On a personal note, I do not remember a time Before Fred, as it were. Atypically of my generation and entirely unprompted, I grew up watching his black-and-white films on television and immersing myself in the music of the Great American Songbook, so much of which he introduced on stage and screen. It was probably Astaire who first inspired my love of theatre, as many of his films dealt with the world backstage, albeit a highly romanticized one with stages and dressing rooms that would scarcely fit inside a real theatre. More than that, a true alchemist, he showed us the theatre of the everyday, rendering magically, vitally dance-like the most prosaic activity or object. There was no demonstrative or demonstrable demarcation between his dancing and nondancing selves—dance was a natural, unpremeditated, effortless form of expression, a state of being no less.

It was, however, not as a dancer so much as a storyteller and musician that Astaire captured my imagination. He could make you "see" music, its shape and narrative, its intricate inner workings, by virtue of his unusual corporeal eloquence and the syncopated rhythms of his feet.[2] His technique, though sublime, is seldom obvious and always exercised in the illumination of character and plot, the distillation of wit and pathos.

As for Adele, I had no cinematic evidence of her purportedly superior alchemy, her famed sparkle. Yet, in reading about her and listening to her sing the Gershwins' "Funny Face" or "So Am I," her personality emerged just as vividly— an intriguing amalgam of impish soubrette and inspired clown.

While there have been exclusive studies made of the Astaire-Rogers partnership, its essence and impact (notably by Arlene Croce in 1972 and Hannah Hyam in 2007), no such study has been undertaken of the crucial partnership that preceded and, in many ways, made possible this iconic screen pairing. The story of Fred and Adele Astaire is an extraordinary one and deserves to be told for its own sake and not merely as the prologue to Fred's more famous solo career. What follows is not so much a chapter in the history of dance as the story of a social and theatrical era told from the perspective of two of its defining characters. The research it has involved has been a fascinating voyage of discovery, my flight in this time machine of the imagination a privilege.

ABBREVIATIONS FOR ARCHIVAL COLLECTIONS RESEARCHED

AAC   *Adele Astaire Collection, Howard Gotlieb Archival Research Centre, Mugar Memorial Library, Boston University*

FA/MS   *Fred Astaire Manuscript Collection, University of Southern California Archival Collections*

HRC   *Helen Rayburn Collection (taped interviews), Howard Gotlieb Archival Research Centre, Mugar Memorial Library, Boston University*

RKO/UCLA   *RKO Studio Files, UCLA Performing Arts Special Collections*

SHU   *The Shubert Archive, New York*

INTRODUCTION

MOANING MINNIE AND GOODTIME CHARLIE

You've got a lot
Of personality N. T.
A thousand laughs I've found
In having you around.
—George and Ira Gershwin, "Funny Face"

If Fred Astaire had been the first or only child of Johanna and Frederic Austerlitz we might remember him very differently, or not at all. For he literally followed in the footsteps of his older sister Adele, co-opted by circumstance, rather than obvious ability or burning ambition, into an extraordinary adventure. Had he never entered films, he would still have a secure place in entertainment history as one half of a legendary partnership and as an innovator in dance and musical theatre. The shows written for the Astaires' singular talents changed the very shape of the American musical. Their first major collaboration with George and Ira Gershwin, *Lady, Be Good!* in 1924, was, according to Gershwin biographer Howard Pollack, "one of the quintessential American theatrical works of the 1920s" and "the work that finally severed musical comedy from operetta."[1] In the previous year, the Astaires had become ambassadors of the American musical, transforming the London musical stage and firmly establishing the international supremacy of the indigenous Broadway musical. Their final collaboration, *The Band Wagon* in 1931, began, in Brooks Atkinson's words, "a new era in the artistry of the American revue,"[2] through the imagination of its dance narratives, the pungency of its satirical sketches, and the technological audacity of its scenic transitions. Along the way the Astaires played a significant role in fashioning the rhythm and soul of the Jazz Age on both sides of the Atlantic.

In the prologue to his play *The Clandestine Marriage*, the great eighteenth-century actor-manager David Garrick lamented the inherent ephemerality of live performance, contrasting the nature of his craft with that of his contemporary William Hogarth

> But he who struts his hour upon the stage
> Can scarce extend his fame for half an age;
> Nor pen nor pencil can the actor save,
> The art, and the artist, share one common grave.

Had Fred Astaire not entered films, knowledge of his revolutionary contribution to musical theatre and popular culture would perhaps, in the twenty-first century, be largely the preserve of stage and social historians. He might not have attained the universal, lasting renown that screen stardom confers and of which Garrick could not have dreamt.

Adele Astaire, one of the first true pop icons of the twentieth century and, for the duration of their professional partnership, a bigger star than her brother, retired from show business in March 1932 to marry Lord Charles Cavendish, plunging both Forty-Second Street and Shaftesbury Avenue into mourning. Except for one aborted foray into films in 1937,[3] she made no attempt to resurrect her glittering career as a performer. Never having been prey to the precisionist zeal that drove her brother to rehearse endlessly, she neither regretted her retirement nor envied Fred's subsequent success in Hollywood. She led an interesting and worthwhile posttheatrical existence, though one apportioned an unusual measure of tragedy, but she has, since her death in 1981, passed into comparative obscurity. It is Fred's name that remains in the mainstream cultural consciousness, and it is Ginger Rogers who has been immortalized as his most famous dancing partner.

From a more optimistic and, I think, truer point of view than Garrick's, Edith Hall argues "that there is something distinctive about the immanent presence of live performance in the human memory. Far from being an ephemeral art, which happens, comes to an end, and vanishes without a trace, a compelling theatrical experience can leave a much deeper impression on the memory even than the printed word or painted image."[4] The impression left by the stage partnership of Fred and Adele on individual memory, and on the cultural landscape of the early twentieth century, was such that in their lifetimes they were often invoked as an illustrious part of show business folklore and as the archetypal Broadway success story.

In early 1934 it was rumored that a film portrayal of Fred's life was being devised by RKO, for which Joan Crawford would be borrowed from MGM to play the role of Adele. This particular film never came to fruition, but in 1951 Alan Jay Lerner wrote a screenplay based loosely on the success and dissolution of the Astaires' partnership, which MGM produced under the title *Royal Wedding* (or *Wedding Bells* for the British release). This featured Fred himself and a felicitous third choice of costar in Jane Powell.[5] Apart from this vaguely biographical evocation of Fred and Adele, there were, scattered throughout popular culture in the half century following Adele's retirement, various references to the Astaires that testified to the team's legendary status. In Warner Brothers' *Gold Diggers of 1933*, producer Barney Hopkins (Ned Sparks) confidently tells his latest discoveries, Brad Roberts (Dick Powell) and Polly Parker (Ruby Keeler), that they "could make a swell team. Like the Astaires!" Ironically in hindsight, one of the film's featured players, who appears in this scene, is the young Ginger Rogers (*Gold Diggers* was released seven months before RKO's *Flying Down to Rio*). The eleven o'clock number in Hugh Martin's score for the show *Look Ma, I'm Dancin'* in 1948, contended: "We'll never dance like Adele and Fred Astaire." Three decades later, the song "I Don't Need Anything But You" from the Broadway hit *Annie*, included the verse "They're two of a kind / The happiest pair now / Like Fred and Adele, they're floating / On air now." A 1982 film adaptation of Agatha Christie's *Evil under the Sun* contains a scene in which Hercule Poirot (Peter Ustinov) makes a nocturnal examination of the hotel register. Among the signatures of previous guests he discovers the names of Fred and Adele Astaire between those of Ivor Novello and Cole Porter. In 1987, a BBC television dramatization of Dorothy L. Sayers's *Gaudy Night* interpolated a scene in which Lord Peter Wimsey (Edward Petherbridge) and Harriet Vane (Harriet Walter) are at a tea dance. As Lord Peter gracefully conducts the slightly awkward Harriet around the dance floor, he gallantly assures her that she is "doing beautifully. Light as a feather. Quite in the style of Fred and Adele, I think."

As far as we know, no footage exists of Fred and Adele performing together on stage. All we have are a few tantalizing seconds from the end of a 1930 short entitled "Backstage on Broadway." The context is a mock rehearsal of the ill-fated production *Smiles*, presided over by producer Florenz Ziegfeld. In the clip Ziegfeld calls for his dancers and, on that cue and to a piano accompaniment, Fred and Adele, led by costar Marilyn Miller, step jauntily from out of the wings and toward center stage, only to be told by Ziegfeld, "I don't mean my ten-thousand-dollar-a-week dancers." The chastened headliners pause, make their apologies, and, smiling, shuffle arm in arm back into the wings.[6] Frustratingly, this footage has been shot from the side of the stage, and our view of the Astaires is partially obscured by Miss Miller. It is a priceless fragment of Broadway history but an exceedingly meager glimpse of a glorious artistic pairing. The main purpose of this book, then, is to recapture something that was not documented on film—the complementary gifts and combined charisma that made the Astaires the toast of two continents—and to penetrate the essence of a rare personal and professional union. Fred and Adele's success was, I believe, as much a triumph of personality as it was of Terpsichorean virtuosity.

Intro.1 Adele and Fred in the 1920s.

Primarily what made Fred and Adele such an effective team was that, creatively and temperamentally, they were perfect foils for one another. Adele was born with, and retained until her death at the age of eighty-four, "star quality," an ineffable sparkle Ellen Terry dubbed "that little something extra." Brought up on Thackeray's *Vanity Fair*, she had Becky Sharp's wit, satirical gift, and untameability without her ruthlessness. Her early stage idols were Ziegfeld beauties and accomplished comediennes and provide clues to her own professional identity and aspirations. Among them were Hazel Dawn, Ina Claire, Billie Burke, and Lillian Lorraine. Adele was an exuberant gamine who, as one reviewer witnessed in 1919, danced "like a lilac flame."[7]

Her artistry was intuitive and sometimes dangerously improvisatory. During a matinée performance, producer Vinton Freedley sat up in one of the boxes waving a $10 bill at Adele, hoping thus to intimidate or bribe her out of her usual practice of making her fellow actors "corpse" by ad-libbing or doing something a little extra on the side. Adele, of course, merrily defied him and continued her popular antics. On Boat Race Night, during the London run of *Lady, Be Good!*, she boldly exchanged badinage with the rowdy Varsity crowd in the stalls, and when one obstreperous undergraduate threw a chocolate at her, she swiftly returned fire, planting the offending sweet squarely on his shirtfront, to her brother's intense delight.

Audiences and critics alike adored this element of daredevil spontaneity in her performances, the sense that with Adele onstage *anything* could happen—and often did, since her capacity for extemporaneous mischief and her readiness to raise a laugh knew no bounds. In *Lady, Be Good!*, dressed as a spurious senorita at one point and obliged to establish her cultural credentials, she had to describe how a matador "grabs the bull by the horns." One night, she said, allegedly by accident, "The matador comes forward and he grabs the bull by the balls." The whole orchestra fell off their seats and a full five minutes of laughter resounded throughout the theatre. A review of *Stop Flirting* in London spoke of her "schoolgirl abandon and frolicsome devilment [which] make you wonder what her next trick will be. When it comes it is a fresh trick and an unexpected one, too."[8] Audiences also relished Adele's ability to "hypnotize" them, to pick people out individually in the darkened auditorium and fix her eyes on theirs, making them believe she was speaking and singing directly to them. At times, indeed, she did speak directly to members of the audience, greeting them by name if they were regulars and ad-libbing pleasantries across the footlights. Everyone wanted to get down the front.

By all accounts Adele was a natural clown, a wonderful madcap, outrageous, and dazzling. She could suggest infinite mischief with a turn of the mouth or a lift of the eyebrow. At least one London critic was convinced that she had been stolen at birth by fairies, who brought her up and taught her all their secrets. The notoriously waspish Broadway critic George Jean Nathan was utterly captivated by her, comparing her peculiar charm to "a dozen Florestan cocktails filtered through silk." His reviews of the Astaires' early Broadway shows read like open love letters to Adele. Certainly his are among the most colorful and original descriptions of her: "As unconscious as a peach short-cake, as careless about it all as a United States senator's necktie"; "She has the air of a Peck's Bad Girl being blown hither and thither by a hundred powerful electric fans. . . . [She is] a figure come out of Degas to a galloping ragtime tune." Nathan even devoted an entire essay to expounding the proposition that Adele's dancing was far more theatrical and watchable than George Bernard Shaw's *Back to Methuselah*, which opened on Broadway the same week as the Astaires' *For Goodness Sake*.

Offstage, Adele displayed the same careless exuberance that defined her onstage persona. She carried with her, and ignited in others, a sense of excited expectancy. She delighted in shocking people and could do so with such casual and ladylike composure that the intended targets of her outrageousness were never certain whether they had heard correctly. Those who knew her best interpreted this propensity to startle as a defense mechanism or an indication of a deep-seated shyness. One of her closest friends in later life, Sybil Connelly, described Adele as "a wayward child trying to find her way through the mists." From similar first-hand observations, she does seem to have had about her an

Intro.2 Miss Adele Astaire, in "Funny Face"
The Stage

MISS ADELE ASTAIRE,
in " Funny Face."

aura of wanton innocence as well as a naughtiness definitively of the 1920s. She once attended a costume party, hosted by Elsa Maxwell, dressed as an angel, complete with wings, a blonde wig, a halo, and a copy of *Lady Chatterley's Lover*. She had a positive genius for profanity, which she exercised liberally and without sacrificing a trace of gentility. The piquancy of her tongue was to her younger brother a source of both mortification and furtive pride. Surprisingly for one exposed at such a tender age to the rough backstage milieu, and who spent the majority of his leisure hours at the racetrack and in pool rooms, Fred seldom indulged publicly in bad language. "Oh, he'd 'JC' it and 'GD' it all the time," Adele said, "but he never used my words"[9]. He certainly never swore in the presence of women—with one exception. In his letters to Adele, he does employ the occasional coarse turn of phrase. It is as though he was making an effort to keep pace with her racier idiom. It is also a demonstration of how, with his sister, Fred was at his least guarded and better able to express a different side of his personality, something of the faint hoodlum element that James Cagney discerned in him.

There was a different side to Adele's personality, too, a calmer, more contemplative one. The girl once held to have put "all the flap in flapperdom" was an avid and discriminating reader who enjoyed the company of intellectuals. In London during the 1920s, she formed friendships with several leading writers of the day and could hold her own in spirited literary debate. Despite her bookishness, however, she was always an inventive speller and had superior facility with the spoken word than with the written word. By contrast, Fred's remarkable ortho-graphic and grammatical accuracy belied the limits of his formal education and reading habits.

Exactly two years and eight months younger than Adele, Fred was a famous workhorse and worrier. His sister's nickname for him was "Moaning Minnie" on account of his habitual, indeed unfailing tendency to fret and foresee disaster. He in turn, Adele said, "always called me 'Goodtime Charlie' because I was up and out at everything, and I loved parties and he didn't. 'Moaning Minnie' and 'Goodtime Charlie'—that was us." While Adele's star was the more radiant, Fred supplied the team's creative energy, choreographic brilliance, and discipline. From about the age of sixteen he assumed much of the managerial burden of the partnership, including the negotiation of contracts and salaries and the selection of songs and other material. In an unpublished passage in the longhand manu-script of his autobiography, *Steps in Time*, Fred compared himself and Adele as child performers: "The difference between Adele's acting and mine was the dif-ference between a pert girl with dazzling eyes who wanted to be an actress and a small boy who went through the motions conscientiously, afraid he would forget his lines."[10] This self-comparison, it seems to me, is the key to Fred's precocious work ethic and sense of responsibility. Throughout their joint career, he was tor-mented by a persistent notion that he was somehow a liability to his brilliant and beguiling sister and that he must compensate for his lack of luminosity by ever-increased application and concentration. But even as an adolescent vaudevillian, he was noted as contributing to the team an appeal and charisma all his own: "Fred is plentifully supplied with magnetism, is a clean cut, wholesome looking chap, full of pep, and his work has a finish to it that removes it far from the ordi-nary."[11]

In an interview with Helen Rayburn in 1979, Adele painted a frank and loving portrait of her brother's complex character, declaring, "I just feel there's nobody in the world like him," and praising his dignity, anger, softness, sweetness, loyalty, and stubbornness[12].

On the stage, as later on film, Fred masked a seething powerhouse of perfec-tionism with an appearance of elegant effortlessness, and a shy and serious dis-position beneath an urbane insouciance. He also made a charming virtue of boyish awkwardness. In and out of the theatre, he projected a warm affability and was known as a prankster with a pixie sense of humor, but whereas his sister was in her element amid the social swirl of Bright Young Things, he was more of a reluctant reveler, though just as sought-after at parties and by society hostesses. He was an intriguing combination of confidence and insecurity, supremely in con-trol of what he was doing yet needing constant reassurance. Less combative and more circumspect than Adele, he nevertheless had greater drive and ambition. Gentle, diffident, and in occasional need of his sister's forthright defense against

Intro.3 Fred in 1914.
Antoine Dutot Museum and Gallery

bullying theatre managers and stage directors, he was, in his own way, no less tough than she. And in spite of his gentle nature and slight build, there was never anything effete about Fred. He was a good baseball player in his youth and loved the rough-and-tumble—the street games and high jinks—of the Midtown neighborhood in New York where he spent part of his boyhood. From his late teens he also reveled in the masculine camaraderie of the dressing room and the turf.

In public, Fred was normally as reticent as Adele was outspoken. He submitted courteously to the interviews he abhorred, avoided controversy, and conducted himself at all times with gentlemanly discretion and restraint. While one could argue that his autobiography is itself an exercise in gentlemanly discretion, he was anxious in the opening chapter to dispel the impression that his public reticence denoted unworldliness. In a paragraph excised from the final version, he claimed to "know more about a lot of things than people might think. I know a hell of a lot more about show business than I'll admit and that goes for many other things such as sports, politics, women, children, critics."[13]

The even greater reserve with which he managed his private life provoked a similarly false impression, which he was less eager to rectify. Adele's romances featured regularly in the gossip columns, with many wealthy and titled young men, alternately and sometimes simultaneously, rumored to be her fiancé. The relative scarcity of colorful copy surrounding Fred's amatory exploits, however, has led most biographers to infer that, before his well-publicized marriage in

1933, he lacked the time, impulse, or assurance for romantic involvement. However, it was not that Fred's love life was any less active than his sister's, merely that he was more discreet.

The dichotomous relationship between Fred and Adele to some extent reflected the contrasting personalities of their parents. Their father, Frederic, or Fritz, was an Austrian immigrant and employee of the Storz Brewing Company. He was a gregarious and laid-back individual with a passion for music and theatre. Although a man of thwarted ambition and unexceptional deeds, who derived vicarious satisfaction from his children's success, he had an air of cosmopolitanism and bohemianism more suggestive of the Ringstrasse and its café society than of downtown Omaha. It was from Fritz, his wife once claimed, that Fred and Adele inherited their talent: "He was musical. Music was as natural to him as breathing, and they were born with a sense of rhythm."[14] She also recognized in her children a style and mannerisms that were unconsciously but innately Viennese. Fritz was obviously very dear to both children, whose infant career he guided from afar, and who simply accepted his necessarily occasional presence in their lives. Adele ascribed to her father an inferiority complex yet an extraordinary prescience and belief where his children's future was concerned:

> I think the reason he wanted us to go on the stage was that it was what he wanted to do but never could. His life was rather a disappointment all the way along because he never came up to his brothers, who were high-ranking officers in Franz Josef's Imperial Army. . . . He was what you'd call a loser. But I don't see how anybody could take two children like that, who could do a little dance and be cute, and say they're going to be great. How could you know?[15]

Ann Astaire, as she became known, had no such theatrical ambitions. She was the product of a rigid Lutheran upbringing that had instilled in her a Victorian sense of propriety. A gentle, intelligent, and demure woman, she defied the conventional image of the Stage Mother.

In another unpublished excerpt from his autobiography, Fred described her as "amusing and playful with us, if strict, but she was wallflower-shy about almost everybody else, especially theatrical people."[16]

Yet, for all her social timidity, she was an extremely independent woman. Not only did she undertake, while still in her twenties, the daily hardships and logistics of launching her talented progeny onto the vaudeville circuit, virtually as a single parent, but in the 1920s and 1930s, when it was rare for a woman to travel unaccompanied, she made annual trips to Europe on her own. Undoubtedly, if somewhat to her discomfort, Ann's progressive independence helped foster her daughter's free-spirited behavior and her son's attraction to strong-minded women.

Intro.4 Ann Astaire. Taken before a party at St James's Palace, London given by the Prince of Wales for Fred and Adele in 1928.
Adele Astaire Collection, Howard Gotlieb Archival Research Centre

On the whole, Adele was more like her father, having inherited his sociability and what she called his "friskiness," while Fred had his mother's shy and gentle demeanor, a streak of her puritanism, and all of her obstinacy.

Fred and Adele's letters home from London in August 1923, reporting on their adventures with the Prince of Wales, are quite revealing of their incongruous personalities. Fred writes to his mother at two o'clock in the morning, sleepless with exhilaration after a visit to the chic Riviera Club, where he and Adele had been invited to join the Prince's party. His account of the evening is suffused with excitement yet presented in diligent detail and with an endearing mix of self-effacement and awe:

> Well, you cannot imagine the wonderful treatment we get from this Royalty. The Duchess of York is so sweet and bashful like a little school girl and the Duke a perfectly wonderful boy. I danced with the Duchess several times and she seemed to enjoy it as much as I did. The Mountbattens are lovely too and we talked of America and their trip and everything and they are all like Mary Elizabeth and Jimmy to us,[17] kidding and all that stuff all the time and not at all like the great personages one would expect them to act like. As for the Prince, well mother darling the Prince and I are like old friends. He calls me Freddie this and that etc. They all wanted me to play the piano, so I sat down and

played and sang a little, and they all appreciated it as if I had done something great.

Adele's version of the same "shindig" was dispatched a few days later and is written in an earthier, more hurried style, rippling with gaiety and innuendo. She begins with the assertion: "Think 'the' prince likes me—however I'm going to try and vamp his brother Prince George—he is an innocent, unsuspecting youth and I could easily take advantage of him—ahem!" With equal indiscretion she muses on the dizzying attentions of the heir to the throne: "No one will be good enough for us to meet anymore—there (four-flushing 'nouveau-riche' at home, I mean)."

Such differences in behavior and temperament between brother and sister were used to good effect in forming their onstage relationship and were cleverly captured by George Gershwin and Desmond Carter in the song "I'd Rather Charleston," which was added to the London production of *Lady, Be Good!*

Dick (Fred):
I've seen for days,
That you've got some ways
That must be checked,
In you I never can detect
The slightest signs of intellect.
You're mad on dances;
Think of the chances you neglect.
You never seem inclined to use your mind;
And it's quite plain to see
That I'm the brains of the family.
Take a lesson from me.

Susie (Adele):
I'd rather Charleston.

Dick:
Charleston?
Think of what you might be.

Susie:
I'd rather Charleston.

Dick:
Charleston?
I'm disappointed in you and your ways.

Susie:
   I'm double-jointed,
   There's no sensation like syncopation.

In Adele's cooey soprano we hear, as Arlene Croce remarked, "something heartless, vague and self-adoring, the very cuckoo-note of a heedless era."[18] In Fred's voice, which continually rises and cracks as he echoes the word "Charleston," we hear the incredulous, heartfelt exasperation of a serious-minded brother vainly endeavoring to contain the whirlwind that is his sister. Ironically, though, it was Fred who in real life was photographed in a London nightclub dancing an "inappropriate" Charleston with Edwina Mountbatten, for which fragrant misdeed Lady Mountbatten was soundly rebuked by Queen Mary. The incident was even reported in the American press under the headline "A Royal 'Spanking' for Gay Lady Mountbatten."[19] At this distance in time, it is easy to forget how scandalous the dance itself was considered, emblematic as it was of post–World War I abandon and indelibly associated with flappers and speakeasy culture. In the same year that Fred and Lady Mountbatten were caught indulging in the new dance craze, the Association of Hotel and Dance Managers in London tried to ban the Charleston in their establishments because of the high injury rate occasioned by its frenetic tempo and fast-kicking steps.[20] In America, the Charleston had already earned the appellation "the dance of death"; its violent, reverberative rhythm was blamed for the collapse of Boston's Pickwick Club in which fifty people were killed.

Although Fred and Adele were essentially divergent but wonderfully complementary personalities, the similarities between them ran deep and were just as central to their successful partnership. They shared an inspired impishness, a vitality and resilience, as well as an affecting vulnerability, qualities celebrated in George and Ira Gershwin's "Hang on to Me," another tune from *Lady, Be Good!,* and particularly in the verse Fred sang to Adele:

Trouble may hound us,
Shadow surround us—
Never mind, my dear,
Don't be downhearted;
When we get started,
They will disappear.
Listen to brother:
While we've each other,
There's no need to fear,
For like Hansel and Gretel,
We will prove our mettle.

Listening to the song more than eight decades after it was first recorded, one can still sense the profound affection brother and sister had for one another. Fred and Adele also had in common a strong but undemonstrative faith in God, readily acknowledging the importance of prayer and spiritual quietude in their lives. Each was generous, headstrong, forward-looking, and disdainful of self-pity.

As one might expect of siblings whose formative years were so closely entwined and whose keen mutual understanding evolved from the countless ordeals, triumphs, and confidences they shared, Fred and Adele were fiercely protective of one another. Once he had overtaken her in height, and because he seemed the more mature of the two, Fred was frequently assumed to be Adele's older brother, an assumption he encouraged by chivalrously referring to her in interviews as his "little sister" and which he usefully exploited in dealing with her legion of suitors. He could never bear to see his sister upset, at one point even pleading with the critics to aim their barbs solely at him. In many respects Fred was more like a father to Adele, by turns stern and indulgent.

For her part, and by her own admission, Adele was a possessive sister, subjecting Fred's girlfriends to unnerving scrutiny. One of these, English actress Renée Gadd, who appeared with the Astaires in the London transfers of *Lady, Be Good!* and *Funny Face*, recalled: "If you didn't pass [Adele's] test, there was no chance of being alone with Fred."[21] Her "passionate affair" with Fred, she insisted, was made possible by her friendship with Adele: "Everybody said she was a bitch, but she wasn't with me. Luckily she thought I was good for Fred."[22]

Like her mother, Adele ill concealed her initial disapproval of Fred's marriage to Phyllis Livingston Potter, a beautiful young society divorcée with a four-year-old son. Again like her mother, she wanted to be the most important woman in Fred's life; with typical candour, she expressed on more than one public occasion a wish that her brother were homosexual, presumably in the belief that he would thereby have been safeguarded against designing women and had more time to spend with her. Nor did her protectiveness lessen with age. Friends have speculated that her inability to accept Fred's second marriage, at age eighty-one, to former jockey Robyn Smith hastened Adele's death.

Incredibly, theirs appears to have been a partnership unmarred by professional jealousy or internal rivalry, a fact I would ascribe to the grace and self-worth instilled in them by their untheatrical mother Ann. Adele always maintained that Fred was the superior dancer, that she got the laughs because he pushed her forward. One of the most moving insights into the strength of Fred and Adele's personal relationship is contained in a letter Fred wrote to his sister in the latter part of 1933. The letter helps to illuminate the essence of the pair's professional success. It begins in indignant response to Adele's claim that Fred

Intro.5   Fred and Adele in London, 1944. Photofest

had been a neglectful correspondent and to her criticism of his decision to accept the lead in the London transfer of *Gay Divorce*, a decision she had unfairly attributed to interference on the part of Phyllis, whom she accused of "running" Fred. After remonstrating with her at length, and pointing out that "Freddie is not a <u>nit wit</u> and never has been" and 'Freddie is doing alright', Fred's anger subsides and he writes: "Well—you always have been one of my biggest problems but please don't change—I love it Delly—and life would seem peculiar without it."

CHAPTER 1

Opening the Bill

There's a right little girl
With the right little curl
For ev'ry right little boy
When she comes, you'll forget
All the others you've met
Sorrow will turn into joy.
—Irving Berlin, "Along Came Ruth"

People are often astonished to learn of Fred and Adele's humble midwestern origins, considering that he became a Hollywood legend synonymous with all that is debonair and urbane, an artist whom George Balanchine likened in rareness and stature to Bach, and she—a girl who danced with the Prince of Wales—became the Duke of Devonshire's daughter-in-law and was related by marriage to Harold Macmillan and John F. Kennedy. Yet, for all their grown-up glamour, some essential constituent of their being remained indelibly of the Midwest and its vaudeville playhouses. In Fred this manifested itself in an indomitable work ethic, in Adele an irrepressible impulse to burlesque pomposity and play the clown, and in both of them a curiously incorruptible and fundamentally American innocence, which their consciously and unconsciously acquired layers of international sophistication could not disguise, nor their show-business worldliness entirely subvert.

Adele and Fred were born at the end of the nineteenth century in Omaha, Nebraska, which, with the completion of the First Transcontinental Railroad in 1869 and the founding of the Union Stockyards in 1883, had become a booming center for transportation, meatpacking, and breweries and the fastest growing city in the United States. As the children of an immigrant father and a first-generation American mother, they were part of that revered mythology of the American Dream, a complex ethos exposed with elegiac lyricism at the conclusion of *The Great Gatsby*, "where the dark fields of the republic rolled on under the night."

Their father, Frederic "Fritz" Austerlitz, was born in Linz, Austria, on 8 September 1868, the third child and second son of Stefan Austerlitz, a self-employed trading agent from Prague, and his wife, Lucie Heller of Saaz, Bohemia.[1] Stefan and Lucie had married in Pilsen in 1862 and four years later moved to Linz. Both were Jewish, but in February 1867, together with their two eldest children—three-year-old Adele and two-year-old Ernst—they converted to Catholicism and were baptized at St. Michael's in Leonding, the church later attended by Adolf Hitler as a boy and where his parents and younger brother Edmund are buried. When Fritz and his brother Otto were born, they too were baptized in the Catholic Church.

The Pillersdorf Constitution, promulgated on 25 April 1848, removed some of the discriminatory legal restrictions on Jews, while the Austro-Hungarian Compromise (Ausgleich) of 1867 granted them full citizen rights. Nevertheless, anti-Semitism[2] remained at least an unofficial fact of life, and nationalistic pamphleteers and polemicists, repudiating the reforms of 1848 and 1867, which had led to Jewish emancipation, stressed the harmful and subversive "otherness" of Judaism within Austrian and German culture. For some Jews, conversion was a pragmatic remedy against very real prejudice and social impediments, and in certain professions, such as the army, there was a known link between conversion and promotion.

From 1881 the Austerlitz family lived in Vienna. When they came of age, all three brothers were conscripted into three-year military service, but whereas Ernst and Otto did well in the army (and eventually changed their surname to Artner, most likely in a further effort to conceal their Jewish roots), Fritz was drawn longingly to Vienna's café society, its artists, writers, musicians, and theatre folk, and to life on the Ringstrasse, the elegant apotheosis of Jewish cosmopolitanism. He dreamt of working as a pianist in the orchestra of an operetta. Exactly why he left Vienna for the New World is uncertain. The story he would later recount to his wife and children was that he had been thrown in the guardhouse after failing to salute his brother Ernst, a superior officer, and vowed on his release to leave Austria and start a new life. This was probably just a colorful fiction he conveniently concocted to explain how he came to the United States and a way of rationalizing a deep and dogged restlessness and sense of disappointment. What is certain is that he arrived in New York on 26 October 1892 on SS *Westernland* from Antwerp and that he is listed in the ship's manifest, preserved in the Ellis Island Database, as "Mr. Fritz Austerlitz, 24, clerk."

Fritz's ambition was to settle in Manhattan and pursue a career as a singer and musician, but all his attempts to find work failed. He did, however, make acquaintances who in years to come would prove useful in establishing his children's career. He also encountered fellow Austrians Morris Kerpeles and Huber Freund, whom he persuaded to employ him as photographer and traveling agent in the

Figure 1.1 Fritz Austerlitz listed in the ship's manifest for the *SS Westernland*, 26 October 1892.
Ellis Island Database

International Publishing and Portrait Company, which the two men planned to launch in Omaha. Unfortunately, their grand scheme collapsed in the economic depression known as the Panic of 1893. Fritz was left to seek whatever employment he could and managed to secure a position as a cook in a saloon run by Fred Mittnacht, the Mountain Liquor House on Broadway ("jug trade a specialty; best whisky—ten cents a drink"). For a man with theatrical yearnings and dandified ways (he had grown an impressive curling moustache and affected the sartorial flourish of a cane), it was a long way from the heady bohemian bustle of the boulevards and coffee houses of fin-de-siècle Vienna. But Fritz, who had natural charm and an easy way with people, discovered a congenial niche in the social life of Omaha's German-speaking community, of which his new employer was an active member. Many of the community's social events were organized by the Lutheran Church, and at one such event he was introduced to fifteen-year-old Johanna Geilus, a beautiful and intelligent girl with a maturity beyond her years.

Johanna was the first of her family to be born in the United States. Her parents, Wilhelmina and David Geilus, had left East Prussia in 1878 and arrived in Omaha with their children, Marie and Daniel. By the time their second daughter was born on 22 December that year, David was working at the Union Pacific shop as a furnace man and molder. An unhappy and frustrated man, who had difficulty in mastering English, he sought solace in alcohol and would disappear for days at a time. His wife, of necessity, learnt to live frugally and to provide for her children, but she was an authoritarian rather than openly affectionate mother. Johanna grew up in a repressive household in which she received little stimulation. Quick-witted and studious, she excelled at the local Lutheran school where, at the end of her schooling, she was kept on to tutor the younger pupils. She liked to make and wear fashionable clothes and developed an appreciation of literature, art, and music. Although she lacked the curiosity and imagination that distinguish the true scholar or artist, she was, like Fritz, a restless soul, even if she did not understand or dared not articulate her sense of longing.

To the dutiful and repressed Johanna, Fritz was a terribly romantic figure—raffish, worldly, and musical. She was fascinated by his stories of old Vienna, finding in them, and in his attentions, a release from the parochial strictures of her home life. At the end of her teaching day she would often sneak away to meet him at the saloon. A shared feeling of incongruity with their circumstances, an awareness of unformulated, unfulfilled aspiration, drew the pair closer, and they soon fell in love. Johanna's parents strongly disapproved of Fritz, mistrusting his cosmopolitan airs, but when Johanna became pregnant, her father reluctantly gave his consent to their marriage.

The wedding was held on 17 November 1894 at the First Lutheran Church of Omaha; Fritz was twenty-six, his bride not yet sixteen. Almost immediately they relocated across the Missouri River to Council Bluffs, Iowa, where Johanna's condition would not cause a scandal and where Fritz found work as a glassware salesman for the Harle-Haas Drug Company. For Johanna, or Anna, as Fritz called her, the romance of her liberation was short-lived. She had a difficult pregnancy and did not carry to term. In the midst of this sadness, she began to recognize in her husband the same weakness for alcohol she had witnessed in her father. When she became pregnant for the second time, she insisted they return to Omaha, where she would be near her family.

Fritz found employment in Omaha with Walter Moise as a salesman of beer, wine, glassware, and cigars, an occupation that, much to Anna's concern, took him regularly to saloons and drinking establishments. The couple moved into a two-story white clapboard house at 1112 South Eleventh Street where on 10 September, 1896 Anna gave birth to a healthy baby girl, named Adele Marie after her two aunts. Fritz, in particular, was besotted with his dark-eyed, dark-haired daughter, and the two formed a special bond. From quite early on, Adele was aware of her father's inferiority complex, the weight of failure beneath the engaging bonhomie, but she remembered him as a dear and easygoing man, with a fondness for schnapps and Turkish cigarettes, who, when he was not traveling for work, would fill the house with music, playing on the piano waltzes by Strauss and Franz Lehár to which Adele would dance. Anna too played the piano, having had lessons as a child, and favored operatic pieces such as "To the Evening Star" from Wagner's *Tannhäuser*.

Anna loved her daughter but desperately wanted a son. Her wish was granted on Wednesday, 10 May 1899, when in their new home at 2326 South Tenth Street, Frederic Austerlitz II was born, blue-eyed and fair like his mother. In later years, Adele gave a graphic, if less than clinical, account of her brother's fragile state at birth: "My brother was born half dead. . . . Fred was born too big a baby and he deflated like a balloon. My grandfather, my mother's father, said, 'Annie, that child will never live.'" Anna was determined the frail little boy would live and devoted herself to building up his strength and immunity.

Figure 1.2 2326 South Tenth Street Omaha, Nebraska. Birthplace of Fred Astaire.
Helen Rayburn Collection, Howard Gotlieb Archival Research Centre

Their mutual devotion to their children was in truth the only thing keeping Anna and Fritz together, that and Anna's desire to maintain respectable appearances. Fritz's drinking, his frequent absences on account of his work (he was now a salesman for the Storz Brewing Company), and rumors of his womanizing placed a considerable strain on the marriage, while husband and wife were increasingly haunted by a sense of individual unfulfilment. The children were vaguely aware of their parents' effectual estrangement, but both remembered their early years in Omaha as happy, untroubled ones. For Fred and Adele these years were a brief prelude of singular normality, the only time when they lived typical midwestern small-town lives.

Adele remembered their home as "very simple and plain, a set of furniture in the dining room, pieces that matched in the living room. We had a carriage and horse." The family had a "hired girl" named Dorothy, who received $5 a week; the employment of such domestic help at that time was not a sign of particular affluence. Anna was a good cook, and whenever Fritz returned from one of his business trips, he and the children were served her special homemade dumplings. Following European custom, Fred and Adele always drank beer with their dinner as children. They attended the Kellom School at Twenty-Third and Paul Streets and on occasion visited their cousins, the Prochnows, who had a farm just outside the city. There they enjoyed running around with the ducks, cows, chickens, and pigs, riding one of the sows like a horse.

Fred recalled his mother as strict and diffident about herself but also gentle and usually ready to play with them. Although she had her work cut out with Adele, who was bright, boisterous, and consciously brimming with charm, Anna did her best to discourage precocity and boastfulness in her children, thereby giving them a valuable formative sense of proportion. Adele, who loved to dance for her father and to show off, was enrolled in the local dance school run by Willard Chambers. She quickly stood out from her classmates for the naturalism of her style and the exuberance of her personality, and was soon featured in recitals and at private parties, including several at the house of Adolph Storz, the son of Fritz's employer, Gottlieb Storz. Fred was also enrolled in Chambers Dancing Academy because his mother believed it would increase his strength and develop his frail physique.

The legend attached to Fred's first dance steps was perhaps the inspiration behind the seminal scene in Stephen Daldry's film of 2000 in which northern schoolboy Billy Elliot, hovering on the periphery of a little girls' dance class, tries on a pair of ballet slippers and earnestly imitates the barre exercises performed, somewhat lackadaisically, by the diminutive ballerinas. Whether Fred found his true calling after this fashion or not, he did demonstrate some aptitude and affinity for dance—if not the outstanding natural ability of his older sister—and he could dance *en pointe* (more successfully than she, claims Adele, who had a much lower instep than her brother). This was a rare talent for a male and one he shared with no less a dancer than Nijinsky.

In Adele, and to a lesser extent Fred, Willard Chambers perceived the potential for a professional stage career and persuaded Fritz and Anna that their children's promise would best be nurtured in New York, where they could receive proper training and direction and possibly attract the attention of booking agents in search of a new child act. That the Austerlitzes not only entertained a proposal of such life-altering and logistical magnitude but also acted so readily on it is extraordinary. In part, and at least subconsciously, their decision to venture into the unknown was motivated by selfish reasons. It was for Fritz the chance vicariously to fulfill his theatrical ambitions and for Anna the chance to escape the despondency of a failed marriage and lead an independent life without the need for a divorce. The children themselves, especially Fred, understood little of what was happening, but they were excited at the prospect of traveling to the great metropolis. Everything else they took calmly and unquestioningly in their stride, with childhood's characteristic easy acceptance of the exceptional.

Adele was eight and Fred just five when, in January 1905, they left Omaha with their parents and set out by rail for the East Coast. Fritz was to return to Omaha and continue in his job with the Storz Brewing Company in order to finance the hazardous adventure, but owing to the contacts he had made thirteen years earlier in New York and his avid, up-to-date interest in the theatrical business, he was instrumental in stage-managing their introduction to The Profession. A subscriber to the weekly theatrical trade paper the *New York Clipper* (later absorbed into *Variety*), Fritz spotted in that useful publication an advertisement for the extravagantly named Alviene Master School of the Theatre and Academy of Cultural Arts. Then located in the Grand Opera House on the northwest corner of Eighth Avenue and Twenty-Third Street, the school had been founded in 1894 by Claude M. Alviene and his wife Neva C. Irwin, the former toe dancer La Neva. It purported to be the first institution in America to offer specialized courses in all aspects of theatre arts, drawing its teaching staff from the professional ranks of vaudeville, opera, and ballet and guaranteeing to produce young graduates thoroughly equipped for a career in show business. This was the school Fritz selected for Adele and Fred.

In his autobiography Fred describes Alviene as "a kindly, fatherly man with white hair,"[3] although he was barely thirty-five at the time. He and Adele were led by their parents up a narrow flight of stairs in the Grand Opera House to a door that opened onto a large ballroom with a stage at one end. Here they met Mr. Alviene, who looked over his two new charges. At the end of a brief interview, in which Adele had been the main focus of discussion, Alviene gently tapped Fred's tiny head and, smiling, said, "We're going to make a big star out of you."[4]

At Fritz's insistence, the family then went to Luchow's on East Fourteenth Street, a celebrated German restaurant frequented by people like O. Henry, Victor Herbert, Ignacy Jan Paderewski, Lillian Russell, and the great comic duo Joe Weber and Lew Fields. The dining room was handsomely appointed with carved-oak paneling, huge mirrors, etched glass, murals, and skylights. The chairs were upholstered in red velvet, and the chandeliers bathed the tables and surrounding oil paintings in golden and amber lights. A violinist moved among the tables playing music by Strauss and Brahms.

Fritz, seated in a corner with his family, wallowed in an atmosphere he had known and adored in Vienna. Dining at Luchow's became a traditional treat when Fritz visited his children in New York. On this first occasion, Fred, who had hardly spoken since leaving Claude Alviene's school, suddenly looked at his father and exclaimed, "Papa, Mr. Alviene said he's going to make a big star out of me." He had clearly been turning this statement carefully over in his mind. Adele later said she would never forget the tears in her father's eyes as Fred, with an affecting, wide-eyed solemnity, repeated Alviene's words.

On arriving in New York, the family had checked into the Herald Square Hotel, but when Fritz returned to Omaha, Anna needed to find more permanent and affordable lodgings. One of the services the school provided was securing suitable accommodation for its students, and Mr. Alviene recommended a

Figure 1.3 Postcard showing the interior of Luchow's Restaurant.

nearby boarding house on Twenty-Third Street. There Anna and her children made their new home in one large front room on the second floor with a broad bay window. It contained a bed for Anna, two small cots for Adele and Fred, and sufficient room for Anna to give the children their lessons in grammar, arithmetic, history, and geography. There was a bath at the end of the hall, and the family ate their meals downstairs. Routinely, Adele and Fred were tutored in the morning and began their dancing and acting lessons at two o'clock. (Among their classmates at Alviene's were the Dolly Sisters). On Sundays, with Anna, they would take the trolley car to Central Park and play or take a boat on the lake. Afterward they would go to Macy's Department Store and buy cakes and cookies.

Dinner was at six o'clock and bedtime at eight. Every night before they went to sleep, Anna made sure the children said their prayers and would then read to them for half an hour, often from a curious combination of the Bible and *Vanity Fair*. She could also entertain them for hours by sitting in the bay window and inventing stories about, and conversations between, the passers-by outside. There were times, however, when the stress of single-handedly looking after two young children in a dauntingly big city, and keeping them amused, proved too much. To punish their misbehavior (in Adele's case being even noisier than usual and in Fred's unscrewing the tap and splashing water around) Anna would occasionally walk out on the children, leaving them alone in their room. She did not go far, normally around the block a few times to regain her courage and composure, or maybe to a museum for an hour; but Adele, being older and more aware than her brother, was terrified, thinking her mother was never coming back and that she and Fred would be left to fend for themselves in New York. As a form of punishment, this mental anguish Anna subjected her eight-year-old daughter to seems bizarre and cruel, but it is worth remembering that at twenty-six, she was scarcely more than a girl herself and had had her own childhood curtailed by marriage. And while she never begrudged her children the sacrifices she made for them or the enforced nomadic existence she led, she resented her stage-struck husband and the ambitions that had placed her in so alien and vulnerable a situation— even though these very ambitions facilitated her own bid for independence and a purposeful life.

In addition to preparing and supervising the children's regular lessons, Anna assumed charge of their cultural education, realizing that one of the best ways for them to learn about the theatre, stage technique, and style was through exposure to the cream of the profession. In this, Anna was both a discerning and a liberal guide, introducing Adele and Fred to most forms of entertainment from burlesque and variety to legitimate plays and ballet. By the time they were thirteen and ten, they had seen performances by Ethel Barrymore, Laurette Taylor, and John Drew Jr; Lillie Langtry's vaudeville debut at the age of fifty-three in *Between Nightfall and the Light* at the Fifth Avenue theatre in 1907;[5] and Anna Pavlova in her first season at the Metropolitan Opera House in 1910, dancing *The Dying Swan* and, with Mikhail Mordkin, the *Autumnal Bacchanal*. Although they saw the doyen of Broadway, George M. Cohan, at the height of his career, Adele remembered people doing imitations of him better than she remembered the man himself. One performer who did fire her imagination and leave a lasting impression was Hazel Dawn, when she sang, danced, and played the violin in Ivan Caryll's show *The Pink Lady* at the New Amsterdam in 1911; Dawn was an original member of the *Ziegfeld Follies* in 1907, and Adele idolized her, thinking her "the most lovely, graceful creature" she had ever seen.[6]

But the artist who had the most significant influence on Fred and Adele in those pre-adolescent years was the Danish ballet star Adeline Genée. In early 1908 she appeared for the first time in America in a musical extravaganza produced by Florenz Ziegfeld, *The Soul Kiss* at the New York Theater, and was billed "The World's Greatest Dancer." Of the show's 122 performances, Fred and Adele saw nearly a quarter, almost always from the end of the third row in the balcony, where they could intently study Genée's graceful agility and discreetly practice her movements. Genée's costumes were in the style of the 1830s; as Adele remarked, "She never wore a tutu, she always wore her dresses long, and she wore her hair in three blonde curls."[7]

Figure 1.4 Adeline Genée in
The Soul Kiss, 1908.

Theatre spoke rhapsodically of her captivating stage presence and the delicacy and lyricism of her dancing:

> Her dainty blonde personality, when in repose, is of the type that suggests the apt though overworked comparison of "Dresden china." But when she dances and smiles and smiles through her dancing, in every ethereal poise and pirouette, then we must fly for similes to the breeze-born petals of the rose—to the thistle-down, and the sprites and sylphs of the sunbeam.[8]

The same critique points to another quality, a Thespic substance underlying the ethereal poise: "But Genée, besides being a classical elève of the ballet school, is an accomplished pantomimiste, and an intelligent actress as well. Thus the scope of her expression is infinitely widened, both as to her individual joy in the dance and the interpretation of an idea or a role." It was probably this quality above all that left its mark on Fred and Adele, young though they were, and that they would themselves embody as they grew into seasoned performers. The interpretation of an idea and the exposition of character would, moreover, become the central tenets of Fred's choreographic philosophy on film.

Theatre in the wider sense lay all around Adele and Fred. Before Charles Frohman built his Empire Theatre on Broadway at Fortieth Street in 1893, the pulsating heart of New York's theatre district had been West Twenty-Third Street, home to the Grand Opera House, Koster and Bial's Concert Hall, and continuous vaudeville at Proctor's Theatre. ("After breakfast go to Proctor's, after Proctor's go to bed.") Opposite Proctor's was the Hotel Chelsea, itself an enclave of bohemia, whose turn-of-the-century residents included Sarah Bernhardt and Lillian Russell. The boarding house recommended by Alviene was of course popular with people in the business, and Adele recalled that at the time they moved in, one of their fellow residents was appearing at Wallack's Theatre in George Ade and Gustav Luders's comic opera *The Sho-Gun*; another sewed theatrical costumes. She also recalled that every Saturday a beautiful open carriage drew up outside the boarding house and two decoratively adorned ladies got in; on much later reflection, she realized that they were probably high-class prostitutes. As well as being a fascinated observer of the adult world, its foibles and everyday tragicomedies, Adele made her own theatre. One of her favorite pastimes was to entertain the neighborhood children with lurid tales summoned up from her prolific imagination: "I was very lonely in some ways. I liked to scare other children. It was awful. I'd say, 'You know that house there—the most horrible people come out at night with knives.' I made up these stories to scare them. . . . I loved to read aloud—I thought my voice sounded so dramatic." This infant taste for melodrama and the macabre makes one think of Margaret O'Brien's character in *Meet Me in St Louis*.

Around this time, Anna began to devise a suitable stage name for the children. She wanted one with immediate star quality, a euphonic, less "foreign" and unwieldy surname than Austerlitz that would look for all the world as though it belonged on a theatre marquee. There are several theories as to how the name Astaire came to be selected, one being the existence, on Anna's side, of an Alsace-Lorraine uncle with the surname L'Astaire. However, in the program for the Alviene School, Adele and Fred are variously billed as "The Austers," "The Astiers," "The Astares," and "The Astairs," which suggests that the name did not instantly propose itself but evolved. Whatever the precise derivation or inspiration, it was a brilliant choice, a name redolent of American affluence (rather like Astor) and continental chic, a name impossible now to dissociate from an image of showbiz supremacy. Anna herself adopted the new nomenclature as a symbol of her autonomy, her own evolution. She abbreviated her first name at the same time, so that from the chrysalis of Johanna Austerlitz, Ann Astaire definitively emerged.

Patriarchal convention determined that the younger Fred should receive first billing, but Adele was indisputably the leader on and off the stage. And from the start of their training, their relationship as performers, and the contrasting individual attributes they brought to the partnership, were firmly established: Adele was the one who could dazzle effortlessly through sheer force of personality and with the confidence of innate talent; Fred was the more industrious, striving to keep up with and not disgrace his sister, but with gifts of his own awaiting discovery. Under Claude Alviene's patient tutelage, the children devoted equal time to dancing and acting. Fred's most potent memory of their dance classes was of the mesmeric metronomic effect of Alviene beating time with a stick on the back of a wooden chair, which either triggered or chimed with the acute sense of rhythm and love of complex rhythmic interplay for which Fred would become famous. His principal memory of the dramatic side of their studies was, for him, less enthralling. At a school recital, he and Adele performed a scene from Edmond Rostand's *Cyrano de Bergerac*. The difference in their ages and heights dictated that Adele should play the swashbuckling poet-warrior and Fred, reluctantly following in the pre-Restoration stage tradition of female impersonation, the fair Roxanne, complete with the embarrassing encumbrances of a long blonde wig and satin dress. Adele played Cyrano with a dashing, Fairbanksian brio.

In the autumn of 1905, Alviene decided the children were ready to make their first professional appearance. He created an act for them and secured a booking at Pavilion Beach in Keyport, New Jersey, an amusement park that had opened two years earlier. For an end-of-pier vaudeville debut, "The Wedding Cake Act," as it was called, was elaborately conceived and technically demanding. The custom-built set pieces were two large wedding cakes, six feet in diameter, two feet high, and equipped with musical bells and flashing electric lights. The routine was designed to run an average of twelve minutes—the standard for vaudeville—and began with Adele and Fred, a miniature bride and groom, posed atop the separate illuminated cakes. Adele was dressed in white satin and Fred, fatefully, in top hat and tails. They danced on the cakes and up and down the musical stairs that magically appeared, playing "Dreamland Waltz" with their toes. Each had a solo; Fred's was a buck and wing executed on his toes. After an exit and quick change, they returned to the stage fantastically costumed, Fred as a lobster and Adele as a glass of champagne, to perform an eccentric final duet on the musical cakes.

The Keyport engagement was not the most auspicious theatrical beginning. The cumbersome wedding cakes and attendant technical paraphernalia engulfed the stage when they arrived and did not endear Ann and her children to the overstretched stagehands and electricians. And because of the time-consuming and audible process of setting up the cakes, the act was assigned the least enviable spot on the bill—number one. When the matinée began at three o'clock, Adele and Fred found themselves playing to a nearly empty theatre. A typical vaudeville bill consisted of eight separate, unrelated acts and was brutally hierarchical; exactly where one appeared in the bill was crucial and, therefore, the driving obsession of performers. Opening spot, referred to as "the doormat," was a "dumb act"—animals, acrobats, *tableaux vivants*, or hapless dancers forced to give their all in the face of desultory attention and noisy latecomers. The second spot fared little better and was usually allocated to newcomers or minor singing acts. Third on the bill might be a comedy sketch, "tab" (tabloid edition of a Broadway success), or "flash act" (a showy song-and-dance number backed by a chorus and enhanced with special effects). The fourth and fifth spots were reserved for solid performers such as established comedy teams. Sixth, the challenging post-interval slot, required a "class" act, such as the ballroom sensations Vernon and Irene Castle, whom the Astaires were to emulate and profoundly admire. The coveted penultimate or "featured" spot was reserved for the top act of the evening, the star turn or headliner. The last act, known as the "chaser," might again be a dumb act and had the dual responsibility of clearing the theatre and keeping entertained those patrons who had remained steadfastly to the end; early moving pictures became effective chasers.

It was years before the Astaires attained headliner status, and their climb to the solid, respectable middle of the bill was slow and arduous. Yet the very things that could make vaudeville such a demoralizing business were also what made it an invaluable training ground. Speaking of his own days in small-time vaudeville, George Burns once quipped that the virtue of this form of entertainment was that it gave inexperienced performers somewhere they could be bad. The prevalence of vaudeville and its twice-daily and upward format allowed for the necessary luxuries of failure, development, and a certain amount of experimentation.[9] The many months spent opening the bill or occupying equally undesirable spots taught Fred and Adele the importance, as performers, of economy, timing and pace, and personal magnetism. The relative brevity of the vaudeville act meant there was precious little time in which to warm up an audience. An incorrigibly restive or disengaged house was ruinous—they had to be won over, and their sense of humor, belief, and delight inveigled at the outset.

There was virtue, too, in the discipline of repetition. The Astaires would spend twelve years honing three basic vaudeville routines, a grueling schedule of practice and performance that instilled in Fred his often-cited perfectionism and in Adele an abhorrence of rehearsal. Larry Billman makes the vital point that during these years Fred "began to think of his work as 'Work' rather than some charismatic 'Art' he created magically."[10] But alongside the repetitive toil were inspiration and observation, and Fred, particularly, dedicated his non-working hours to watching the headliners from the wings, examining with critical wonder the alchemy practiced by the old pros, in an effort "to further my ham education."[11]

No act, of course, could flourish without publicity, a fact appreciated by Ann, at whose instigation, no doubt, Keyport's local newspaper proclaimed: "The Astaires are the greatest child act in vaudeville." Out front at their Keyport debut was Claude Alviene, who was encouraging about their performance but believed the children could benefit from extra training. He suggested they be enrolled for lessons in the ballet school of the Metropolitan Opera and, at the same time, helped secure further bookings for them, beginning with Young's Pier Theatre in Atlantic City in January 1906. Intermittently over the next two years, Fred and Adele performed "The Wedding Cake Act" with dates in New Jersey and Pennsylvania and moving as far west as Minnesota. On 30 March 1907, they appeared in a left-corner inset on the cover of *Variety*, alongside other vaudeville entertainers of the day—the Elinore Sisters, May and Kate, who portrayed Irish immigrant women; Jack Norworth, soon-to-be lyricist of "Take Me Out to the Ball Game" and "Shine On, Harvest Moon"; and singing comedienne Jeanette Dupre.

Fritz continued to offer guidance and to follow their progress keenly from afar, but it was Ann who, from day to day, acted as the children's manager, costumier, tutor, and constant companion. In view of their tender years, she was highly protective of them and did not permit them to fraternize too much with the adult performers. "She wanted us to be polite," Adele said, "but she didn't want us to get into conversation with any of the grown-up actors for fear of us getting spoiled. She wanted us to be children." It was by no means a normal childhood, but Ann wanted Fred and Adele to have a routine that imposed some stability and regularity. Being young and attractive, she herself was subject to unwanted attention from predatory booking agents and stage managers, which built into her an intense resentment of men in general and her husband in particular. But she swiftly learnt how to look after herself and insulate her children from the more sordid aspects of show business and the life of itinerant players.

It has been alleged by Adele's unpublished biographer, Helen Rayburn, that by this time Fritz was living in Omaha with a young woman who called herself Mrs. Austerlitz and gave birth to his child in 1908. Rayburn bases this assertion on apparent testimony from the Astaires' cousin Helene Geilus (to whom Fred dedicated his autobiography) and Omaha historian Harold Becker, but local records furnish no corroborative indication of this de facto relationship or the existence of an Astaire half-sibling. Wherever the truth about his domestic arrangements lay, Fritz's guiding interest in his children's career did not wane. As well as finding them a new teacher, he introduced them to Frank Vincent, head booking agent of the prestigious Orpheum Circuit, and negotiated a twenty-week contract at a salary of $150 per week plus train fare.

The new teacher was Ned Wayburn. The slogan of his School of Dance, which started out at 115 West Forty-Second Street (he later purchased a building on West Forty-Fourth Street, which he converted into a school and miniature theatre), promised "Health, Beauty, Fame, Popularity, Independence." Wayburn had acquired his early training in movement at the Hart Conway School of Acting in Chicago but started his career on the Keith Circuit as a blackface ragtime pianist and monologuist. He made his Broadway debut at the Herald Square

Figure 1.5 Adele and Fred at the time of "The Wedding Cake Act".
Adele Astaire Collection, Howard Gotlieb Archival Research Centre

Theatre in February 1899, as a performer, composer, and costume designer in a broad farce entitled *By the Sad Sea Waves*. He was to stage more than 200 vaudeville acts and 300 spectacles for producers such as Oscar and William Hammerstein, Marcus Klaw and A. L. Erlanger, Lew Fields, the Shuberts, and Florenz Ziegfeld, including six editions of the *Ziegfeld Follies* between 1916 and 1923. He would also choreograph an Astaire musical, unhappily Fred and Adele's most ignominious flop, the Ziegfeld-produced *Smiles*.

In his history of the early development of tap dancing, Mark Knowles credits Wayburn with "the first official use of the word 'tap' in reference to percussive American show dancing."[12] In 1902, Wayburn had created a novelty act for the New York Theatre Roof called *Ned Wayburn's Minstrel Misses*, featuring a chorus line of sixteen girls in light clogs with split wooden soles, and in the publicity for the show he described the hybrid of clog, jig, and buck dancing performed as "tap and step dancing." It was at Wayburn's school that Fred learnt the rudiments of tap dancing and syncopation; he was even instructed by Wayburn himself in some buck-and-wing steps. Fred was amazed that such a large man was so light and nimble on his feet—indeed Wayburn stood at six feet two inches and weighed over 200 pounds. There is a photograph from 1923 showing Wayburn teaching a young woman the Charleston—a stout, bespectacled bear of a man who looked nothing at all like a dancer or dancing master.

Wayburn's influence extended beyond techniques of dance. It was he who gave Adele and Fred their first proper vocal training and who impressed on them that "the indefinable factor called personality" was intrinsic to the formation of an individual dance style. In his manual *The Art of Stage Dancing*, published at the height of the Astaires' fame in 1925, he wrote:

> I cannot emphasize too strongly the importance of *personality* in a successful stage career. Along with the actual mastering of the dancing steps and acquisition of health and a beautiful body, comes just as surely the development of personality. And since each individual has a distinct personality it is advisable to select the type of dancing best suited to that personality. It is because of this quality that the performance of stars like . . . Fred and Adele Astaire leaves a lasting impression. Every step, every movement is designed to drive home the characteristics of their individuality. Even more important than the actual dancing steps they do is the manner in which they execute them—the individuality which gives expression to all that they do.[13]

Wayburn also taught the children not to neglect the hands and upper body in mastering their dance steps, for like the ancient pantomime dancers of the Greco-Roman world, he believed in the importance of *cheironomia*, the rhythmic and expressive use of the hands:

> The hands give expression or emphasis to the thought that it is desired to convey, both in speaking and in the pantomime of the dance and the screen. . . . While you acquire the necessary dance steps to make you a perfect dancer, also learn the hand and arm movements that complement your steps and perfect the picture into its most pleasing possibilities, movements that shall develop the idea of the dance you are portraying and carry it across the footlights.[14]

In *Steps in Time*, Fred misremembers the date he and Adele became students at Wayburn's school, placing it around 1910 or 1911. In fact, their enrolment preceded their engagement on the Orpheum Circuit and must have occurred at least as early as February 1907, because they were photographed for an article on Wayburn's school that appeared in the *New York World* on 3 February 1907 under the heading "New York's Theatrical Incubator: Tots Who Are Being Taught to Be Actors and Actresses and Can't Wait for Graduation Time."

The Astaires' twenty-week tour commenced at the Majestic Theatre, Des Moines, in July 1908 and took them, in the week of 6 December, to Omaha, where they received a warm home-town welcome at the Orpheum Theatre on South Sixteenth Street and Adele was presented across the footlights with a white Pomeranian puppy she had admired in the window of a local cigar store. On the same bill in Omaha were comedian Ben Welch, the Trapnell family of acrobats, Harry Foy and Florence Clark, and headliner Violet Black. The children received enthusiastic notices in most towns they played; Fred was singled out for his "surprisingly powerful voice";[15] and their success ensured a further twenty weeks in 1909, which included bookings along the West Coast. For this second tour, the Alviene act was refined and the weighty wedding cakes eliminated. Still a few months shy of his tenth birthday, Fred began making small choreographic suggestions of his own. The *Saint Paul Dispatch* declared Fred "one of the most remarkable toe dancers now appearing on the vaudeville stage. Freddie is still a mere boy, but his toe dancing is on a par with that of any dancer before the public. He is also a clever entertainer and has a sweet voice."[16]

Billman contends that in February 1909 the Astaires appeared on a bill in San Francisco headlined by Spanish dancers Eduardo and Elisa Cansino, a slightly

Figure 1.6 Fred dancing *en pointe* at the age of eight.

older team of dancing siblings (their father, Antonio, was one of the pioneers of flamenco and creator of the bolero). But this cannot be so, as the Cansinos did not emigrate from Madrid until 1913, arriving in the United States on SS *Prinz Friedrich Wilhelm* on 12 January. It was about two years after that, and in Toledo, Ohio, that the Astaires first encountered the Cansinos in vaudeville and, Fred "watched Eduardo at every show. He was a marvelous dancer and together he and his sister were exciting performers. We worked with the Cansinos for a number of weeks. Eduardo spoke enthusiastically about our dancing and we were flattered and encouraged."[17] The Cansinos were best known for "La Cuchipanda," a variation on the tango combining graceful body and arm movements, which the Astaires sought to incorporate in their ballroom routines. Adele, approaching eighteen, became infatuated with Eduardo, whom she called her "first real love," while nearly thirty years later Fred danced in two films with Eduardo's daughter Margarita or, as she was then known, Rita Hayworth.[18]

This second tour came under the scrutiny of the New York Society for the Prevention of Cruelty to Children (NYSPCC), more popularly referred to in vaudevillian circles as the Gerry Society after its principal founder, Elbridge Thomas Gerry. A Columbia-educated attorney whose grandfather was among the signatories to the Declaration of Independence, Gerry had been legal adviser to the American Society for the Prevention of Cruelty to Animals. His involvement in the Mary Ellen Wilson case of child abuse, which he took to the New York State Supreme Court in 1874, led directly to his establishment, with the support of Henry Bergh (founder of the ASPCA) and philanthropist John D. Wright, of the NYSPCC. Its mission was "to rescue little children from the cruelty and demoralization which neglect, abandonment and improper treatment engender; to aid by all lawful means in the enforcement of the laws intended for their protection and benefit; to secure by like means the prompt conviction and punishment of all persons violating such laws." Gerry's reforming zeal was not limited to protecting children from exploitation and long working hours in the unhealthy environments of mines, mills, and factory sweatshops; his crusade aimed to rescue child performers from what he deemed the morally corrupting influence of the stage.

The New York society prompted the rapid formation of affiliates across the country, and by 1910 there were two hundred and fifty in operation; the agents of these societies were nicknamed "Gerrymen," whose responsibilities included the rooting out of underage performers, which in New York itself meant children under sixteen appearing professionally. These officers and their leader's good intentions struck fear and loathing into the hearts of many theatrical youngsters whose families' livelihoods depended on their performing careers. Critic George Jean Nathan once defined the Gerry Society as "an organization which, by preventing children predisposed to become actors from following their inclination, hopes thereby in time to preserve the drama."[19] Anti-Gerry campaign groups inevitably arose, and desperate stage parents found ways of circumventing the law, such as borrowing or forging birth certificates and—a more extreme measure—passing their children off as midgets. In a process the opposite of that applied to Dickens's Infant Phenomenon in *Nicholas Nickleby*, every effort was made to make Fred and Adele appear older, with nine-year-old Fred being put into long trousers, even though their real ages had been published in reviews and articles. After their first performances in Los Angeles in February 1909, the Gerrymen intervened, and their booking was canceled. Ann thereupon initiated a campaign of her own, appealing to newspaper critics to help publicize their plight and finally obtaining a hearing before the local chapter of the Society. She pleaded convincingly the children's dedication and well-being and the excellent care and tuition they were receiving, and the society relented.

Another crisis soon followed, however, which no amount of cunning or entreaty could forestall. Adele was fast developing into a young woman, while Fred remained on the awkward cusp of puberty. As dancing partners, the difference in their heights and maturity now bordered on the ludicrous. And it was not merely the physical discrepancy that was noted. One manager's report had stated: "The girl seems to have talent but the boy can do nothing," a judgment that haunted Fred throughout most of his stage career. It was clear, too, that both children had outgrown "The Wedding Cake Act." Ann and Fritz agreed that the best solution would be a period of retirement in which Fred and Adele would continue to train but otherwise live as "normal" children. Rather than return to Omaha, Ann, Adele, and Fred moved to a rented house in El Dorado Place, Highwood Park, a residential area of Weehawken, New Jersey, just across the Hudson River from Manhattan's theatre district. For the first time in nearly five years the children attended public school. They became pupils at Alexander Hamilton Grammar School, where it was discovered that his mother's assiduous home tuition had placed Fred slightly ahead of his peers—a fact that might have astounded Elbridge T. Gerry.

Although they did not perform professionally for the next two and a half years, Adele and Fred did participate in school recitals, and on 17 December 1909 they appeared in an evening concert or Musicale at the Studio in Louisa Place, Weehawken, "given by the junior pupils of Miss Nellie E. Andrews, kindly assisted by Miss Anna Bohrmann Soprano, and Mr. Herbert Stroh Violinist." Fred played the triangle and Adele the triangle and xylophone.

Inside the little program for the concert is printed:

Vesper Hymn, Matthews
Cadet's March, Smith
Frederic Astaire

Figure 1.7 "Musicale", Weehawken, New Jersey, December 1909. Adele front row, far left; Fred front row, second from right.

Waltz, Curlitt
Adele Astaire

The children still had the real stage in their sights. For Christmas that year Fritz gave Adele a small red diary published by the Storz Brewing Company. Inside Adele drew two portraits of herself alone and center stage: one in a blue dress and blue ballet slippers, standing *en pointe*; the other striking another ballet pose with an orchestra conductor below the footlights. The rest of the diary is filled with drawings of "fashionable" ladies and actresses, including another of her idols, Billie Burke, whom she might have recently seen in Somerset Maugham's *Mrs. Dot* at the Lyceum. There is just one journal entry or short story, which is composed in rhyme and reads not unlike an Edwardian music-hall song. The spelling is highly idiosyncratic, the punctuation haphazard and, despite the rhyme scheme, the piece is set out as ordinary prose:

> Lots of girls that I no have love affairs, som are highly colord some are plain. Mine was quite a short one didn't last a week, don't think I will get engaged again. When I told Mama there was a young man after me

she said let me meet him so I brought him home to tea. All the family
eid him up and rather good at that and William and myself whent in the
parlor for a chat. I sat over here Willy over there he was on the sofa I was
on the chair every time he spoke to me I was most polite. Ma kept pop-
ping in to see that everything was right. At half past eight he said he
must be leeving didn't seem at home somehow all the family around to
watch us say goodnight. Willy's got another girl now. . . . After he had
been there an hour or more, he said will you play something. Well I did
my best—sure played the swanny river—although I thought it grand he
didn't seem to like it well—I only play one hand.

By the summer of 1911, Fred had gained a few inches in height, and he and
Adele were anxious to return to vaudeville. Ann paid Ned Wayburn the huge
sum of $1000 (in four installments) to write and stage a new specialty act, one
that would reflect the children's maturity and display their improved abilities,
including their acting and comedic skills. After at least six drafts, Wayburn produced a skit entitled "A Rainy Saturday" (or more familiarly "The Baseball Act"),
which he explained was "a natural story, which should get some laughs and the
children can interpret it and hold the audiences in the vaudeville houses."[20] The
scenario featured Adele as Rosie Bloom and Fred as her little brother Robbie, a
pair of rather knowing and faintly insolent children (Robbie says "Damn it!" at
one point and speaks of his father having a hangover.) Ann also featured as the
voice of their offstage mother. Rain has washed out Robbie's baseball game and,
obliged to entertain themselves indoors, the children re-enact their parents'
marital quarrels, make believe how Rosie's first beau will propose to her, and
stage a short series of domestic scenes: Father's belated and drunken homecom-
ing from the club; Mother's scolding reception of him; a breakfast table scene in
which Mother refuses to speak to Father; and a happy ending in which Mother
and Father kiss and make up. There were two musical numbers: a waltz to follow
the proposal scene, "You Don't Belong to Me," and a solo by Fred, "When Uncle
Joe Plays a Rag on His Old Banjo."

In his letter to Ann outlining the concept, Wayburn gave very specific instruc-
tions about the children's costumes and where they should be purchased:

I want Freddie to wear a gray base-ball uniform the same as the N.Y.
Giants traveling uniform at the opening of the act. It is gray with a faint
black stripe in it—and it wants a black cap, black stockings, black belt.
Across the breast of the shirt have them put THE LITTLE GIANTS in
black letters. The shoes should be made by J. Miller, West 23rd Street
opposite the Grand Opera House—tell him I sent you. Have them
made with gray uppers to imitate base-ball shoes, but the foot and soles

must be for dancing and be flexible—so he can do the waltz. Get the
uniform made by A. G. Spalding and Bros West 42nd Street, near 5th
Avenue. Adele should be dressed in a dainty little summer frock with
her hair in a single braid. . . . In that scene [Father returning home from
the club] I want Freddie to wear a silk hat large enough to come down
over his ears and an old prop dress coat.[21]

Rather than commute to Manhattan by ferry each day for rehearsals, the
family moved to a brownstone boarding house on West Forty-Fifth Street
between Times Square and Eighth Avenue on the south side of the street, not far
from the old Hotel Astor. The neighborhood abutted Hell's Kitchen and witnessed turf wars between rival gangs, into which Fred and his companions were
sometimes unwittingly drawn. While they were living there, the artist's model
and chorus girl Evelyn Nesbit used to come and visit someone in the house
across from theirs. Although Nesbit had attracted notoriety in 1906 when her
husband, Henry Kendall Thaw, murdered her ex-lover Stanford White during a
performance at the Madison Square Roof Garden, she was a heroine to Adele:
"I wanted to be just like her. I just thought she was so beautifully dressed and
carried herself with such assurance." After one year the family would move again,
to the residential Calumet Hotel on West Fifty-Seventh Street between Eighth
and Ninth avenues. This was next to the Church of Zion and St. Timothy, where
Fred met the stagestruck Reverend Randolph Ray, who had observed his unmistakable dancer's technique and rhythm in the course of a street ballgame and
who later confirmed Fred in the Episcopal faith at his new parish, the Church of
the Transfiguration or, as it was known to theatre people, "The Little Church
around the Corner."[22]

In contrast to the precocious and knowing characters Wayburn had written
for them, Adele and Fred were still largely innocent of the facts of life, thanks to
their mother's prim reticence on the subject. Adele recalled: "We had some kit-
tens when we lived in Weehawken and I said, 'Mommy, where did they come
from?' I was about thirteen I guess, and she said, 'Oh, they were nourished.'
That's all she would tell me. She never told us a thing. I learned [about sex] from
the telephone operator in the hotel." Fred derived his knowledge of such matters
from a similar source: "Bellhops were always my friends. I used to sit on the
bench with them in hotel lobbies and enhance my education. And I don't necessarily mean theatrically."[23]

When the new act had been fully rehearsed, Ann discovered that the children's two-year layoff had not done them any favors. She was unable to get a
booking agent to consider them. Wayburn came to the rescue by arranging for
them to premiere "A Rainy Saturday" at a benefit he was sponsoring at the
Broadway Theatre. The reviews and audience reaction were positive, and the

Figure 1.8 Adele and Fred, 1911.
Antoine Dutot Museum and Gallery

performance sparked the interest of agents. Ann accepted an offer for Fred and Adele to appear at Proctor's Fifth Avenue Theatre, on the corner of Broadway and Twenty-Eighth Street, for the week of 19 February 1912. Proctor's housed high-class vaudeville and was a prominent venue for the Astaires' first professional appearance in New York City. What is more, the bill was to be headlined by Douglas Fairbanks, who, between engagements in the legitimate theatre, was making a brief vaudeville tour in a sketch called "A Regular Businessman."

Everything augured well for Fred and Adele's official return to the stage, but when they arrived at the theatre for the first Monday matinée performance, it was to find themselves listed on the bill as the "doormat," the opening act, and because of the show's unusual length, without even a preceding newsreel to subdue the audience. Far from qualifying as a dumb act, the new routine was heavy with dialogue and proceeded for several minutes before the first musical number. They resolved to make the best of it, but they ended up playing to row after row of empty stalls and an inattentive balcony. The jokes were lost, and the dances were greeted with the sparsest applause. At the end they sneaked in a single bow, but as in every actor's nightmare, the applause ceased while they were still "out there," leaving them stranded in an excruciatingly vast no-man's-land between the footlights and the wings, compelled to make their exit to thunderous silence.

All Fred and Adele could hope for was a later position on the evening bill. After a rest and a light dinner, they returned to the theatre at seven o'clock and hurried to the notice board on which was posted the order of acts. Their names no longer opened the bill. Instead, "A Rainy Saturday" had been canceled. For "the greatest child act in vaudeville" it was the beginning of their lowest ebb.

CHAPTER 2

Over the Top

Show me a step
Full of the pep,
Show me and I'll take a chance.
I love to spin around until I'm all out breath,
Vernon Castle myself to death—
Twirl me about,
Tire me out
Because I'm simply crazy to dance.
—Irving Berlin, "I Love to Dance"

After the unqualified failure of their vaudeville comeback and New York debut, bookings were scarce for the Astaires and confined to the grinding, unglamorous assembly line of the small-time circuits, which meant lower pay for more frequent performances (three shows a day and four on Saturdays), playing rougher, often converted theatres in small towns or rural areas. Weeks would elapse between engagements. During these fallow periods, the children performed at private functions to supplement their erratic income. Two particular low points were the Monticello Theatre in New Jersey, where they were drowned out by a chorus of catcalls from the balcony and pelted with pennies, and a drunken New Year's Eve party at which their act counted for nothing.

With the help of agents Lew Golder and Jo Paige Smith, Fred and Adele obtained bookings on the United Booking Office circuit with occasional forlorn forays into the Gus Sun houses, the epitome of small, small time. For the next two years they played, in Fred's words, "every rat trap and chicken coop in the Middle West" and were introduced to the dispiriting practice of "split" weeks.[1] Instead of a full week of six performance days (Monday to Saturday) in a single location, the split-week formula, invented by Gus Sun, entailed two or three days in one town and three or four days in another, with a train journey in the middle. One of the many drawbacks of playing split weeks was that an act was seldom in one place long enough to attract reviews and publicity. This could, of course, have its advantages if the act flopped, but it made it extremely difficult to establish any kind of reputation and to progress.

Split weeks on the small-time circuits were not designed to enhance a performer's self-esteem, though they were certainly character-building. There were constant stark reminders of one's lowliness in the showbiz food chain, from thefleabag hotels to the primitive conditions backstage. In Coffee Cup, Indiana, Fred and Adele experienced the ignominy of sharing the bill with just one other act, a team of trained seals who occupied the "star" dressing room, the only downstairs accommodation, while the Astairs had either to climb a ladder to the vertiginous heights of the Number 2 dressing room or change in the alley.

Fred's most vivid impressions of these years were not of the hardships he and Adele endured but of his own inadequacy, his lack of stage presence. He refers to himself at this time as "still a detriment to my sister" and as being "in a sort of blank stage."[2] He did not seem to resent Adele's spontaneity, her charismatic self-possession as a performer, and her intuitive way with an audience. Nor did he try to compete with her. Early in their career Fred and Adele realized that the key to their partnership was to exploit not only the combination of complementary talents but also that of contradictory temperaments. They respected their differences even when frustrated by them. Ironically, Adele believed she was something of a detriment to her brother because she lacked his discipline and creativity, his choreographic instinct and inventiveness. "I wouldn't do anything that made me work all the time. I was a lazy slob . . . I want things to come to me without having to work for it."[3]

When they were grown up and earning good money, Fred would often have to bribe his sister with gifts to get her to rehearse. Adele's laxity in regard to warm-up and rehearsal was an endless cause of energy-sapping worry and irritation for Fred, although he conceded that she could get away with a certain carelessness, which he could ill afford: "She had style, and everything she did it was because Adele was doing it that made it work."[4] For him, punishing, repetitive practice was the only way to compensate for his perceived deficiencies and to cultivate what ability he knew he had. His capacity both for work and for self-censure became a defining trait and was engendered by his vaudeville training.

Ann's thrift and good management of their meager finances allowed the children to enjoy a decent annual vacation. They spent four summers between 1911 and 1914 at the Delaware Water Gap, then a fashionable resort, on the border of New Jersey and Pennsylvania. Sometimes dubbed nature's "Eighth Wonder of the World," the Delaware Water Gap was considered the second largest inland resort town in the United States in the years following the Civil War. It catered primarily to prosperous, middle-class city dwellers escaping the oppressive heat and humidity of New York for the resort's scenic beauty and cool mountain air. The Astaires stayed at one of the area's best hotels, Water Gap House on Sunset

Hill, built in 1872 and advertised in the *New York Times* as "A Mountain Paradise
... commanding views for thirty miles in every direction of the grandest scenery
east of the Rockies. . . . Now the Finest Equipped, Best Appointed, and Largest
Hotel in this Region, entertaining refined high-class patronage."[5] President
Theodore Roosevelt had stayed there during a motor tour of the Pocono
Mountains in August 1910. For Ann, it was important that the children mix
socially with the hotel's affluent clientele and aspire to the same sort of
refinement. She impressed on them that they belonged in Society.

Away from the tawdry treadmill of small-time vaudeville, Fred and Adele
swam and rode canoes on Lake Lenape, a reservoir at the base of Mount Minsi
that supplied water to the area's other large hotel, Kittatinny House.

It was at the Gap that Fred discovered two lifelong passions, horses and golf.
Water Gap House had its own stables, and nearby was the nine-hole Caldeno
Golf Course. One summer the Astaires' fellow guests included "America's
Sweetheart," Mary Pickford, and company, on location to film the George
Sand fantasy *Fanchon, the Cricket*, directed by James Kirkwood. The Astaires
watched some of the filming from the sidelines and met Pickford and her two
dangerously flighty younger siblings, Jack and Lottie, who had minor roles in

Figure 2.1 Adele and Fred on Lake Lenape, Delaware Water Gap.
Antoine Dutot Museum and Gallery

Figure 2.2 Adele, Ann, Fred, and Fritz at Delaware Water Gap, August 1913.
Adele Astaire Collection, Howard Gotlieb Archival Research Centre

the picture. Fred remembered Jack as "all over the place" but "a good ballroom dancer."[6] Jack Pickford would later marry the Astaires' future Broadway costar Marilyn Miller.

In August 1913, Fritz joined his family at Delaware Water Gap, and a momentous decision was made. It was clear that the children's career was languishing in the devitalizing void of small-time vaudeville and that "The Baseball Act" had run its dubious course. A radical solution was needed, which Fritz provided in the form of a new teacher, Aurelio Coccia, whom Fred would describe as "the most influential, as far as dancing goes, of any man in my career."[7]

Born in Rome in 1868, Coccia had come to the United States at the turn of the century, finding work as a dancer with the Barnum & Bailey Circus before entering vaudeville in 1907. He and his wife, Minnie Amato, founded a successful dance troupe that toured the country with "A Night in the Slums of Paris," an eighteen-minute pantomime. This act introduced American audiences to the brutal and languid apache dance, which had its origins in the violently seedy subculture of the Paris underworld of the Belle Époque. Street gangs of young dandified ruffians, known as les Apaches, haunted the eastern faubourgs of Paris and were identifiable by their workers' caps, red neckerchiefs, and tight, flared trousers. The apache dance was essentially a duet between a *pierreuse* (prostitute) and her pimp in which the man hurled the woman around the stage with savage panache. Coccia taught the dance to Gloria Swanson for the 1924 film *Humming Bird*, in which he briefly partnered her, and explained at the time:

> The apache dance is cruel, fierce, and wild. Many people believe that it has been exaggerated by dancers, but that is not so. One night in Paris, while making the rounds of the cafes in the Montmartre district in search of colour for my dance, I was fortunate enough to witness a little triangle drama between two apache men and a girl. One of the apaches, seeing the woman with his rival, picked up a bottle and smashed it to fragments on the floor. He deliberately cut his hand with a piece of glass, advanced to the defiant girl, seized her with his bloody hand, and began to dance to the strains of the notorious Mattischiche. It was a fascinating sight.[8]

This exponent of a dance of such eroticism and sadism, however stylized, may seem a strange choice of instructor for fourteen-year-old Fred and sixteen-year-old Adele, but Coccia was a great headliner and inspired showman with choreographic flair, who schooled the Astaires in a number of new dance styles and rhythms such as the Argentine tango and revolutionized their act. He agreed to see the children perform and, on recognizing their tremendous promise, to train them intensively for six months. The radicalism of his approach, however, initially met with horrified resistance from Fred and Adele. Fred had overhead Coccia say to Ann: "They'll have to forget what they know and start all over again." This had a devastating effect on the normally resilient pair, who, for the first time in their young lives, lost their passion for performance. It was only their mother's cajolery and remonstrance, and economic imperatives that convinced them to submit to Coccia's program of study. After a while, they began to appreciate that his methods were not as drastic as they had sounded and that his intention was to develop and refine their existing techniques rather than nullify everything they had learnt previously. But Coccia had not exaggerated how hard he expected them to work under his care.

At the same time as he was training them, he was compiling a more sophisticated and streamlined act for the Astaires, one that would transform them from a cute and clever kiddie act, who could sing a little, dance a little, and handle dialogue, into fully fledged specialty dancers. The result was an act of self-proclaimed freshness with an emphasis on dance and dance styles: "New Songs and Smart Dances." Coccia discarded the entire baseball dialogue, which he felt was too slow and somewhat stale, reconstructed the dances from "A Rainy Saturday," and added new ballroom routines set to new musical arrangements. To open the act, he dreamt up a dramatic crowd-pleaser, a little exchange that was quite literally arresting. Offstage and in blackout, Fred would call to Adele: "Stop! Stop! Don't you dare move; you're under arrest!" She would reply in song: "What have I done to you?" and Fred would continue: "Stop! Stop! I've got you covered. See that badge on my chest?" At which point the music to "Love Made Me a Wonderful Detective" would swell as Fred pulled Adele into the spotlight and they went into the first of a series of numbers, including a tap dance, an adagio, and one number with Adele singing to Fred's piano accompaniment.

The opening song was written by Ted Snyder of Watterson, Berlin & Snyder Inc., future composer of "The Sheik of Araby" and co-writer, with Bert Kalmar and Harry Ruby, of "Who's Sorry Now?" Snyder also gave the Astaires permission to use Irving Berlin's "I Love to Quarrel with You." The "New Songs" component of the act demanded an up-to-the-minute and constantly changing repertoire. In 1915, for instance, Fred and Adele incorporated the new fox-trot song by Gordon Strong, "The Charlie Chaplin Glide." From the age of fourteen, Fred assumed responsibility for the musical side of the partnership and became one of the throng of entertainers of the time who frequented the publishing houses of Tin Pan Alley in search of fresh material. Out of this early experience he developed an enviable capacity for recognizing and exploiting the best popular music. Two of the most successful selections he made in this youthful phase were from the world of musical comedy—Jerome Kern's "They Wouldn't Believe Me" (from *The Girl from Utah*), a song he sadly never recorded, and Cole Porter's "I've a Shooting Box in Scotland" (a tiny gem from the extremely fleeting *See America First*). The latter song Fred did resurrect on LP, sixty years later, with Bing Crosby, although this duet, recorded in London in 1975, does not include all of the delightful period lyrics of the 1916 first verse:

> Nowadays it's rather nobby
> To regard one's private hobby
> As the object of one's tenderest affections;
> Some excel at Alpine climbing
> Others have a turn for rhyming
> While a lot of people go in for collections.
> Such as prints by Hiroshigi,
> Edelweiss from off the Rigi,
> Jacobean soup tureens,
> Early types of limousines,
> Pipes constructed from a dry cob,
> Baseball hits by Mister Ty Cobb,
> Locks of Missus Browning's hair,

Photographs of Ina Claire,
First editions still uncut,
Daily pranks of Jeff and Mutt,
Della Robbia singing boys,
Signatures of Alfred Noyes,
Fancy Bantams,
Grecian vases,
Tropic beetles,
Irish laces,
But my favorite pastime
Is collecting country places.

Fred was to become famous for his screen collaborations with Berlin, Kern, and Porter, among others, and for introducing more standards than any other performer. He would also prove himself a capable tunesmith, never to reach anything like the Olympian heights of the composers who wrote for him, but good enough to have Johnny Mercer provide a lyric for one composition ("I'm Building Up to an Awful Letdown" in 1936), which made the hit parade, and to have Benny Goodman record another ("Just Like Taking Candy from a Baby" in 1940). In some ways songwriting was Fred's first love, a source of intense pride as well as regret.

One of the publishers Fred made the rounds of was the New York branch of the Detroit firm Jerome H. Remick & Co., whose catalogue included such best-selling (and rather lunar-centric) songs as "Shine on Harvest Moon" (1908), "By the Light of the Silvery Moon" (1909), "Oh, You Beautiful Doll" (1911), "Moonlight Bay" (1912), "When You Wore a Tulip" (1914), and a string of ragtime tunes. In the days before radio and widely available quality recordings, the frontline of music sheet sales was manned by the "song-pluggers," pianists employed by the publishing houses and music stores to demonstrate and "put over" a song. Occupying one of the fifteen piano cubicles in Remick's premises on West Forty-Sixth Street in 1914 was George Gershwin, who had left school at the age of fifteen and, having ably convinced Remick's office manager of his sight-reading and transposition skills, become, supposedly, New York's youngest song-plugger, earning $15 a week.

Gershwin's extraordinary rhythmical sense, his improvisational skill, and his affinity for rag and Harlem stride marked him as no ordinary plugger. He seemed even then to have the pulse of modern Manhattan in his veins and at his fingertips. Composer Vernon Duke gave this account of Gershwin's distinctive playing style:

To anyone who has not heard Gershwin play, his piano magic is hard to describe. His extraordinary left hand performed miracles in counter-rhythms, shrewd canonic devices, and unexpected harmonic shifts. The facility for abrupt yet felicitous modulations, the economy and logic of the voice-leading, and the all over sureness of touch were masterly in their inevitability.[9]

There was also a dance-like quality about his playing, very similar in essence to Fred's natural *eurythmia* (good time or proportion; gracefulness). "There was no exhibitionism or showmanship," observed composer and conductor Dimitri Tiomkin. "Rather, you were reminded of some blithesome person who seems to dance as he walks. It was musical magic."[10] Interestingly, choreographer Hermes Pan defined Fred's everyday walk as "a loose rhythmic saunter that looks as if it's, in a way, dancing. I remember Gershwin wrote music especially for that."[11]

The piano cubicle at Remick's may have been the "tinpantithesis" of Aeolian Hall or Carnegie Hall, where Gershwin later premiered his own concert pieces, but, like small-time vaudeville for the Astaires, it was a valuable training ground of sorts. "Every day at nine o'clock I was there at the piano," he said, "playing popular tunes for anybody who came along. Colored people used to come in and get me to play 'God Send You Back to Me' in seven keys. Chorus ladies used to breathe down my back. Some of the customers treated me like dirt. Others were charming. Among the latter was Fred Astaire."[12] Adding to George's disaffection was Remick's unwillingness to publish his own songs or let him play them to customers. The first of his compositions they did publish was "Rialto Ripples" in 1917, after he had been with them for three years.

Sharing fundamentally the same ambitions and frustrations, George and Fred struck up an immediate friendship and had a deep respect for one another's talents. George even admired Fred's self-taught jazz piano style: "I had a sort of knocked out slap left hand technique and the beat pleased him. He'd often stop me and say, 'Wait a minute, Freddie, do that one again.' In what sounds like a line of calculated prescience straight out of a Hollywood biopic, the young Gershwin remarked to Fred one day: "Wouldn't it be great if I could write a musical show and you could be in it?"

Aurelio Coccia was not the only important influence on Fred and Adele during this transitional stage of their development. There were also the husband-and-wife exhibition dancers Vernon and Irene Castle, possibly an even greater sensation than the Astaires became at their zenith.

Their dancing career was comparatively short-lived, but their impact socially and on the history of popular dance was profound. They destigmatized "close" dancing, freeing it from the charge of vulgarity and investing it with genuine elegance and respectability and a chaste romanticism far removed from the elemental nature of the apache dance. And like the Astaires in the 1920s and 1930s,

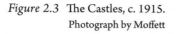

Figure 2.3 The Castles, c. 1915.
Photograph by Moffett

they personified a spirit of modernity. The cultural critic Gilbert Seldes made this appraisal of their "inspired rightness":

> That these two . . . determined the course dancing should take is incontestable. They were decisive characters, like Boileau in French poetry and Berlin in ragtime; for they understood, absorbed, and transformed everything known of dancing up to that time and out of it made something beautiful and new. Vernon Castle, it is possible, was the better dancer of the two; in addition to the beauty of his dancing he had inventiveness, he anticipated things of 1923 with his rigid body and his evolutions on his heel; but if he were the greater, his finest creation was Irene.
>
> No one else has ever given exactly that sense of being freely perfect, of moving without effort and without will, in more than accord, in absolute identity with music. There was always something unimpassioned, cool not cold, in her abandon; it was certainly the least sensual dancing in the world; the whole appeal was visual. It was as if the eye following her graceful motion across a stage was gratified by its own orbit, and found a sensuous pleasure in the ease of her line, in the disembodied lightness of her footfall, in the careless slope of her lovely shoulders. It was not—it seemed not to be—intelligent dancing; however trained, it was still intuitive. She danced from the shoulders

down, the straight scapular supports of her head were at the same time the balances on which her exquisitely poised body depended.

There were no steps, no tricks, no stunts. There was only dancing, and it was all that one ever dreamed of flight, with wings poised, and swooping gently down to rest.[13]

Vernon Castle was born William Vernon Blythe in Norwich, England, in 1887 and Irene Foote in Fort Worth, Texas, six years later. They met in 1910 when Vernon was appearing at the Broadway Theatre in *The Summer Widowers*, produced by Lew Fields and directed by the Astaires' then mentor Ned Wayburn. Vernon was regarded as an eccentric dancer and comic actor at that time, with a special line in gentleman drunks. Very late in the show's run, Irene gained a replacement bit part, sharing a dressing room with nine-year-old Helen Hayes. She joined Vernon again the following year in *The Hen Pecks*, and at the end of the show's first season they were married. When Vernon was offered a role in a revue in Paris, he made his acceptance conditional on Irene's inclusion. *Enfin . . . une Revue* was not a huge success, but the Castles had one vigorous dance routine, to the tune of Berlin's "Alexander's Ragtime Band," that won critical plaudits and attracted the notice of Louis Barraya, the proprietor of the Café de Paris, who hired them as a specialty dance act. The Castles became the rage of Parisian high society, performing such American dance crazes as the turkey trot, grizzly bear, and Texas Tommy. They were tipped liberally by the Café's wealthy patrons and invited to dance at private gatherings. At a magnificent supper party at London's Ritz in July 1912, given by Anthony J. Drexel in honor of a Russian grand duke, they shared the floor with Nijinsky and Karsavina.

Back in New York, their rise was meteoric. They danced nightly at the Café de l'Opera, and they appeared in vaudeville, with their own twelve-piece band, and in two Broadway shows, one of which, *Watch Your Step*, featured Irving Berlin's first complete score. Adele recalled that she and Fred had seen the Castles in *Little Girl, Little Girl*; by this she must have meant *The Sunshine Girl* at the Knickerbocker Theatre in 1913, which included the number "Little Girl, Mind How Your Go." In late 1913, the couple opened Castle House on East Forty-Sixth Street, a combined club and select dancing school. The following year saw the opening of the dance palace Castles by the Sea at Coney Island's Luna Park and two nightspots in their name at the Forty-Fourth Street Theatre, the rooftop Castles in the Air and the basement Castle Club.

Vernon was a natural choreographer. Their most famous dance, however—the Castle Walk—was created more or less impromptu at a late-night birthday party for actress Elsie Janis. This dance was a variation on the one-step; as Irene explained, "Instead of coming down on the beat as everybody else did, we went up. The result was a step almost like a skip, peculiar-looking I'm sure, but exhilarating and fun to do." This idiosyncratic routine was as celebrated in the pre-war era as the Astaires' run-around was in the 1920s. The Castles were shrewdly marketed by their socially well-connected agent Elisabeth Marbury, and their role as trendsetters extended well beyond their graceful ballroom moves. Irene's tastefully spare dress designs, lightly corseted figure, and what became known as the Castle Bob (a hairstyle described by one newspaper columnist as "a cross between an ancient Greek runner and a child's bob") were fashion innovations copied by millions of women.

Fred said that he and Adele idolized the Castles but did not seek to imitate them, being concerned to find their own distinctive style: "They were ballroom dancers, but we were more specialty dancers. Our own personality came through in some way that was considered unique. But they were inspiring to us, in just the same way as people come to me now and tell me that they were inspired by something we did."[14] Adele was more forthright and effusive about the extent to which, as youngsters, they consciously patterned their emergent style on the Castles:

> They were our ideals. We tried to do the Castle Walk and all those things. We tried to ape them a lot. Oh we thought they were wonderful. . . . Her clothes were made by Lucile. She had beautiful clothes. Naturally I tried to copy everything she had at my tender age. . . . They were so smooth and they were both tall and thin and lithe. Fred and I just went goo-goo over them. When they were really tops in New York, society flocked around them like bees to honey.[15]

Vernon Castle, who had enlisted in the Royal Flying Corps in 1916, was killed in 1918 when his plane crashed during a training flight at a military airfield near Irene's birthplace, Fort Worth. In 1921 Fred staged some dances for Irene's return to the vaudeville stage at B. F. Keith's Theatre in Boston, and in 1939 he and Ginger Rogers, in their final RKO film together, portrayed the Castles in *The Story of Vernon and Irene Castle*, with Irene Castle listed as "technical adviser."

In the three or four years that witnessed a nation-wide mania for the Castles, Fred and Adele were criss-crossing the country with their "New Songs and Smart Dances," making a slow but steady assault on the peaks of vaudeville. Along the way, they appeared on bills with some of the biggest names in the business, learning from the wings and gaining in confidence and status from small triumphs of their own. Early in the life of the new act, at the Opera House in Davenport, Iowa, they shared a bill of three acts with thirty-six-year-old Bill "Bojangles" Robinson, the first solo black performer in "white" vaudeville.[16] Fred said of

Robinson: "The great Bill interested me, not only for his incomparable dancing but for his good nature and likable personality—in addition to his ability as a pool player. He often watched our act. His first words to me were 'Boy, you can dance!' That meant a lot to me. We discussed dancing and compared steps."[17] What distinguished Robinson's dancing was the clarity and crispness of his taps and the fact that in contrast to the flat-footed buck-and-wing style, he danced on the balls of his feet while keeping the rhythm swinging and giving "lightness and effervescence, a symmetry of phrasing, and a knowing delight to his audiences."[18] Fred later paid tribute to Robinson on screen in "Bojangles of Harlem" (*Swing Time*, 1936).[19] The number is, however, something of a dual tribute, in that Fred is dressed in the style of the character Sportin' Life, whom John W. Bubbles (the stage name of "rhythm tap" pioneer John William Sublett)[20] played the year before in Gershwin's *Porgy and* Bess. Fred's percussive heel-drops in this number also clearly owe more to the younger Bubbles than to Bojangles.

In Chicago in November 1914, the Astaires experienced a highlight of their vaudeville career when they played the Palace Theatre. It was a big-time engagement with a strong bill, and the stars were felicitously aligned: they had a fine conductor, who knew instinctively what they required, and an obliging stage manager, who allowed Fred to sprinkle his beloved rosin on the stage to prepare the floor for sure-footed dancing. One handicap remained—they had the dreaded opening spot, but there would be a newsreel to precede their act and settle the audience, so they felt they had a fighting chance. They stopped the show at their first performance and received six long curtain calls. For the evening performance they were moved up the bill to number three, just ahead of Eddie Cantor and Lila Lee.

Unfortunately, the Astaires never played the Palace in New York, the ultimate destination for the big-time aspirant ("to play the Palace" meant simply to have made it to the top). But from then on, although occasionally they reverted to opening status, the Astaires gradually took their place in the middle and higher orders of the bill and scored bookings in other major cities. In December that year, they were called in as a replacement act at the Orpheum Theatre in New Orleans, where they were given the solid number five spot and earned $350 a week, their highest salary yet. Next month, in Flatbush, New York, they were again number five in a bill headlined by Sophie Tucker.

As the act improved and their fortunes increased, some things remained outside Fred and Adele's control, and they found themselves caught up in wider events. By now, Europe was at war, and while this had little impact on the daily lives of most Americans, it involved the Astaire family in a slightly surreal incident. When the *Lusitania* was sunk by a German U-boat on 7 May 1915, sparking fierce anti-German sentiment and precipitating America's entry into the war, the Astaires were performing in Canada. Their next booking was at the New Brighton Theatre in New York, but as they crossed the border to return to the United States they were woken at four o'clock in the morning and had their luggage seized and detained by the War Department. At some point, Fritz had given Ann postcard photographs from his brother Ernst for safekeeping. Ernst was, of course, serving in the Austrian army, which made him a German ally. Someone on the train had overheard the Astaires discussing the postcards and reported them to the authorities. Eventually the seizing officials satisfied themselves that the two young vaudevillians were not German spies and the Astaires were allowed to proceed, but the temporary confiscation of their trunks, containing their costumes, cost them the Brighton engagement (though they did appear there two months later).

The other, more costly, event in which the Astaires became embroiled was the White Rats' strike of 1916. The White Rats were a trade union that began in 1900 with eight men, led by George Fuller Golden, who modeled themselves on the British Water Rats, a benevolent society of music-hall actors who had helped Golden when he was out of work in London. Later, headliners like George M. Cohan, Eddie Foy, and Weber and Fields joined their ranks. The Rats' principal aim was to protect vaudeville performers from unfair treatment by the Association of Vaudeville Managers, a monopolistic syndicate that kept wages low and determined where actors could work. The Astaires were not members of the White Rats, but the strike of 1916, which started spontaneously in Oklahoma City, spread nationally and affected nearly everyone in the business; performers faced being either blacklisted by management or labeled traitors by their more militant colleagues. The strike left the Astaires stranded in Detroit without work, train fare back to New York, or—at one critical stage—sufficient food. Nor was Fritz in a position to support them. Nebraska's vocal temperance movement had for years wanted a total ban on alcohol. Finally in 1916, voters approved a statewide prohibition amendment, putting Fritz and many other brewery employees out of a job. When their money ran out, Fred tried unsuccessfully to sell one of his songs to Remick's, while Ann pawned her diamond engagement ring and a fur coat to put food on the table. Actors around the country were in similarly dire straits, and the strike collapsed within months.

With the resumption of work began the Astaires' most successful season in vaudeville, and their last. During their week at Shea's Theatre in Buffalo, in June 1917, Fred took out a full-page ad in *Variety*, headed "Fred and Adele Astaire: Here's the Proof!!" The page displayed a central photo of the pair surrounded by their clippings from Seattle to New Orleans. Words such as "sprightly," "youthful," and "fresh" figure repeatedly in these notices. Adele predictably receives the lion's share of praise, with the *Denver Times* insisting "there is no more bewitching miss in vaudeville."

Figure 2.4 Adele, 1916.
Adele Astaire Collection, Howard Gotlieb
Archival Research Centre

Fred, in his autobiography, quotes other reviews from Boston and Washington, which emphasize his role as an adjunct to his sister's superior talent, but in fact the critics were taking note of his individual qualities too. In September 1916, *Variety* declared: "That boy alone is like a streak of artistic lightning on his feet."

At the bottom of Fred's full-page ad was printed the question "What has the East in store for them?" A great deal, as it happened. The week after the ad appeared, the Astaires played Detroit's Temple Theatre and there, on 28 June, 1917, received a telegram from producer Charles Dillingham: "Will be glad to see your act when you play New York which I understand is week after next." It would be more than two years before they were featured in a Dillingham show, for the very same week Fred and Adele received another life-changing telegram—from Rufus LeMaire, a prominent theatrical agent and later casting director for MGM, who offered them a contract for a musical show to be produced by Lee and J. J. Shubert. The Astaires' vaudeville days were over. They were now Broadway bound.

Appropriately, perhaps, Fred and Adele were to make their Broadway debut on the site of Castles in the Air, which had now been converted into a conventional playhouse, christened the Forty-Fourth Street Roof Theatre and intended to rival Ziegfeld's famed Roof Garden above the New Amsterdam Theatre. The show that was to launch the new space, an escapist extravaganza, was also intended to surpass Ziegfeld for sheer beauty and novelty. The novelty was announced in the original title *The Nine O'Clock Revue*. It was hoped that the later curtain time would lure a more fashionable crowd who would enjoy dining before the show in the theatre's basement restaurant. The beauty was to be chiefly supplied by former Ziegfeld girl (and Alviene alumna) Justine Johnstone, around whose purely ornamental talents the show was constructed. Johnstone had made her Broadway debut in *Watch Your Step*, with Vernon and Irene Castle, and had been featured in two editions of the *Follies*. Her acting and musical abilities were limited to say the least—she had rarely been required to do more than strike ravishing, statuesque poses onstage—but, in an all-too-familiar Broadway scenario, she had won the ardent attention of Lee Shubert, who expressed his admiration by creating for her a starring vehicle, unperturbed by, or blind to, her shortcomings as a performer.[21] Fortunately there was genuine talent on hand, drawn partly from the ranks of vaudeville, as in the case of the Astaires.

Ned Wayburn had tried to interest the Shuberts in the Astaires as far back as 1908, but the moguls had little use for a child act, and the Gerry Society would have made it impossible for Fred and Adele to appear in a Broadway musical at that age. The Astaires were paid a standard salary of $250, but they were shocked by some of the conditions stipulated in their first Broadway contract. They were guaranteed only twenty weeks of work during a theatrical season. They would not be paid during the rehearsal period, nor for a rehearsal called after the show had opened. The management reserved the right to lay off performers during Holy Week, the week before Christmas, and the week before a presidential election, and if the show were to be performed on any of those dates, the cast would receive only half of their normal salary. Moreover, any performer under contract to the Shuberts was expected to take part, on request and without compensation, in the popular Sunday Night Concerts staged by the Shuberts at the Winter Garden Theatre. As Adele put it, "Everybody was 'invited' to come and do a stunt on Sunday night." These concerts may not have been lucrative for the performers involved, but they were nevertheless a valuable experience for Broadway novices like the Astaires, who would be seen alongside such stars as Al Jolson.

The Astaires were given three dance numbers in the show (one in the first act and two in the second) and were to perform in various comedy skits as well. The revue comprised twelve tableaux. With the United States now in the war, it was renamed *Over the Top* and included a spectacular visual recreation of American aircraft attacking a German trench. Fred and Adele's duets, to the music of Sigmund Romberg, were of a less extravagant and jingoistic nature and were, in running order, "The Gown Dance," "Where is the Language to Tell?," and "The Justine Johnstone Rag."

According to Fred, the lengthy rehearsal period was characterized by confusion and indecision, culminating in a hectic out-of-town first night at the Shubert

Theatre in New Haven, where the show's raggedness was indulged by a raucous audience consisting mainly of Yale undergraduates. The New York opening on 28 November 1917 met with mixed reviews, but most critics singled out the Astaires as a rare highlight in an otherwise mediocre entertainment, with the honors divided almost evenly between brother and sister. Louis Sherwin of the *New York Globe* wrote: "One of the prettiest features of the show is the dancing of the two Astaires. The girl, a light, spritelike little creature, has really an exquisite floating style in her caperings, while the young man combines eccentric agility with humor."

From the critics' descriptions of their dancing, it emerges that what was unusual and captivating about the Astaires was their eccentric variations on ballroom steps, their ability seamlessly to combine consummate grace and rhythmic movement with "something novel in the way of grotesquerie."[22] It is apparent, too, that the Astaires impressed the critics not merely with their Terpsichorean style and uncanny agility but equally so with their personalities, particularly their air of youthful wholesomeness and their infectious delight in what they were doing. In those early days, the critics did not always spell the Astaires' names correctly (e.g. "Ted and Adele," "The Alstaires"), but they liked what they saw of this young dancing couple.

Against expectations, the chic nine o'clock starting time had a negative effect on the box office, and after a few weeks the Shuberts decided to raise the curtain at the more traditional time of 8.30. One of the principals, comedian T. Roy Barnes, became quickly disenchanted with the show after its lackluster critical reception and asked to be released from his contract. He was replaced by Ed Wynn, whose inventive and zany comedy style lifted the show out of the doldrums. *Over the Top* had a modest run of seventy-eight performances at the Forty-Fourth Street Roof, but the post-Broadway tour, under the title *Oh, Justine!*, fared better.

At the Garrick Theatre in Washington, D.C., Charles Dillingham finally had a chance to see the Astaires and discerned in them something special, the makings of true Broadway stars. He visited them backstage after the show and told them he wanted to produce a show for them. Inhibiting Fred and Adele's joy at this announcement was the fact that they were under contract to the Shuberts for a further season. Dillingham was prepared to wait and to top any salary offer made by the Shuberts, who were themselves anxious to retain the Astaires' services and to capitalize on their growing star power. As they were happily to discover, Dillingham was a very different impresario from the Shuberts or any of his other rivals. Adele described him as a gentleman and "a very intellectual and classy manager."

In June 1918, the Astaires began rehearsals for their second Shubert production, which opened at the Winter Garden Theatre on 25 July. This was the latest edition in an established series of revues known as *The Passing Shows*, the Shuberts' answer to the *Follies*. It also marked the Broadway debut of silent film star Nita Naldi, who was among a chorus of "Alluring Vampire Girls." Frank Fay and Charles Ruggles were the comedy stars, Sigmund Romberg again wrote the music, and Fred and Adele had several numbers, together and apart. Adele was given an opening solo, backed by "a Bouquet of Winter Garden Steppers," with a song that perfectly captured her irrepressible personality, "I Really Can't Make My Feet Behave."

Fred had a dance number with Sam White and Lou Clayton in a scene in the second act set in Child's Restaurant at Fifty-Ninth Street. The three of them, dressed as waiters, slid up and down the long tables serving pancakes and coffee, a lively routine to "Trombone Jazz" that proved an audience favorite. Fred and Adele's first duet in the second act was a number they both loathed intensely, inanely titled "Twit, Twit, Twit." Much to their embarrassment, they were forced to flit about the stage in feathered costumes, as Miss Robin and Chanticleer, surrounded by a flock of Dancing Birds.

Animals were a recurring theme in the show and not always in performance. The stage director, J. C. Huffman, had a short temper and a caustic tongue. He believed screeching and bellowing at his cast, and sometimes belittling them, were the most effective means of getting his point across. During the dress rehearsal in Atlantic City, Fred and Adele were doing their tango specialty, which

Figure 2.5 Costume sketch by Cora MacGeachy for Adele performing in 'I Really Can't Make My Feet Behave' from *The Passing Show of 1918*.
The Shubert Archive

they had performed countless times in vaudeville. At one point Fred became aware of a problem with the spotlight and stopped the orchestra, provoking, as he says, "a volcanic eruption from J. C.," who proceeded to berate him for his impudence. Adele, who maintained that she was the fighter in the partnership, stepped forward. "You don't understand, Mr. Huffman," she protested. "We've been doing this dance for years. My brother and I know exactly how it should look. Why, this dance is almost sacred to us." After a painfully protracted silence, Huffman, summoning all his acerbity, hollered: "Alright, young lady. May we now go ahead with the Dance of the Sacred Cow?"[23]

The Astaires could at least feel vindicated by a second sweep of glowing notices trained on their contributions. And for once, Fred was possibly more the focus of attention than Adele. For example:

> In an evening in which there was an abundance of good dancing, Fred Astaire stood out. He and his partner, Adele Astaire, made the show pause early in the evening with a beautiful loose-limbed dance. It seemed as if the two young persons had been poured into the dance.
> —*New York Times*, 26 July 1918

> Fred Astaire . . . is a master dancer, a rattling eccentric comedian and in his biggest scenes was assisted by a dancing girl, Adele Astaire.
> —*Chicago Daily News*, 14 May 1919

But battles had still to be fought with management. At the end of the New York run of 125 performances, which coincided with the end of the war, the Astaires agreed to accept half salary for a time since ticket sales were suffering as a result of the Spanish influenza pandemic. Yet when business improved in the course of the post-Broadway tour, their salaries remained at half the normal rate. Fred sent the following letter to J. J. Shubert from Boston on 12 December 1918.[24]

> Dear Mr. Shubert,
>   In view of the fact that you asked us to alter our contract by accepting half during the last few weeks in New York on acct. of the Influenza epidemic, we ask you now that business here is big, to *please* see that we receive our full salary on Xmas week to partly make up for our losses.
>   Can assure you this will be greatly appreciated, especially at Xmas time.
>
>   Respectfully and confidentially yours,
>   Fred and Adele Astaire

Two days later he received this implacable response:

> Dear Sir & Madame,
>
> I am in receipt of your favor of the 12th inst. I am very sorry but I cannot make fish out of one and fowl of another regarding the Christmas week. I would rather make it up in some other way, but I cannot make any exception to this rule. I trust you will appreciate my position in this matter.
>
> Yours very truly,
> JJS.[25]

The brothers' ruthlessness gained them power and prestige but little personal popularity.

One of the Astaires' last acts while under contract to the Shuberts was to entertain the soldiers at Fort Sheridan, Illinois, presenting, along with the rest of the company, abridged versions of their numbers from the show. On 12 September 1918, the last of three national draft registrations was held for men aged eighteen to forty-five. This included Fred, who was now nineteen years and four months old. His registration card identified the Shuberts as his employers and the Winter Garden as his place of employment. He was classified A1 for active service, but the war ended before he was called for duty. In June 1919, the Astaires' contract with Shuberts ended. Despite the brothers' efforts to renew it, the way was now clear for Fred and Adele's new alliance with Dillingham.

3

Dancing Comedians

It's the Whichness of the Whatness and the Whereness of the Who
That explains most everything to us
And you must admit the whole thing is ridiculously simple
As well as simp-l-y ridiculous. Ah, ha, ha, ha, ha!
Don't forget it, or remember to forget that you forgot
It will save you lots of trouble if you do
So get this in your head and you will have it in a nutshell
It's the Whichness of the Whatness and the Whereness of the Who!
—William Daly, Paul Lannin, and Arthur Jackson, "The Whichness of the Whatness"

"Charles Dillingham took a loving interest in us personally," said Adele.[1] The fifty-one-year-old impresario lavished an unusual amount of time and care on the Astaires, considering their relatively minor and non-speaking status in their first Dillingham musical. It was not simply that he believed they were "going places" and was eager both to nurture and exploit their star potential. Dillingham took a genuine delight in their youthful company, treating them almost as his own children, although sometimes flirtatiously and occasionally with a lover's wounded sensibility. Fred and Adele remembered him as a debonair Father Christmas—bald, plump, and jovial, with a hearty laugh, but tall and stylish in dress. In manner he was not unlike their father, Fritz, with an easy charm and ready wit, teasing and confidential, a princely practical joker. Typical of Dillingham's humor is a story included in *Bartlett's Book of Anecdotes*. He and his great rival, Florenz Ziegfeld, were among the pallbearers at Houdini's funeral in 1926. As the casket was hoisted, Dillingham whispered across to Ziegfeld: "Ziggy, I bet you a hundred bucks he ain't in here!" At the Astaires' first meeting in Dillingham's office above the Globe Theatre, which he built in 1910, "C. B." was full of playfulness and amiable banter, putting on a "show" for them in effect—a display of intimate, egalitarian bonhomie and imperial largesse—before sending them off in his Rolls-Royce with the instruction to take it any place they pleased: "Just tell the chauffeur that Mr. Ziegfeld says it's o.k."[2]

The son of an Episcopalian minister, Charles Bancroft Dillingham had literary ambitions. He served on newspapers in his native Hartford and in Chicago
before being made drama critic for the *New York Evening Post*. In 1896, he wrote
and produced *Ten P.M.*, a play that, although it failed, brought him to the attention of Charles Frohman, New York's leading theatrical manager, who hired him
as a press agent and production assistant. Two years later he became tour manager for Shakespearean actress Julia Marlowe, and by 1902 he had begun producing plays in his own right with *The Cavalier* at the Criterion Theatre. Apart
from building his own theatre at Broadway and Forty-Sixth Street, named in
honor of Shakespeare's "Wooden O" and with the innovation of a retractable
roof, from 1915 to 1922 Dillingham managed the Hippodrome, a temple of
spectacle and reputedly the world's largest theatre. There, in 1916, he introduced
mass American audiences to Anna Pavlova and her partner Alexandre Volinine,
the Bolshoi Ballet's premier danseur, in *The Big Show*. In 1906, he made history
by installing Broadway's first moving illuminated sign in front of the
Knickerbocker Theatre, a revolving red windmill powered and lit by electricity
to advertise Victor Herbert's operetta *The Red Mill*. Dillingham would produce
more than 200 shows in his lifetime, including notable straight plays as well as
musicals. In 1905, he presented the American premiere of George Bernard
Shaw's *Man and Superman*, and he later imported Clemence Dane's *Bill of
Divorcement* (1921) and the drawing-room comedies of Frederick Lonsdale,
among them *Aren't We All?* and *The Last of Mrs. Cheyney* (both in 1925).[3]
It was Dillingham who in 1914 staged Irving Berlin's first complete Broadway
score and "The First All-Syncopated Musical," *Watch Your Step*, featuring the
dancing of the Castles. He produced nine musicals by Victor Herbert and nine
by Jerome Kern.

In Adele's eyes, Charles Dillingham was a more "exclusive" producer than
Ziegfeld, but not purely in theatrical terms. As she saw it, he was personally a
more refined character and socially better connected. Among his intimate friends
were Elsie de Wolfe, Averell Harriman, the Astors, and the Vanderbilts, and
under his paternal auspices Fred and Adele were introduced to high society.
Dillingham enjoyed showing off his two protégés at parties, where, as a novelty,
they danced for his aristocratic friends and taught them some of their steps.

As well as glittering New York parties, Dillingham would take the Astaires to
Atlantic City, to the Traymore Hotel or the Ritz, where, as Adele recalled, "he'd
just sit for the weekend with us and we'd look out over the sea and he'd say,
'Do you see that bird sitting on the beach?' He wanted to show us how good his
eyesight was. I'd say, 'Yes,' and he'd say, 'Well, I see it, too.' He never had children.
I think he really loved our company."[4] Whenever Fred and Adele were away from
New York, on vacation or on tour, Dillingham wrote to them regularly, and at
Christmas he presented them with extravagant gifts. When the Astaires met

him, he was married to the young actress Eileen Kearney, his second wife, but he had been Charles Frohman's devoted and inseparable companion until Frohman's death aboard the torpedoed *Lusitania*.[5] The two men had at one time shared living quarters and jointly owned a country retreat, maintaining, as Kim Marra defines it, "a Damon and Pythias friendship."[6]

Ann Astaire actively encouraged her children's close friendship with Dillingham, especially as it afforded them contact with a gracious way of life she felt was rightfully theirs. She also continued to ensure, within the family's means, that they vacationed in fashionable watering spots where Fred and Adele could relax and, equally important, mix with the "right" sort of people. Before rehearsals for *Apple Blossoms*, their first contracted show for Dillingham, began in August 1919, the Astaires spent several weeks at Galen Hall in Wernersville, Pennsylvania, a first-class hotel and sanitarium. Here they encountered a slightly younger pair of siblings, the offspring of a once wealthy Philadelphia Main Line family, who became their lifelong friends and who, like Dillingham, represented an entry into a more exalted social stratum. James and Mary Elizabeth Altemus were the children of Lemuel Coffin Altemus, a textile entrepreneur, and the former "Bessie" Dobson, who became president of the Pennsylvania Council of Republican Women. Their parents divorced in 1911, three years after their father was declared bankrupt, so that Bessie Altemus, in common with Ann Astaire, was effectively a single mother, used to genteel poverty and the need to keep up appearances. The Altemus and Astaire children had much in common, too. Temperamentally, thirteen-year-old "Liz" was more like Fred, mature and well-behaved, while "Jimmy" had Adele's devil-may-care love of adventure and mischief. It was from the Altemus children that Fred and Adele gained a greater sense of social prerogative and confidence.

Apple Blossoms was a calculated gamble on Dillingham's part. He believed audiences and critics would welcome a return to the graceful world of operetta as an antidote to ragtime's freneticism and "ragged" rhythms—"Relief from the jazz of Broadway musical comedies."[7] The book, by future film producer William LeBaron, was based on *Un Mariage Sous Louis XV* by Alexandre Dumas (père) and the score was provided by Fritz Kreisler, the most distinguished violin virtuoso of the day, and Victor Jacobi, the Hungarian composer of *Szibill*.

The settings were by the Viennese architect and designer Joseph Urban, who had been influenced by the Vienna Secessionists and the New Stagecraft, a movement that he helped establish in America; it was inspired by the designs and theoretical writings of Edward Gordon Craig (Urban's exact contemporary), Adolphe Appia, and Max Reinhardt.[8] Known for his bold and dramatic use of color and light, Urban had designed more than fifty productions for theatres and opera houses in Vienna and throughout Europe, including the Opéra de Paris. He first came to America to create the Austrian Pavilion at the 1904 World's Fair in St. Louis; he went on to become art director of the Boston Opera Company, to design productions for the Metropolitan Opera in New York and the Ziegfeld Follies, and to design the Ziegfeld Theatre, whose auditorium was encircled by "the world's largest oil painting," an immense and densely textured mural painted by Lillian Gaertner under Urban's direction and evincing the influence of Gustav Klimt.[9]

Like the production itself, the Vienna-born Kreisler was something of a calculated gamble owing to his brief period in the Austrian army in 1914. He had made his American debut at Steinway Hall in New York in 1888, at age thirteen, and in the same year undertaken his first tour of the United States. A subsequent series of American tours in 1901–3 brought him wide acclaim. In London in 1910, he premiered Edward Elgar's Violin Concerto, which Kreisler had commissioned and which Elgar, whom he considered the greatest living composer, had dedicated to him. At the outbreak of war, Kreisler was drafted into the Austrian army as a lieutenant; his service in the trenches on the Russian Front lasted a matter of weeks before he was wounded and honorably discharged, whereupon he returned to the United States to resume his concert career. But when America entered the war in 1917, Kreisler and his music became targets of fierce anti-German sentiment, forcing his gradual withdrawal from public life.

Kreisler deplored the crude nationalism that now branded Austro-German art Hunnish and alien. Years later he said:

> I believe that humanity lived more gracefully, more abundantly, and more deeply appreciative of what the arts meant for human uplift, during the period before 1914 than it could during and after the ravages of two world cataclysms. It has filled me with pride and joy that, while science, alas, has been mainly diverted during my lifetime to purposes of destruction, art, and especially the art of music, has been a healing factor, a powerful stimulus to overcoming national animosities, a harbinger of peace and international brotherhood.[10]

His work on *Apple Blossoms* played a healing, indeed salvational role in his career, coming as it did in the midst of his musical exile. The show's New York opening on 7 October 1919 preceded his first reappearance on the American concert platform by nearly three weeks and marked the beginning of his rehabilitation.[11] In the audience on that opening night, and showing their support of Kreisler, were Sergei Rachmaninoff, violinists Mischa Elman and Jascha Heifetz, and Walter Damrosch, conductor of the New York Symphony (who would commission Gershwin's Concerto in F and *An American in Paris*).

Fred and Adele could boast the unique distinction of counting among their rehearsal pianists, in the same rehearsal period, Kreisler himself and George

Gershwin. They had only two dances in the show, one in the prologue, the other in the second act. The first was an entirely new number performed to Jacobi's work "On the Banks of the Bronx" inside the ivied walls of Urban's garden setting for Castle Hall School.

The second, set in a ballroom, was their familiar tango routine, which, since their altercation with J. C. Huffman in *The Passing Show*, they referred to as the "Sacred Cow" dance. For this, Kreisler suggested they use his bravura concert piece "Tambourin Chinois," which he composed around 1905. It had an Oriental ambience, popular at the turn of the century, but with a middle section more reminiscent of Vienna. As the Astaires carefully plotted the dance to fit the music, Kreisler insisted on playing for them from the orchestra pit. On another day, when the regular rehearsal pianist was unavailable, George Gershwin lent his services. Fred, in his autobiography, says George was at the time still working at Remick's, but Gershwin had resigned from his job as a song-plugger in March 1917 and had his first complete book musical up and running: *La-La-Lucille!*, then playing at the Criterion. (The young co-producer of this show, Alex A. Aarons, was soon to become a crucial figure in the Astaires' lives.) Gershwin was also just months away from having his song "Swanee" recorded by Al Jolson for Columbia Records, after which, he said, "Swanee" penetrated the four corners of the earth."[12]

Not all their experiences in rehearsal were as pleasant. Fred G. Latham, an Englishman, was a director who, like Huffman, trusted in the efficacy of

Figure 3.1 Garden setting by Joseph Urban for the Prologue of *Apple Blossoms*, 1919.
Joseph Urban Papers, Rare Book and Manuscript Library, Columbia University

bellowing at and belittling his cast. Early on in rehearsals, and in front of the whole company, he had exploded at Fred for being a minute late for a full run-through. Fred lost his temper and yelled back twice as loudly. Latham was apoplectic with fury, and it took Dillingham's intervention to defuse the situation. Fred was gently commanded to apologize. With a menacingly seraphic smile, Latham said to him: "My dear boy, you don't have to apologize. I'll be bawling you out enough between now and when the show opens that you'll get rather used to it. But I warn you now, don't ever raise your voice to me again." Sixty-six-year-old Latham was not accustomed to having his directorial authority violently questioned and certainly not by a callow youth such as Fred. In London, before the Astaires were born, he had managed Drury Lane Theatre and the Adelphi, and in 1900 had come to America as tour manager for Sarah Bernhardt and Coquelin. Fred's display of temper also astounded his sister, since ordinarily Adele was the fighter of the family, the one who could be relied on to protest and answer back.

Apple Blossoms was greeted most warmly by the first-night audiences in Baltimore and New York, but a touch less so by the critics who felt the show was charming if unexceptional—save in one respect. The Astaires were consistently singled out for the highest praise; their two divertissements were thought to have overshadowed the singing and acting of the "real" stars, John Charles Thomas and Wilda Bennett—a critical scenario that would repeat itself over the next few years. As Fred phrased it: "We killed 'em in the first act and 'panicked 'em' in the third."[13]

> In all frankness we must admit that to us, the most stirring event was the dancing of the Astaires. [It] is remarkable . . . [and they] had more fire and abandon than their associates.
> —Heywood Broun, *New York Tribune*

> Fred Astaire and his pretty sister, Adele, danced as though they were twins and scored the biggest hit they've ever made.
> —Charles Darnton, *Evening World*

The post-Broadway tour, on which they embarked in the autumn of 1920, brought Fred and Adele more such accolades:

> The loudest and longest applause of the evening went to the Astaires— Fred, and his sister, Molly [*sic*]—whose dancing furnished the most exciting moments of the evening. Theirs is the kind you never grow weary of—it's too refreshing.
> —*Boston Record*

Two brilliant dance artistes feature in the production. They are Fred
and Adele Astaire, joyous sprites of Terpsichore, both of them. Their
dancing was graceful, vivid and original, and they received many
recalls.

—*Toledo Blade*

On one leg of the tour, the Astaires themselves were upstaged, but not from
within the ranks of *Apple Blossoms*. Between 11 and 13 October 1920, they made
their final appearance in their hometown, Omaha, at the Brandeis Theatre, a
beautiful Art Nouveau playhouse. It should have been a triumphant occasion for
them, but it coincided with Enrico Caruso's appearance at the City Auditorium,
as part of his last tour. Caruso received the largest audience ever assembled in
Omaha for a musical event, and consequently all the press attention the city
could muster. Only one local reviewer—writing for the *Omaha World-Herald*—
cited the Astaires: "Next to the star [John Charles Thomas], those of the cast to
evoke the heaviest applause were the dancers Adele and Fred Astaire, who began
their stage career in this city."

The first two rows of the Brandeis Theatre were filled with Ann's relatives, but
there was one family member who had seen the show in New York—Fritz
Austerlitz. With their own financial security assured in the short term (they were
being paid $550 a week by Dillingham), Fred and Adele were anxious for their
father to share in their success and to see his children fulfill his dreams for them.
They believed that with superior employment opportunities in New York, Fritz
could re-establish himself in the East and be more than an occasional visitor in
their lives. Ill health, failing fortunes, and a strong sense of pride made Fritz
reluctant to join his family at their expense, but he finally acquiesced. He rejoiced
in the show's Viennese associations and in his children's performances, but he
did not remain long in New York. In what could have been his father's epitaph,
Fred succinctly explained: "He attempted several business ventures but nothing
much materialized."[14] Deeply aware of his failures, personal and professional,
Fritz could not bear to stay and be provided for by his children.

The next Dillingham production to which the Astaires were assigned was *The
Love Letter*, a second operetta intended to repeat the formula and commercial
success of *Apple Blossoms*. To that end, many of the main contributors to *Apple
Blossoms* were reassembled: Edward Royce was director, Victor Jacobi composer,
William LeBaron librettist and lyricist, Joseph Urban designer, and John Charles
Thomas star. Fred and Adele were given more responsibilities, with three dances,
one in each act. But *The Love Letter*, although it had the same essential creative
ingredients, was a flop when it opened at the Globe on 4 October 1921, with a
run of just thirty-one performances. The book was adapted from Hungarian
dramatist Ferenc Molnár's play *The Phantom Rival*, which David Belasco had

successfully staged at his New York theatre in 1914. As a musical vehicle, however, it proved cumbersome, and the comedy was weak.

Short-lived though it was, *The Love Letter* had far-reaching and positive consequences for the Astaires, not least as the genesis of the "run-around," a novelty routine that became their signature exit step and an astonishing crowd-pleaser. Fred said: "It was like striking oil—that little stunt handed to us by Teddy Royce."[15] The concept was simple but ingenious: shoulder to shoulder, Fred and Adele would jog, or rather lope, around the stage in a widening circle, with their arms extended as though they were grasping the handlebars of a bicycle—all the while looking purposeful in their imaginary journey and accompanied by an incessant 'oom-pah, oom-pah' beat. As the music quickened, so would the pace of their revolutions. They would sustain several circuits before exiting into the wings. Royce conceived the idea as the finish to a "nut" dance, a dance both intricate and absurd, which would devolve naturally into the loping strides of the run-around. He asked Jacobi and LeBaron to compose a suitably nonsensical number and they came up with "Upside Down," the first of many nutty numbers over the years to give rise to this "circuitous" hilarity.

That Royce should have devised such an inspired piece of pantomime is not surprising in view of his British music-hall heritage. A small, slender, dapper man who was himself an accomplished dancer, he was born in Bath, the son of E. W. "Teddy" Royce, "first low comedian, ballet master, and principal dancer" at the Glasgow Colosseum and, in the 1870s and 1880s, member of the famed burlesque quartet at London's Gaiety Theatre, which also comprised Nellie Farren, Kate Vaughan, and Edward Terry. Royce Jr. originally trained as a scenic artist and then as a dancer, but he was soon staging productions at the Savoy, the Aldwych, and Daly's Theatre. Of his directorial work on Edward German's comic opera *Merrie England* at the Savoy in 1902, the *Observer* described him as "Mr . Edward Royce, jun. (the clever son of Teddy Royce, the old Gaiety favourite), who by his excellent arrangement of the dances and stage grouping in *Merrie England* established himself as one of the most able and inventive 'producers' of the day."[16] The first Broadway show Royce choreographed was *The Doll Girl*, produced by Charles Frohman at the Globe in 1913.

Another happy consequence of the unhappy *Love Letter* was Fred and Adele's introduction to Noël Coward. Coward saw the show in the last weeks of his first visit to New York. He was accompanied by the young classical pianist Lester Donahue and wrote afterward: "I hadn't realized before that such rhythm and taste in dancing were possible."[17] Coward had been in the States for five months, chancing his arm as a playwright, infiltrating New York society, making friends such as Alfred Lunt and Lynn Fontanne, writing one play (*Sirocco*), and finding inspiration in the family of Laurette Taylor and J. Hartley Manners for another (*Hay Fever*).[18] He was insistent that the Astaires in turn should chance their arms in London: "You two will be a tremendous success there—you must come as soon as possible."

The opportunity to go to London was nearer than Fred and Adele could have imagined, but for the moment they were in the throes of a flop; their only consolation was that, once again, they personally had triumphed, albeit to the ill-concealed displeasure of John Charles Thomas.

> The Astaires . . . made the high score of the evening, getting four encores for their entertaining singing and "nutty" dancing to "Upside Down," and revealing in this and other whirlwind numbers that they have developed a penetrating comedy touch with their lips as well as their always ambitious feet.
>
> —*New York Herald*

> They completely stopped the show after the star had made an entrance, and Mr. Thomas, evidently not relishing this, walked off the stage without so much as looking at them. A specimen of theatrical bad manners.
>
> —*Billboard*

> Their rendition of "Upside Down" was so appreciated that they stopped the show and left Mr. Thomas and Miss [Carolyn] Thomson stranded in the middle of the stage rather embarrassed, while they returned to take still another bow.
>
> —*New York Times*

The third seminal event during the fleeting life of *The Love Letter* was Fred's chance encounter with Alex A. Aarons, the thirty-year-old producer of *La-La-Lucille!* The two men met in Finchley's men's store, where Aarons, a part owner of the shop, was waiting on Fred. Aarons professed himself an admirer of the Astaires and voiced his opinion that they should be doing a more contemporary, intimate, and manifestly American musical comedy like Jerome Kern's *Oh, Boy!* of 1917.[19] Fred thought his advice presumptuous, if unexpectedly shrewd, until Aarons revealed his identity as a novice impresario and the son of composer-producer Alfred E. Aarons, who was general manager for theatrical magnates Klaw and Erlanger.[20] Before Fred left the store, Aarons asked what his and Adele's future commitments were and whether they would consider doing a show for him. As bait he dangled the possibility of a score by George Gershwin.

Fred and Adele's immediate commitments were to Charles Dillingham. There was still the post-Broadway tour of *The Love Letter* to do, after which they were contracted to Dillingham for one more show. *The Love Letter* was moderately well received on the road, but it was an expensive production to transport and barely broke even. After an engagement at the Tremont Theatre in Boston and shortly before Christmas, the rest of the tour was canceled. Just as the company was given two weeks' notice, Aarons cabled Fred: "MY FATHER SAYS LOVE LETTER CLOSING. ARE YOU AVAILABLE PLEASE WIRE." He now had a specific project in mind for the Astaires. Dillingham, on the other hand, did not. The tour's premature end meant he did not have another show ready for them to rehearse.

Fred decided to approach Dillingham in a businesslike manner about Aarons's proposition and ask that he and Adele be temporarily released from their contractual obligation to him. In *Steps in Time*, he typically glosses over the gravity of the interview and the pain it caused Dillingham, making the producer's compliance with his request sound rather more cordial and forgiving than it was. Fred's formality of manner had hurt Dillingham as much as his consideration of the offer from Aarons, but as Dillingham had no work for the Astaires in the short term, he reluctantly agreed to lend them out, with the proviso that their program credit read "Fred and Adele Astaire appear by arrangement with Charles Dillingham."

There was but the briefest interval between the closing of *The Love Letter* in Boston and rehearsals for *For Goodness Sake*, as the new Aarons production was titled. For the first time in their Broadway career, Fred and Adele were given substantial speaking parts; their characters, Teddy Lawrence and Suzanne Hayden, formed a romantic subplot within the story. Hopes of the show being a bona fide Gershwin musical did not materialize, as Gershwin was under contract to George White for the *Scandals* of 1922. The featured composers were William Daly and Paul Lannin, both of whom were primarily conductors and orchestrators —Daly had been musical director on *Apple Blossoms* and *The Love Letter*. The lyricist was Arthur Jackson. Gershwin, however, did supply three "additional" numbers, while his older brother Ira, writing under the pseudonym Arthur Francis (which he concocted from the names of his youngest brother and sister), contributed lyrics to five songs. "All to Myself" was the first song written by the Gershwins that the Astaires performed. Fred and Adele also sang Ira's lyrics in "Oh, Gee! Oh, Gosh!," but their biggest hit was with an entirely non-Gershwin tune, the show's dedicated "nut" number "The Whichness of the Whatness," which ended of course in the run-around.

Fred called *For Goodness Sake* "probably the most potent hop forward in our careers up to that point,"[21] but it was also important in terms of his individual development. The dance director, Allan Foster, who had worked on a number of the Shuberts' *Passing Shows* (though not that of 1918), invited Fred's choreographic input, which Latham and Royce had not been inclined to do. From then on, Fred would exercise greater artistic control over his and Adele's dances, while the dance director assumed more of an editorial or advisory role. Fred would choreograph only his and Adele's routines, never those of the chorus. He was, his sister affirmed, instinctively creative, and "he knew what looked right and what looked wrong."

The other principals in the cast were John E. Hazzard, Marjorie Gateson, Charles Judels, Virginia O'Brien, and Vinton Freedley, who was soon to quit the stage and enter into partnership with Alex Aarons. "Freedley," Adele said, "was a rich man and a thwarted actor. He wanted to be an actor but never quite made it, so he became a manager. But you know, what always amazes me is that in those days—in *our* days anyway—all our money came from Wall Street backers. We never had to have auditions. I never had an audition in my life, neither did Fred. They wanted us, they knew what we could do, and that was it."[22]

When *For Goodness Sake* had its first try-outs in New Haven, Dillingham wired Fred to say he had heard it was a great show, adding at the end of his telegram, "It better be!" He was there when it opened at the Lyric Theatre, New York, on 20 February 1922. And someone else was in the audience that night whose presence they valued even more highly: an ailing and delighted Fritz, who had now moved to New York. As before, Fred and Adele stole the show, but this time it was a hit show:

> The two Astaires are the principal assets of *For Goodness Sake*. They speak a little, act a little, and dance quarts. They are as nice a twain as one could wish to see. They pirouette through the mazes of this musical comedy with energy, yet restraint, and the dances they exhibit are always clever and artistic.
>
> —*New York Morning American*

> As they amble into view and mix with the youngsters they don't look as though they were anything more than somebody's children. But when they dance—oh, boy, and likewise girl! With ease, grace, rhythm, charm and humor, youth becomes a wonderful thing, and you realize all this in watching the Astaires.
>
> —*Evening World*

> Somewhere, sometimes, perhaps there may have been a more charming juvenile team than Fred and Adele, but certainly not in the memory of anyone in the audience that filled the Lyric Theatre.
>
> —*Evening Sun*

During these years, 1919–22, the Astaires' dance style emerged more distinctively and was recognized as distinctively theirs by the critics. Although they were originally hired by Dillingham in a specialty capacity, they quickly established themselves not as a specialty dance act but as dancing comedians. In addition to their agility (one reviewer in St. Louis hailed Fred as "a marvel of gutta-percha suppleness") and technical virtuosity, what set them apart from their peers and gave their style substance and distinction was their combination of eccentricity and gracefulness, as well as the articulacy of their movements. The critic for Philadelphia's *Sunday Ledger* mused: "But those Astaires! Why is it that they, who really have nothing essential to do with the unfolding of the romantic story, should have their little singing and dancing duets stand out as the acting part of *The Love Letter* that probably will linger longest in the memory?" And Alexander Woollcott characterized Fred as "one of those extraordinary persons whose senses of rhythm and humor have been all mixed up, whose very muscles of which he seems to have an extra supply are downright facetious."[23] The Astaires appeared to transcend the thin fabric of the story lines in which their duets were interpolated and to weave more compelling and amusing narratives in dance by virtue of their silent eloquence and somatic timing.

Words like "nutty" and "whirlwind" were commonly applied to their eccentric convolutions and the glorious, climactic silliness of the run-around. Although there is no footage and little recorded detail of their choreographed routines, we know their steps were often intricate but executed with a sprite-like rapidity and ease. The *New York Herald* described them in *The Love Letter* as dancing about "like fireflies" and looking as though they had been taken "from the quaint cartoons of Maxfield Parrish," while the *Philadelphia Inquirer* likened them to a pair of "ragtime pixies: impish, imaginative, young, wholly captivating."

Adele was the more obvious and winning clown, but Fred was developing comedic instincts of his own, particularly as a pantomimic comedian. One perceptive critic, writing in New York's *Illustrated Daily News* in 1919, observed of his performance in *Apple Blossoms*: "The boy Astaire looks like Wallace Reid and dances as Charles Chaplin might if he only could," thus identifying in Fred an idiosyncratic comedy style tinged with pathos, a certain subtlety and poetry to his physical humor, even at its most slapstick, and the surfacing of an alternative heroism that was endearing, even desirable. In fact, twenty-year-old Fred did not resemble Wallace Reid, a tall, athletically built matinée idol who would have been perfect casting for Jay Gatsby. But the critic's imaginative mergence of "the screen's most perfect lover" and the Little Tramp, in describing Fred, pinpointed a duality in the Astaire persona that was central to his enduring popularity—his appeal as a romantic urchin, best summarized in James Agate's later depiction of Fred as "this waif with the sad eyes and twinkling feet."[24]

These qualities were further delineated, some years later, by English author Graham Greene, with reference to another iconic cinematic hero. In his *Spectator* review of the 1936 film *Follow the Fleet*, Greene pronounced Fred, with his "quick physical wit," "the nearest approach we are ever likely to have to a human Mickey Mouse. . . . If one needs to assign qualities to this light, quick, humorous cartoon, they are the same as the early Mickey's: a touch of pathos, the sense of a courageous and impromptu intelligence, a capacity for getting into awkward situations."

The thing that truly distinguished the Astaires as dancers and as a unified stage presence was sheer likeability, and an almost tangible sense of delight in what they were doing. It is said that the Shinto goddess Ame-no-uzume-no-mikoto danced on an upturned tub to the merriment of the other gods and in order to induce the Sun from her hiding place. She became patron deity of professional actors and dancers who, like her, "lighten the hearts of men, comfort them in distress, and make the sun shine again."[25] Following then in an ancient and sacred tradition, what Fred and Adele seemed immediately and spontaneously to convey was an infectious sunniness and a conviction that all was right with the world. "When they dance," Robert Benchley exclaimed, "everything seems brighter."[26] *And* they were engagingly, touchingly young.

It was also during these years that Adele, who had been considered the more radiantly gifted half of the Astaire partnership from their earliest days in vaudeville, came fully into her own as a stage personality. It is no mean analytical or imaginative feat for the theatre historian to try to encapsulate that personality or to distil from a rare mix of qualities the quintessence of Adele's powerful fascination. She was possessed of neither outstanding physical beauty (Cecil Beaton wrote in his diary that she looked like "Felix, the Cat with her large amusing head on a minute exquisite little body") nor an especially good singing voice (her "cooey soprano," as Arlene Croce styled it, which, like the evocatively shrill tones of Binnie Hale, Beatrice Lillie, and Gertrude Lawrence, was very much of its era).[27] But her looks and voice were just the baser metals she alchemized into gold. We know from contemporary reviews and other first-hand testimony that she was a sublimely natural dancer and a born clown, but in the immoderate paeans written about her star quality—onstage and in life—what the modern reader senses, vicariously yet vividly, is not Adele's Terpsichorean talent or comic genius but rather her magnetism, an energy and irresistibility memorialized by various revered men of letters as little short of a fifth force of nature.

What was the key to her extraordinary appeal? It was not one dominant attribute but the anarchic coexistence, in one petite, sweetly brazen figure, of a seeming mass of bewitching, opalescent contradictions. Underlying the irruptive element of danger and incorrigible gaiety with which she imbued her performances was a fundamental vulnerability. She was, to quote Beaton again, "a delightfully brittle puppet," but one who emanated warmth across the footlights, who captured hearts by enabling each member of her audience to experience something in the nature of a personalized and joyful benediction. When she danced she created the effect of "a lilac flame."[28] When she was not dancing she was seldom still, her pert features and quicksilver form lit by an interior flame of inextinguishable mirth: "Miss Astaire is the freedom of youth and grace personified, an airy bubble of personality from her agile toes to her wildly tossing curls" (*Boston Advertiser*).

She did not fit any current mold of showgirl or musical star. In contrast to the formalized, idealized loveliness of the Ziegfeld Girl, for instance, Adele was boyishly pretty and lithe, exuding both a *gaminerie* and grotesquerie. Yet she had a singular facility to be clownish and eccentric and, at the same time, seductive, as was noted of her antics in *The Love Letter*.

> Adele is a real comedian and made every bit of her fun in a legitimate way. One couldn't help laughing over the comic play of her features— it was a delight—and her smile was delicious.
>
> Miss Astaire, in particular, has a range of facial expressions and a gaminerie which are captivating.
>
> —*Boston Transcript*

It was undoubtedly this artless fusion of oddity and allure that within a year or two would captivate writers like Bernard Shaw, J. M. Barrie, and P. G. Wodehouse and, closer to home, moved two of the theatre's most trenchant critics to cast off their sophisticated armor and declare exuberantly their tender devotion to this dancing sprite.

One of these lettered and unlikely swains was the hard-drinking, banjo-playing satirist Ashton Stevens, on whom the character of Jedediah Leland in *Citizen Kane* is supposedly based. The brother of actor Landers Stevens and uncle of director George Stevens (both of whom worked with Fred on the 1936 RKO film *Swing Time*),[29] he was known as the "dean of American drama critics." The two principal papers he wrote for were the *San Francisco Examiner* and later the *Chicago Herald-American*, both owned by William Randolph Hearst. When Sarah Bernhardt visited San Francisco a month after the 1906 earthquake and gave a benefit performance of Racine's *Phèdre* at the open-air Hearst Greek Theatre in Berkeley, it was Ashton Stevens, together with photographer Arnold Genthe, who escorted her through the ruins.

In the *Chicago Herald-Examiner* on 18 June 1922, accompanied by a large sketch of Adele, a full-page article appeared under the heading "Falling in Love with Adele Astaire. In Which It Is Told How the Well-Known Heart of Ashton

Stevens Is Stricken by the Deftest of the Dancing Girls." Stevens, then in his fiftieth year, proclaimed:

> You haven't any idea of Miss Astaire's comic importance to this universe of ours unless you have seen the last act of *For Goodness Sake*. . . . It is here that the pliant body of Miss Astaire takes on rigidity and angles; she assumes a slanting partial paralysis which slays boredom where it sits. . . . And you haven't any idea of Miss Astaire's human importance to this universe of ours unless she has taken you by the hand and played with you and given you things and brought out your latent youth.

The other prominent critic who declared himself in thrall to Adele and made extravagant claims for her comic and "cosmic" importance was the brilliant, iconoclastic, unsentimental George Jean Nathan, the man who in 1930 demolished the play *Tonight or Never* with a one-sentence review ("Very well, then, I say 'Never'"), whose celebrated acerbity inspired the character of Addison De Witt in *All About Eve* and who passionately promoted the dramas of Sean O'Casey and Eugene O'Neill. Fourteen years Adele's senior, Nathan began reviewing professionally in 1906, the year the Astaires properly entered vaudeville. In 1914, he and H. L. Mencken became co-editors of the monthly literary magazine the *Smart Set*, which they fashioned into a mature, fearless, and unsolemn forum for new and established writing talent, helping to introduce readers to the work of Dorothy Parker, Aldous Huxley, James Joyce, Ezra Pound, and Ben Hecht, to name a handful of their contributors. Ten years later, with their mutual publisher, Alfred A. Knopf, they founded the *American Mercury* as "a serious review—the gaudiest and damnedest ever seen in the Republic."[30] In speaking of the collaborative success of their differing temperaments and of their shared ethos concerning the *Smart Set*, Mencken wrote:

> We differ radically in many ways. For example, Nathan is greatly amused by the theatre, even when it is bad, whereas I regard it as a bore, even when it is good. Contrariwise, I am much interested in politics, whereas Nathan scarcely knows who is Vice-President of the United States. But on certain fundamentals we are thoroughly agreed and it is on the plane of these fundamentals that we conduct the *Smart Set*, and try to interest a small minority of Americans. Both of us are against the sentimental, the obvious, the trite, the maudlin. Both of us are opposed to all such ideas as come from the mob, and are polluted by its stupidity: Puritanism, Prohibition, Comstockery, evangelical Christianity, tin-pot patriotism, the whole sham of democracy. Both of us, though against socialism and in favor of capitalism, believe that capitalism in the United

States is ignorant, disreputable and degraded, and that its heroes are bounders. Both of us believe in the dignity of the fine arts, and regard Beethoven and Brahms as far greater men than Wilson and Harding. Both of us stand aloof from the childish nationalism that now afflicts the world, and regard all of its chief spokesmen, in all countries, as scoundrels.[31]

That a self-avowed elitist and skeptic like Nathan, a boulevardier critic with an enthusiasm for Strindberg and Ibsen, should expend so much of his critical energy in extolling the wonder of Adele Astaire may seem curious. But he was not merely a highbrow who despised popular entertainment. Nor did he arbitrarily distinguish between high and low art. What he detested and fought against was sham and cheap sentiment. A clue to his most deeply held dramatic principles is found in inscriptions written to him by his friend and mutual disciple Sean O'Casey, in copies of O'Casey's books that he gave to Nathan:

To George Jean Nathan, Poet-Critic & Champion of the truth as it is in the Drama, from Sean O'Casey, his comrade in the fight that Drama may have life and have it more abundantly.
— New York, 1934 (*Windfalls*)

From Sean O'Casey to George Jean Nathan, comrade in arms for righteousness, deep sorrow, the loud, reckless laugh, the stirring dance, and the gay song in the theatre; the voice of man speaking his best, in good round terms, finding lovliness [*sic*] in the murk of a dark night, or the sunniness of a fine, fair day.
— Devon 1945 (*Drums under the Windows*)

In her own way Adele was a purveyor of theatrical truth and vitality, the very things Nathan valued above all. In her absurdity, unpredictability, bold irreverence, unconventional beauty, ability to be moving without being mawkish, and intuitive understanding that the "reckless laugh, the stirring dance, and the gay song" are a serious and necessary business, Nathan had discovered the epitome of drama and was prepared to risk a charge of philistinism to say so:

I enjoy Miss Adele Astaire's dancing very much more than Mr. George Bernard Shaw's *Back to Methuselah*. If the purpose of theater is to entertain, then I say that the Astaire girl entertains twice as greatly as Shaw's play. If the purpose of theater is to instruct, surely Shaw's play has nothing especially new or profound to tell us, so he and Miss Astaire are even-Steven on that count. If the purpose of theater is to give us beauty, it would surely take an expert comedian to find as much in Shaw's play as in the Astaire dancing flapper. . . .

Although Miss Astaire dances herself half to death before the music show, *For Goodness Sake*, is half over, the impression is quite the opposite. Here is a girl with the grace of Irene Castle, the humor of Ann Pennington, the charm of Marilyn Miller and the variety of Dorothy Dickson rolled into one. She is at once nimble and funny, easy to look at and pleasantly impudent. She is no beauty; she makes up her eyes with a pint or two of shoe blacking; she has little color-sense in the selection of costumes. But in her is all the "theater" that *Back to Methuselah* lacks. . . . A swirl of skirts . . . the lightning of a pair of electric little legs . . . the rain of a 1000 dancing slippers. . . . And all without a touch of the droopy-eyed, sentimental humbug or set grin or undulating arms of the conventional dancing girl. In the midst of a dance as rhythmical as the waves in Havana harbor, the Astaire jocosely lifts a thumb to her small pug nose and wiggles her fingers at the orchestra leader. In the midst of a waltz as graceful as a waving willow tree, she seizes the fraction of moment to wind her right foot back of her and to imbed its toe in the seat of her partner's trousers. A droll clown, an extraordinarily engaging dancer, an exceptionally interesting music show figure.

Figure 3.2 Adele in satirical mode.
Adele Astaire Collection, Howard Gotlieb
Archival Research Centre

Thus, stroking my whiskers, I sum up. I would rather see Adele Astaire dance once than see Part I of *Back to Methuselah*. I would rather see her dance twice than see Part II of *Back to Methuselah*. I would rather see her dance three times than see Parts I, II and III of *Back to Methuselah*, with the Theater Guild's free *entr'acte* coffee thrown in. If this be ignorance, make the most of it.[32]

Nathan's ardent interest in Adele was not expressed wholly in print. He eventually arranged to meet her after a performance and was soon squiring her around town. Adele was flattered by the gallantry of this worldly and influential intellectual, in whom she acquired a mentor and surrogate father as much as an admirer:

I had a need for someone with sophistication. I appreciated it. I also loved having someone I could talk to and learn from. I learned a lot from George. Also from his friend Mencken, whom I got to meet. I loved him. He was so darling and comical in a cynical way which just fascinated me.

We had an eight-month romance. My mother hated him. She'd read one of his books where he wrote that he wished all girls were orphans. Mama never got over that. And she was furious when I went to Europe and he followed me.[33]

Fred, too, distrusted Nathan, and Nathan did little to endear himself to Fred or to Ann by making Adele the cynosure of his critical regard. In his review of *The Bunch and Judy*, he wrote as an afterthought: "The agreeable young person [Adele] has a brother, Mons. Fred, who serves as her partner and who is himself a fellow of no mean foot. He is, in point of fact, similarly an excellent dancer. But men dancers do not especially interest me. A dance without skirts is to me not a dance."[34]

In 1926, Nathan dedicated his book *The House of Satan* to Adele with a strange, vaguely hieroglyphic inscription. When they were together in the Swiss mountains, Adele had written with a stick in the snow the words "I love you." A sudden beam of sunshine had caused the snow to melt and the letters to run together. Nathan made a design of the distorted inscription and had the printer insert it as his book's dedication. Ultimately, however, Ann and Fred were right to distrust Nathan. Although his chief asset as a suitor was that he was "all subtle attention,"[35] he divided his attention between multiple women. Having offered various excuses for broken appointments, Nathan told Adele that the French ambassador to Washington, the poet-dramatist Paul Claudel, was in town and he must meet with him. Adele found out subsequently that the French ambassador was Lillian Gish.

The New York summer heat affected business at the Lyric, and *For Goodness Sake* went on the road to Chicago. In August 1922, Dillingham invited Fred and Adele to Atlantic City to discuss his new venture, but Fred, hoping that Aarons would be able to arrange a London production of *For Goodness Sake*, delayed his reply. In the interim, Dillingham adopted Fred's earlier businesslike approach and sent him the following letter: "In accordance with our contract of 27 May, 1921, I am giving you formal notice that I shall exercise my option on your services for the season 1922–1923. You will be required for rehearsals some time in August."

The Astaires' success with Aarons compelled Dillingham to star them in his new show, *The Bunch and Judy*, but to Fred and Adele's disappointment they were not to enjoy outright star billing or to be the only brother-and-sister act. Their co-star was to be "Dutch" dialect comedian Joseph Cawthorn, but when he fell down a fire escape and broke his kneecap the day before the show was due to open at the Forrest Theatre in Philadelphia, he was replaced by vaudeville head-liner Johnny Dooley, whose sister Ray was already in the company.

The story, by Anne Caldwell and Hugh Ford, concerns a musical-comedy star, Judy Jordan (Adele), who abandons her stage career to marry a Scottish lord, thus foreshadowing events in Adele's own life. The score was by Jerome Kern and included, as the now obligatory nut number, "How Do You Do, Katinka?" Fred Latham again directed with Edward Royce arranging the dances.

Despite being their first starring vehicle, the show was in many ways a step backward for the Astaires. With Latham and Royce in charge, Fred reverted to a choreographically subordinate role. Adding to his discontent, and symbolic of his feelings of creative constraint, was the fact that in a number called "Pale Venetian Moon," part of an operetta (a show within a show) staged in the first act, he was forced to wear a powdered wig, which he loathed, while the song itself was too high for him. Another dance caused more than sartorial discomfort. Fred and Adele had at one point to dance atop a baronial banqueting table held aloft by a dozen members of the chorus. The table was long and narrow and difficult for its bearers to lift at an even angle so as to avoid tipping its human cargo overboard, which happened countless times in rehearsal. It happened in the midst of a disastrous dress rehearsal; as they lay bruised and sprawling on the stage, Adele looked at her brother and remarked wryly: "This is a hell of a way to become a star."[36]

By the time the show opened in New York on 28 November 1922, everyone involved seemed to know they had a flop on their hands. The critics were surprisingly lenient, although most were agreed that its offerings were desultory and uninspired. Even Kern's music was unusually mediocre: "[The score is] out of Mr. Kern's own well-beaten paths . . . on occasion quite grandiose, again sparkling and lilting, but rarely are there heard any of those wistful strains characteristic heretofore of this gifted composer" (*New York Ledger*). The most favorable notice Fred and Adele received would not have convinced them of their arrival as stars, since the reviewer, Heywood Broun, misspelled their name: "The Alstairs are distinctly attractive even when they are not in motion, and once they begin to dance they are among the immortals" (*New York World*).

Fred says *The Bunch and Judy*, or *The Bust and Judy*, as it was forever known to the Astaires, lasted exactly three and a half weeks in New York. In fact it ran for sixty-three performances at the Globe, closing on 20 January 1923. A short tour followed. With the show's failure came the disintegration of the Astaires' relationship with Charles Dillingham. Fred in particular saw their future more with Aarons. While the show was on the road in Boston, Dillingham sent a poignant letter to Adele, indicative of his hurt but no less of his lingering affection, and echoing a song from the show—the "Have You Forgotten Me?" Blues in the second act:

> You and Fred ought to have come up to my house. You know I could not get out of bed ... what I lacked was a little company ... I wish you would write and tell me how things are getting along in Boston ... I suppose you forgot me before you got to New Haven ... I am happy to know that you have a little remorse for not coming in to see me before I was sick ... You could have come in and cheered me up—still, I forgive you and if it is all the same to you, I wish we could get married Easter Sunday. [37]

His efforts at the old banter notwithstanding, Dillingham did not exercise his option on the Astaires' services for the following season, thereby releasing them from their contract. Both parties could see the writing on the wall.

Alex Aarons meanwhile had been in Europe trying to negotiate a deal to take *For Goodness Sake* to London. He was under pressure to succeed, as Fred was seriously considering an offer from Albert de Courville for him and Adele to appear in a revue at the London Hippodrome. De Courville had been responsible for the first American-style revue in London, *Hullo, Ragtime!*, in 1912, and an early champion of syncopated music in England. On 12 February 1923, Aarons wrote to Fred:

> I really think that I can do more for you in London than anybody because I understand your work better than managers who have not seen you and I know better what to give you. Also I believe you are better off with me as I can devote all my attention to you (theatrically). You will be one (or two) of the mob in a revue.

In the end, Aarons finalized a deal with Sir Alfred Butt, the newly elected Conservative MP for Balham and Tooting, who had been director of rationing at the Ministry for Food during the war and who presided over a mini-empire of West End theatres. The terms of the contract were three first-class passages aboard the *Aquitania* for the Astaires and their mother, $1,000 a week, and a minimum eight-week guarantee. The show would be renamed *Stop Flirting*. It was the start of something big—if London's critics were to be believed, of biblical proportions.

CHAPTER 4

Nightingales in Berkeley Square

Let me tell you there are a lot of features
Of the dance that carry you through
The gates of Heaven.
—George and Ira Gershwin, "Stairway to Paradise"

The premiere of *Stop Flirting* at the Shaftesbury Theatre on 30 May 1923 signaled the beginning of London's long love affair with Fred and Adele and of a true transatlantic wonder. In a notable departure from its usual phlegmatic style, *The Times* proclaimed: "Columbus may have danced with joy at discovering America, but how he would have cavorted had he also discovered Fred and Adele Astaire!" Sydney Carroll, writing in *The Sunday Times*, was equally rapturous in his appreciation of the pair: "They typify the primal spirit of animal delight that could not restrain itself . . . the vitality that burst its bonds in the Garden of Eden."[1] Two months later, *Dancing World* enquired of its readers: "Have you seen Fred and Adele Astaire in *Stop Flirting*? Nothing like them since the Flood."[2] Throughout the rest of the 1920s the Astaires were not only leading exponents but also pioneering exporters of one of America's few indigenous art forms. In fact, that most concentrated and glorious decade of their partnership was divided more or less equally between Broadway and London's West End, and it was London that truly made stars of the Astaires.

In the weeks and months leading up to Fred and Adele's London debut, the fledgling BBC made its first broadcast (excerpts from *The Magic Flute* from Covent Garden); Howard Carter unsealed the burial chamber of Tutankhamen; Jack Hobbs scored his hundredth first-class century (against Somerset in Bath); Stanley Baldwin became prime minister; the Duke of York married Lady Elizabeth Bowes-Lyon at Westminster Abbey; and Paris and the world mourned the death of the great Sarah Bernhardt. In the theatre, the first West End production of a play by Eugene O'Neill, the Pulitzer Prize–winning *Anna Christie*, opened at the Strand, and Jack Buchanan was starring in *Battling Butler* at the Adelphi, which was to be the Astaires' first experience of a West End show.

Fred and Adele, together with their mother, arrived in London in the first week of April to begin a five-week rehearsal period. The family settled at the Savoy Hotel (later they leased a flat at 41 Park Lane), with only a brief respite for sightseeing. Very soon Fred and Adele were meeting their producer, Sir Alfred Butt, their director, Felix Edwardes, and the English cast.

Apart from the change of title, significant alterations were made to the imported show in an effort to Anglicize it. Fred Jackson adapted the book, modifying instances of peculiarly "American" dialogue and transposing the action to Bourne Lodge, near Maidenhead. George Gershwin augmented the original score, contributing, in addition to his existing two numbers ("All to Myself" and "Someone"), a new opening chorus, "(I'll Build a) Stairway to Paradise," from *George White's Scandals* of 1922, and two songs from his first Broadway score *La-La-Lucille!* (1919)—"The Best of Everything" and "It's Great to Be in Love."

The new and improved version received its British premiere at Liverpool's Royal Court Theatre on 30 April in the presence of the Astaires' friend and guide Noël Coward. With the exception of a fierce and unforgiving raked stage, which threatened to pitch the dancers over the footlights and into the orchestra pit, Liverpool presented a smooth beginning; the Astaires and company gave an excellent performance to a vociferously receptive audience. They repeated their success at the King's Theatre in Glasgow and the Lyceum in Edinburgh. Their pre-London success did nothing, of course, to allay Fred's habitual fretfulness in anticipation of the West End opening. On the evening of 26 May, he wrote to his father:

> Well pop, we are still all nervous about the opening and can't wait until it has passed.
>
> In front of the theatre, over the entrance there is a great big sign with just our pictures enlarged to <u>three times life size</u> (cut out figures) and also another with just our names and it looks marvellous, but it scares us half to death. I will take pictures of this and send them to you.
>
> Every day some different newspaper man comes to interview us and this makes us all the more nervous. . . .
>
> Oh! if it can only be a big hit and we can do all that they expect of us.[3]

Fred's fears were not entirely unfounded. London did not offer the smooth passage Liverpool had, and its first-night audience proved far more inscrutable, reacting to the first act courteously and with restrained approbation.

However, things changed dramatically in the second act. When the Astaires performed "Oh, Gee! Oh, Gosh!," the house erupted in a thunderous ovation, demanding encore after encore. By the time they executed their signature run-around at the conclusion of the nutty "The Whichness of the Whatness," they had on their hands a palpable hit. At the curtain call, even Adele was rendered speechless by the audience's frenzied response; finally and famously, she managed to stammer out a charmingly ludicrous invitation to tea. The critics, who as always focused chiefly on Adele, were unanimous in their delighted discovery not only of a unique kind of dancing but also of unique personalities.

The Astaires' friendly conquest of London took place on several fronts. To begin with, they spearheaded the American "invasion" of West End musical theatre and were enthusiastically received by the occupied population, including the theatrical fraternity, as John Gielgud's recollected impressions of the young invaders confirms:

> They burst on London with a tremendous success. They were very young and very, very graceful, and Adele was a kind of clown, the sister—rather on the Beatrice Lillie kind of lines; and they used to dance and clown about, and together they made the most enchanting comedy team. At the same time they had about them a sweetness and youth that was extraordinarily appealing. I think they were considered as the sort of young "arrivals" of the season, and we always had a wonderful welcome for people like the Lunts and the Astaires and any great foreign star that came over here. It sort of perked up the whole season as it was then in England.[4]

The hospitality of English actors, who regularly gave parties, and the fanaticism of English audiences were unlike anything the Astaires had known in America. At the stage door each night, between twenty and thirty people would be waiting to greet them and bestow little gifts and mascots on them. Many of these faithful followers the Astaires knew by name. The sense of ceremony that accompanied a night at the theatre was, according to Adele, another novelty for the Americans:

> Nobody ever came to the theatre unless they were in dinner jacket. And on Saturday nights we had all the Irish Guards in full dress tails.... They believed in seeing a show more than once. They came four and five times. And here you'd see the first row was all the Fitzgeralds... and they were so elegant . . . so enthusiastic. It was really a joy to work in England because people really made a fuss of you in those days.

From that time, Fred had a particular method of determining the lifespan of a London show: the moment he caught sight of black ties in place of white ties in the stalls, he knew "the handwriting was on the wall."

The Astaires were not the first American performers to appear in London in an imported Broadway musical; that distinction would seem to belong to Dan Daly, Edna May, and Harry Davenport, the stars of *The Belle of New York*, which transferred to the Shaftesbury Theatre in 1898 and ran for a formidable 697 performances. They were, however, the first of a new wave of musical stars imported from America in the 1920s with whom their British equivalents found it virtually impossible to compete in ability and dynamism. They served as ambassadors of "the American musical itself, in its most confident, thoroughly nativized form."[5] In his history of musical comedy on the West End stage from 1890 to 1939, Len Platt credits the Astaires with establishing "new standards of professionalism and technical expertise" and helping "to secure the crucial identification between 'America' and the 'musical,' which was maintained for the next fifty years."[6] Sheridan Morley says of the Astaires "almost alone they transformed the London musical stage. Not only had audiences simply never seen singing and dancing of such speed and dexterity: people actually working in the London musical theatre had never seen the like of it either."[7] One fellow performer who claimed never to have seen their like was actress Hermione Baddeley. With specific reference to their second London triumph, *Lady, Be Good!*, she commented: "The Astaires were like automatons. They were magic, covering the stage with this terribly smooth, gorgeous rhythm bringing the best of American choreography together—we couldn't believe they were quite human."[8]

In their style and virtuosity, the Astaires influenced the cream of British musical comedy, practitioners such as Noël Coward, Jack Buchanan, Sonnie Hale, and Bobby Howes. Coward and André Charlot enlisted Fred's choreographic assistance with the revue *London Calling!*, produced at the Duke of York's Theatre in September 1923. The two numbers Fred staged were "Other Girls," performed by Noël and the female chorus, and a finale duet for Coward and Gertrude Lawrence to the show's only non-Coward song, "You Were Meant for Me," by Eubie Blake and Noble Sissle. Coward composed two songs for Donald Calthrop's revue *Yoicks!*, which opened in June 1924 at the Kingsway Theatre on Great Queen Street. One of these numbers, "I'd Like to See You Try" (otherwise known as the Fortune Telling Duet) was "arranged by Fred Astaire."

Inevitably, the Astaires also attracted their impersonators. The "run-around" became the most burlesqued item in London. Vera Lennox and Carl Hyson included it as one of the turns in "The Dancing Stars of London," which featured in "The Midnight Follies" at the Hotel Metropole. On April Fool's Day 1924, Adele herself turned up at the conclusion of Lennox's imitation of her. In the 1926 musical comedy *Oh, Patsy*, pantomime artiste Mona Vivian and Hugh

Rene performed impersonations of the Astaires, George Robey, Sophie Tucker, and Cochran star Alice Delysia.

For their part, and because of their proximity to the Continent, Fred and Adele were exposed to some of the best European popular entertainers. On their first visit to Paris, in February 1924, they saw Maurice Chevalier, Mistinguett, and their fellow Alviene alumnae the Dolly Sisters, while feasting on the sophisticated delights of the Folies Bergère, Moulin Rouge, Casino de Paris, and Bouffes-Parisiens.

It is difficult in our "celebrity"-sated era to appreciate what a sensation the Astaires were in London throughout the 1920s. They were photographed by Cecil Beaton and caricatured by Sava. Their social activities were written up in all the smart periodicals. They were invited to contribute articles to the *Sunday Illustrated* and *Daily Express* newspapers on the new dances, their adventures, and their opinions of England. These articles appeared under headings such as "Hoofing It to Fame by Adele Astaire" or "Shall We Tango or Jazz? by Fred Astaire"; undoubtedly they were polished by a copy editor, and some perhaps were ghost-written, but certainly in Fred's case the thoughts and attitudes expressed, even the phrasing, are authentic. Their names and images were used to endorse Tibo toothbrushes, Phosferine, Evan Williams Henna Shampoo, Amami Shampoo, Pond's Cold Cream, Lakerol Bronchial Pastilles, Rayne's

Figure 4.1 Amami shampoo ad with Adele

Dainty ADELE ASTAIRE certainly treats her dark hair " rough." She pushes it back for one clever characterisation and ruffles it on end for another. She is swung about all over the place by her brother . . . she dances and dances and dances. But Amami . . . which Miss Astaire calls "Queen of Shampoos " . . . keeps her hair lovely wherever she goes.

Figure 4.2 Pond's ad with Adele

"Dentelle" Shoes, and Waterman's Ideal Fountain Pen. As so often happens with celebrity, they became commodified.

The Astaires received considerable endorsement of their own—royal endorsement, in fact. One of their most loyal fans was the popular, American-loving Prince of Wales (later and only briefly Edward VIII), who came to see *Stop Flirting* ten times, bringing with him on occasion his younger brothers the

FRED ASTAIRE

The celebrated Artiste writes as follows:—

" *It is a pleasure for me to be able to recommend Lakerol Pastilles. They relieve Throat Fatigue, are refreshing to the voice, and are particularly pleasant to the taste.*"

This is but one of the many testimonials received from Theatrical Celebrities, Doctors, Public Speakers, etc., to the merits of Lakerol Bronchial Pastilles, which are ideal refreshers for the mouth and throat, and which are invaluable in all cases of Summer colds, catarrh, etc.

Lakerol

Bronchial Pastilles

A Free Sample Tin will be sent to all members of the Profession who apply to Messrs. Pastilles Ltd., 124, High St., Shoreditch, E.1

Telephone: Bishopsgate 2381.

1/3 per tin, of all Chemists

Figure 4.3 Lakerol Bronchial Pastilles ad with Fred

Duke of York (who became George VI on Edward's abdication), Prince Henry (created Duke of Gloucester in 1928), and Prince George (created Duke of Kent in 1934). The king and queen did not see the Astaires onstage until their second London coming in 1926. The heir to the throne was a man of massive contradictions—spoilt and generous, democratic and high-handed. In his role as Pied Piper to London's fashionable, slightly louche younger set, he was a source of bemusement and despair to his parents. In 1925, George V wrote to Queen Mary: "I see David continues to dance every night . . . people who don't know will begin to think that either he is mad or the biggest rake in Europe. Such a pity." Under the personal tutelage of Fred and Adele at St. James's Palace, he proved an apt pupil of the new dance steps. With the prince and his close friends Edwina and Louis Mountbatten (his second cousin), whom Adele remembers as "very conscious of celebrities," the Astaires frequented the elegant new nightclubs of the period such as the Kit-Kat Club, Café de Paris, the Riviera Club, Ciro's, and the Embassy Club. It was in one of these nightspots that Fred was photographed dancing an "inappropriate" Charleston with Lady Mountbatten.

In a departure from his customary practice of pursuing married women, the Prince of Wales paid assiduous court to Adele. The Astaires, however, formed a closer relationship with Prince George, who was cleverer than his brothers but also wilder. There is no suggestion that he co-opted either of the Astaires into his

Figure 4.4 Adele and Prince George dancing at the Derby Ball, Grosvenor House, Park Lane, London, June 1933.
Adele Astaire Collection, Howard Gotlieb Archival Research Centre

more dissolute habits, which were said to include an addiction to morphine and cocaine and a string of bisexual liaisons, but the intimacy of the letters he exchanged with Adele reveals a mutual infatuation, which they maintained for a number of years. George's letters to her often begin "Darling" and end with "Very much love."

Fred and Adele were flattered by the royal attention they received, and, as Adele recounts, between them they devised a method of disseminating back home news of their exalted social standing in London, proving that they were no innocents abroad but rather proficient self-publicists:

> We'd write letters home to different people and Fred would say, "Now we'll tell them what we did and who we've seen and who we've met and the parts we've been to. That'll cover that bunch of friends, and I'll write to so-and-so and they'll tell another bunch of friends." So it got in the papers too, of course, and "Cholly Knickerbocker" [a New York gossip column] used to write us up all the time.[9]

The Astaires were also courted by London's literati. Adele in particular became friends with several leading novelists and dramatists of the day. During a convalescent stay at Douglas Shields's nursing home in October 1923, one of Ann

Astaire's fellow patients was sixty-three-year-old Sir James Barrie, who asked to meet her children. He had seen *Stop Flirting* and, like the rest of London, was entranced by Adele, no doubt recognizing in her the feminine equivalent of one of his Lost Boys, something of the wayward child described by Sybil Connelly. A month or two later, over dinner at his flat in Adelphi Terrace House in the Strand, Barrie asked Adele to play Peter Pan during the Christmas season at the Adelphi Theatre. She was excited at the prospect and encouraged by Barrie's assurance that she had the requisite elfin vivacity, but Alfred Butt would not release her from her contract for the required performances. The part went instead to Gladys Cooper.

P. G. Wodehouse and Guy Bolton were similarly under Adele's spell, pronouncing in her "the faculty of making any party from two to fifty-two into a success. Such words as enchanting, delicious, captivating did not seem like tired adjectives from a Hollywood pressbook when applied to her."[10] Wodehouse was keen to fashion one of his stories into an Astaire vehicle, and it would appear, from a letter he wrote to Fred on 3 February 1927, that he envisaged Adele in the role of the wisecracking, good-hearted chorus girl Billie Dore in *A Damsel in Distress*. (Letter in Mugar Memorial Library, Boston University). Like Peter Pan, it was a role that did not eventuate, but it would have been inspired casting.

Adele, meanwhile, fell under the spell of George Bernard Shaw. "He was gorgeous," she recalled. "He was a tall, good-looking man . . . with a voice that could melt ice. He had the most beautiful speaking voice—I wish every actor had a voice like that. It was simply sensational . . . musical Irish."[11] As well as captivating him in turn, Adele could claim the distinction of having momentarily wrong-footed her brilliant idol. Having declared his paltry regard for actors because they would not exist without writers, Shaw was challenged by Adele: "But what about dancers, Mr. Shaw?"—a point he conceded in silence.

John Galsworthy, best known for his three trilogies of novels that began with *The Forsyte Saga*, was so taken with the Astaires in *Lady, Be Good!* that he made mention of the show in his play *Escape*, which premiered four months after the London opening of *Lady, Be Good!* in 1926. In episode 3 of part 1, the title tune of *Lady, Be Good!* is employed by Galsworthy as a warning signal between The Shingled Lady (shades of Adele) and escaped convict Matt Denant:

LADY. Whistle "Lady, be good," if you know it.
LATT. Rather! It's the only tune that's got into prison.

Other literary friends included Somerset Maugham, Hugh Walpole, and A. A. Milne. But of all the correspondence of that time between the Astaires and

London's literary lions, the most touching in its simplicity is a note from Milne's celebrated six-year-old son, handwritten on *Winnie-the-Pooh*/E. H. Shepard letterhead, thanking Adele for her Christmas present.[12]

> It is the only Fire-engine I have ever had and I am very pleased with it.
> I thank you ever so much.
> With Love from
> Christopher Robin

While Adele was being pursued by various men of letters, Fred pursued his ambitions as a songwriter. His latest composition, "You've Such a Lot," with lyrics by his *Stop Flirting* costar Jack Melford (writing under the pseudonym Austin Melford), was sung in *The Co-Optimists* of 1923 at the Prince of Wales Theatre. Billed as "A Pierrotic Entertainment," the Co-Optimists were a type of repertory revue troupe who modeled their format loosely on the once popular end-of-the-pier groups of entertainers. Stanley Holloway was among the featured troupe, and the show also included a song by Noël Coward, "There May Be Days." Initially in company with Coward, Fred sought to further his musical education by enrolling in a course in harmony at the Guildhall School of Music. And on 18 October 1923, he and Adele made their debut as commercial recording artists at HMV Studios in Hayes, Middlesex. The two songs they recorded, "The Whichness of the Whatness" and "Oh, Gee! Oh, Gosh!" were among the first recordings by American artists in London of numbers from a show in which they were appearing.

Less than three weeks before these recordings were made, Fred and Adele suffered the first real tragedy of their lives. Their father died at Galen Hall in Wernersville, Pennsylvania. Ann wrote in her diary that he was fifty-three, but his fifty-sixth birthday was 8 September. The cause of death was cancer of the throat. News of his illness had reached his family in London in July; despite their years of estrangement, Ann immediately returned home to take care of him. On her arrival in New York, she found Fritz had been admitted to St. Vincent's Hospital in Greenwich Village and was shocked by his appearance.

Both Ann and Fritz kept from their children the seriousness of his condition. This is evident from the tone of Fred's letters to his father over the course of the summer. On Sunday, 12 August, he wrote:

> Dear pop—
>   Adele and I were so happy to read your nice letter which mother enclosed. I suppose by this time you are once more a spry old gent. It is

so gratifying to know that mother's trip did you so much good and I know that from now on this little family of ours is going to be happy. Hope you two will go to a good place in the country, not a gloomy old place—as that would make you blue, but someplace where you cannot only rest, but enjoy yourself. . . .

I hope [mother] is well pop, please write and tell me the truth. I'm always afraid she doesn't tell me the real news of herself.[13]

Ann did take Fritz to the country for a rest—to Galen Hall—but he was already terminally ill. He died on 1 October. Ann did not notify Fred and Adele directly. Instead she sent a cable to Sir Alfred Butt, who broke the news to Fred in his dressing room. Butt offered to cancel that evening's performance, but Fred and Adele insisted they would perform.

The concerns Fred had expressed to his father regarding his mother's state of health were justified. On her return to London on 13 October, Ann collapsed in pain. She was admitted to Douglas Shields's private nursing home at 17 Park Lane, where she remained for eight weeks. The exact nature of her illness is something of a mystery. Physical and emotional exhaustion were likely factors, but it is also possible that she underwent surgery for a tumor.

In many respects, Fritz Austerlitz had led a sad, unfulfilled life, a fact underscored by his untimely death at such a distance from his children and at the moment of their greatest success. He had become an increasingly rare presence in their lives, but from the way his children spoke of him and from their frequent correspondence, there is no doubting he was an important influence and a father whom they loved.

Quite apart from their technical brilliance and the freshness of the music composed for them, it was what the Astaires represented to London that made such an impact in and beyond the theatre. Crucially, they first crossed the Atlantic in the spring of 1923, less than five years after the "War to End All Wars" in which England had lost the flower of a generation for the sake, as Ezra Pound phrased it, of "a botched civilization . . . For two gross of broken statues, / For a few 1000 battered books."[14] They were full of youthful expectancy—Adele was twenty-six, and Fred, who had narrowly missed the draft in America, celebrated his twenty-fourth birthday during the tryouts for *Stop Flirting* in Scotland. As Frederick Ashton remarked in 1981, the Astaires had "an immense American vitality."[15] There was a warmth and openness about them as well as something intrinsically joyful and forward-looking.

Their dancing and comedy encapsulated an innocence England had irrevocably lost on foreign fields, which is beautifully elegized at the close of the first act of Alan Bennett's *Forty Years On*. It is the evening of 3 August 1914, and five gilded youths decide to steal away from a stifling ball at Dorchester House because they have conceived a fancy to hear the nightingales down at Kimber. The narrator is Raymond Asquith, his companions Edward Horner, Julian and Billy Grenfell, and Patrick Shaw-Stewart—all five lost their lives in the Great War:

> We climbed out onto the leads among the turrets and towers and the green copper cupola. I remember the weather vane's shrill singing in the breeze, the lanyard slapping the mast as Julian Grenfell broke the square medieval flag above the dark house. I would like to think that up there on the leads at Kimber, where within months I should stand to hear the guns in France, I would like to think that on that summer night in 1914 the shiver I felt was one of foreboding. But if I shivered I fear it was only because it was the hour before dawn and cold up there on the roof. And if I felt a shadow come across the moment, it was only because, young, rich, and as I see now, happy, I could afford melancholy. For another day, another ball had ended and life had not yielded up its secret. "This time," I always thought as I tied my tie. "Perhaps this time." But there would be other nights and time yet, I thought. And so we waited on that short midsummer night and a deer barked and our footsteps were dull on the leads. And then as the light seeped back into the sky, suddenly, just before dawn, we heard the nightingales.

Here the midsummer nightingale's song, evocative of a gentle Edwardian idyll or that demi-paradise immortalized as the Golden Summer of 1914, transmutes into the rumble of the guns in Flanders. This passage in Bennett's play seems to epitomize the violent intersection at which Edwardian romanticism and High modernism meet.

On 19 May 1924, while Fred and Adele were still performing in London, BBC audiences heard an extraordinary live duet between cellist Beatrice Harrison and the nightingales in the woods around her home in Oxted, Surrey, responding to the haunting strains of "Londonderry Air." John Reith, Managing Director of the BBC, observed that the nightingale "has swept the country . . . with a wave of something closely akin to emotionalism, and a glamour of romance has flashed across the prosaic round of many a life."[16] He could just as easily have been describing the wave of "Astairia" sweeping the country. The duet was recreated every spring for the next twelve years, after which the nightingales alone were broadcast, until one night in 1942, when the recording engineer heard an ominous droning competing with the nightingale chorus. The intruding sound turned out to be the start of the 1,000 bomber raid en route to Mannheim, a perversion of the pastoral exactly like the moment in Bennett's play, with the birdsong becoming an urgent plea for life.

Like the nightingales, the Astaires were the sweet voice of life and hope and thus symbolically distinct from both the horror of the Great War and the ennui of its aftermath. In this respect, and for all their jazz-fueled modernity, they were, in essence anti-modernist; that is, they represented something—a defiant New World optimism—counter to High modernism's pervasive sense of the instability of the self and the universe, its concomitant sense of alienation and dislocation from the present.[17] Modernism had its origins in a fin-de-siècle crisis of faith and identity, which Hugo von Hofmannsthal (in his most famous essay, *Ein Brief*) and later T. S. Eliot (in *Four Quartets*) characterized as a terrifying "slipping" or "sliding,"[18] and which manifested itself in a general aesthetic of fragmentation and uncertainty. The year preceding the Astaires' arrival in London had seen the publication of two seminal works in the modernist canon—Eliot's *The Waste Land* and James Joyce's *Ulysses*.

The Astaires, however, seemed unaffected by the modernist crisis and the aesthetic revolt it spawned. And in spite of their association with London's Bright Young Things, they managed to project a wholesomeness and, as Gielgud noted, a sweetness at odds with the self-destructive impulses of the aimless young people satirized in Evelyn Waugh's *Vile Bodies* and of whom G. B. Stern said: "They were suffering not from shell-shock, but from the echo of shell-shock."[19] In contrast to the high-strung hollowness felt by many of their English contemporaries, they expressed musically that quality F. Scott Fitzgerald spoke of when he defined America as "a willingness of the heart."[20]

It is interesting to compare the Astaires with Noël Coward, who in 1921 had prophesied their riotous London reception and who was himself shortly to become an explosive force within British theatre. Just seven months younger than Fred, Coward was a fascinating fusion of nostalgic Edwardianism and chic modernism. His play *The Vortex*, whose characters, "all so hectic and nervy," "swirl about in a vortex of beastliness," had its West End premiere on Coward's twenty-fifth birthday and was an instant cause célèbre.[21] Its three acts were facile and fast-paced, but they did establish a new theatrical voice and dealt with the neuroses, moral inversion, and frenetic hedonism endemic to the period of the Long Weekend between the wars: here in the form of a mother with a much younger lover and a son with a cocaine habit.

Three decades before the Royal Court's kitchen-sink "revolution,"[22] Coward's silk-dressing-gowned pianist Nicky Lancaster is every inch as angry and disaffected as John Osborne's bedsit polemicist (the anti-hero of *Look Back in Anger*)Jimmy Porter; both young narcissists are the casualties of a post-war void, with no world of their own to regret the passing of. Coward himself was sleek and current, and had a talent not only to amuse but also for capturing the Zeitgeist of his generation. Although much of his work, both his songs and his plays, reveals a genuine tenderness and depth of feeling, the brittle carapace of

Figure 4.5 Adele, Noël Coward, and Fred during the London run of *Stop Flirting*, 1923.
Adele Astaire Collection, Howard Gotlieb Archival Research Centre

knowingness and jaded sophistication that, rightly or wrongly, became his trade-mark, and the darker undertones of his mercurial wit, were very different from the sheer joyfulness the Astaires inspired.

Judging from the notices quoted at the beginning of this chapter, with their exuberant references to the Flood, the Garden of Eden, and the discovery of America by Columbus, it is not, I believe, fanciful to suggest that the Astaires' coming was somehow epiphanic, that it was perceived in terms comparable to the sighting of a virgin Paradise, "Where the nightingale doth sing / Not a sense-less, trancèd thing, / But divine melodious truth" (Keats, "Bards of Passion and Mirth", ll. 17–19).

Fred and Adele were seen to provide not merely escapist entertainment of an unusually high order, but a kind of redemption, an antidote to cynicism in a land of lost content.

While London was enchanted by the Astaires' invigorating Americanness and joie de vivre, Fred and Adele became enamored of most things English. Fred, in particular, began to cultivate a whole new style of dress and deportment, with the Prince of Wales and Prince George as his role models. Adele recalled in 1979: "That's when Fred really copied the Prince of Wales. He had to have suede shoes just like the Prince of Wales and he used to try to walk like him and every-thing. He became really so super English." Fred would haunt the rarefied envi-rons of the bespoke menswear establishments on Savile Row and Jermyn Street, which enjoyed royal patronage; he ordered his suits from Anderson & Sheppard and his shirts from Hawes & Curtis (where his photograph is still proudly dis-played), and no doubt he had his hair cut at Geo. F. Trumper of Mayfair and St, James's, an Aladdin's cave of shaving brushes, scent bottles, and other tonsorial accoutrements.

The royal influence was not, however, entirely one-sided. On a visit to Fred's dressing room on 7 August 1924, significant enough to be recorded in Ann's diary, the Duke of York was highly impressed by Fred's numerous pairs of suspenders and his convenient wrinkle of having one pair for each change of trousers. Fred also caused a sartorial stir in London by revealing a few of his anarchic preferences; he flouted convention by wearing a light coat with dark trousers and spurned the voluminous Oxford bags, seen on entertainers such as Jack Buchanan, in favor of narrower and, if you like, more aerodynamic trousers, which showed his dancer's "line" to better effect.

Fred's tailoring was just one aspect of what Benny Green described as "a sort of Englishness by proxy, a demeanour more redolent of Wodehousean persiflage than the homeliness of Omaha."[23] He even began to sound not unlike Bertie Wooster, adapting with ease to British upper-class slang. Toward the end of a letter to his mother, dated 11 August 1923, he writes, in a quaint mix of Mayfair and the Midwest: "Please tell my dear pop about all this—I know he'll be inter-ested as the deuce."[24] Both Fred and Adele to some extent affected English accents, which were swiftly knocked out of them on their return to New York. But Fred, an expert mimic, always retained his facility for aping (when a part required or the mood took him) the clipped tones and drawling vowel sounds of British aristocratic speech.

Not everything English won the young tourists' unqualified praise. There was, for instance, the "rawness" of the cold unrelieved by the lack of central heat-ing. And, coming from syncopated Manhattan, they were dismayed by what they deemed the Englishman's innate lack of rhythm. Giving a journalist his opinion on the blues in England, Fred for once did not pull any punches: "You play it far too slowly—it's a dreary business—the tempo is absolutely wrong. Why, man, the 'Blues' is nigger music[25]—full with life and vivacity. Most of the London bands play it like a slow-step dirge."[26] Adele, meanwhile, shared with *London Magazine* her poor opinion of Englishmen as social dancing partners: "Englishmen, on the whole, don't give much time to dancing, and they haven't got the sense of rhythm that Americans have."[27]

It was not only the Astaires' glamorous transatlantic otherness that the English willingly embraced; a large part of their appeal, I am certain, was based on a comedic eccentricity with which English audiences could strongly identify. Fred and Adele were possessed at times of an almost Barriesque or Wodehousean whimsicality, most discernible in the loping merriment of the "run-around," which proved an even greater audience favorite in London, where it was rechristened "The Oompah Trot" and often culminated in the ribald "Colonel Bogey March." It was not long before ads appeared for the sheet music of the "Oom-Pah-Trot-One-Step Featured in *Stop Flirting*" (price 2 shillings). "The Oompah Trot" made such an impression on the young Frederick Ashton that in 1948 he borrowed it for *Cinderella*, the first major three-act ballet he choreographed for Sadler's Wells, in which he and Robert Helpmann played the Ugly Sisters. As the Sisters made their exit from the ballroom, they circled the stage in an increasingly high-stepping, trotting movement, with heads and ostrich feathers bobbing. The Ashton-Helpmann run-around was preserved on film in the 1960s. There is, of course, no footage of the Astaires performing this popular piece of pantomimic whimsy, but Fred did reprise "The Oompah Trot" with Gracie Allen in 1937 as part of the Academy Award–winning "Fun House" sequence choreographed by Hermes Pan, appropriately for a film adaptation of Wodehouse's *A Damsel in Distress*. The end of "Let's Call the Whole Thing Off" in *Shall We Dance* (also 1937), a number famously executed by Fred and Ginger Rogers on roller skates in a Central Park setting, is another version of the run-around, finishing with the pair, carried away by their own momentum, landing unceremoniously on a grass embankment.

The "English," and indeed ethereal, element in the Astaires' comedic style is also indicated in bewitched critics' depictions of them as a couple of misplaced Spenserian or Shakespearean sprites:

> In their tireless high spirits, their unfailing delight in their own concerns, their litheness and unceasing activities, they almost ceased to be human beings to become, as it were, translated into denizens of an Elizabethan forest.[28]

> [Adele] has wilfully wandered into the absurd world of musical comedy but you feel it is not her natural element. She should be dancing by glow-worm light under entranced trees on a midsummer eve with a rout of elves, after drinking rose-dew.[29]

It was not mere whimsy or an otherworldly eccentricity that struck such a resounding chord; the Astaires were regarded as comedians in the highest sense. In England, far more so than in America, they were valued for the display of mind in their dancing, for the acting ability that animated and made meaningful their rhythmical, eccentric movements. Francis Birrell, writing in the *Nation and Athenaeum*, said they "uttered the least important word with every inch of their bodies, never being content with the employment of the essential extremities—tongue, hand, or foot."[30] The northern Irish dramatist and critic St. John Ervine launched an acerbic attack on young English actresses for their failure to emulate Adele's bodily and facial eloquence: "Compared with her, they are not alive at all. They have never learnt that one must act with one's whole body, but especially with one's face, that features were given to us for the purpose of illustrating our minds."[31] Of Fred, the *Birmingham Post* reported "he has not only winged heels, but winged arms and winged back," and of Adele, "hers is not only the poetry of motion but its wit, its malice, its humour."[32] The *Birmingham Dispatch* provided an account of the mesmeric, transporting quality of the siblings' richly nuanced somatic vocabulary: "Their humour lies in gesture, their attraction in the power to set us dancing with them, to send us in spirit, twirling and striding and frolicking in glorious abandon."[33]

By August 1924 the Astaires had been performing *Stop Flirting* for sixteen months, dividing their London residency between the Shaftesbury, Queen's, and Strand theatres, and touring to Birmingham, Hull, Glasgow, and Edinburgh. It would remain the longest run of any of their musicals. At each performance, they executed eighteen dances, a total of 144 dances (one gross) a week. By the end of the run, they had completed in excess of 10000 dances. Adele had to buy a new pair of silk stockings every day (at a pound a pair) and wore out a pair of shoes a week, while Fred had to have new shoes every fortnight. Adele dubbed the show "Non-stop Flirting."

Whether or not it was attributable to the mental strain of a long run, one evening in Glasgow Fred suffered an uncharacteristic lapse. He walked offstage and went directly to his dressing room, imagining that they had reached the final curtain. He proceeded in leisurely fashion to remove his dress coat, collar, shirt, and tie. Standing half-undressed before his mirror and calmly surveying his reflection, his reverie was suddenly punctured by a shout from the call-boy, alerting him to the alarming fact that he was due onstage in one minute. Frantically he thrust on his shirt, gathered up his coat, collar, and tie, and went on in his shirtsleeves. The situation was salvaged by an impromptu "gag" that he had been assaulted "off" and forced to engage in fisticuffs. Many people in the audience accepted the spectacle of Fred deshabille, and lately returned from street combat, as part of the show.

Apart from fatigue, Fred and Adele were now experiencing acute homesickness. Moreover, they became concerned that if they further prolonged their London engagement, they would risk being forgotten back home.

It was time, they decided, to return to New York. Alfred Butt, however, had no intention of prematurely closing a show whose longevity and profitability were

Figure 4.6 News from home.

guaranteed. He believed *Stop Flirting* could run for at least another two seasons, and the Astaires were contractually bound to appear as long as Butt wanted to keep the show running. To avoid possible litigation and damage to their professional reputation, the Astaire family devised an escape strategy, commissioning Alex Aarons to find a new Broadway vehicle for Fred and Adele and seeking medical confirmation of Adele's imminent nervous collapse. Eventually, recognizing the physical toll the show was taking and the siblings' waning enthusiasm, Butt reluctantly agreed to close *Stop Flirting* on 30 August.

The last night was a memorably bittersweet occasion. The loyal galleryites demanded encore after encore. The audience sang along with each number and, at the final curtain, launched into "Auld Lang Syne." It was midnight before the Astaires were allowed to return to their dressing rooms. This emotional farewell was tarnished somewhat by their discovery that while they had been taking their final bows, their suite at the Savoy had been ransacked by burglars.

On 10 September 1924, Adele's twenty-eighth birthday, the Astaires set sail for New York. Their staterooms aboard SS *Homeric* were awash with telegrams and floral tributes from their many friends in London. One telegram, from Lord "Ned" Lathom, summed up the city's desolate mood at the Astaires' departure: "London is now empty. Life is a blank."

The last eighteen months had been almost an unreal time for Fred and Adele, triumphant and exhilarating beyond anything they had dreamed, and constituting an extraordinary period in London's theatrical and social history. Awaiting the Astaires' arrival in New York was another share of theatrical history—a new show blessed with the first complete score by George and Ira Gershwin. The Aarons-Freedley production bore the regrettable working title *Black-Eyed Susan,* but it would earn its place in history as *Lady, Be Good!*

CHAPTER 5

Fascinating Rhythms

'S awful nice! 'S paradise—
'S what I love to see!
—George and Ira Gershwin, "'S Wonderful"

George Gershwin's prolific and versatile genius ensured that 1924 was a year of milestones for him and for American music. On Lincoln's Birthday, 12 February 1924, Paul Whiteman and his Palais Royal Orchestra presented at New York's Aeolian Hall "An Experiment in Modern Music," a didactically conceived attempt to make "an honest woman out of jazz"[1] and to plot its evolution. The long afternoon program began with a burlesque of the crude, "primeval" sounds of "Livery Stable Blues" (1917) and concluded with Whiteman's special arrangement of Elgar's *Pomp and Circumstance* March no. 1, in which the banjo thumped out the bass line of the "Land of Hope and Glory" trio. The penultimate piece was brand new, Gershwin's *Rhapsody in Blue*, with the composer himself as featured soloist. From the now iconic opening clarinet glissando, played by Ross Gorman as an electrifying metropolitan cri de coeur, the *Rhapsody* was instantly recognizable as an intrinsic part of the American modernist vernacular. It even found its way into *The Great Gatsby*, published in 1925, where it was thinly disguised as "Vladimir Tostoff's Jazz History of the World," "which attracted so much attention at Carnegie Hall last May." In explaining its conception amid the "steely rhythms" of a railway journey, Gershwin said: "I heard it as a sort of musical kaleidoscope of America—of our vast melting pot, of our unduplicated national pep, of our blues, our metropolitan madness."[2]

That year also witnessed Gershwin's first hit show in London, *Primrose*, which opened in September at the Winter Garden Theatre, and three Gershwin premieres on Broadway: *Sweet Little Devil* in January at the Astor; the annual *George White's Scandals* in June at the Apollo; and, on 1 December at the Liberty, *Lady, Be Good!*

This last show, staged by Felix Edwardes (the British director of *Stop Flirting*) was no less a milestone than the first performance of *Rhapsody in Blue*, for it

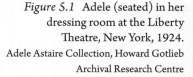

Figure 5.1 Adele (seated) in her
dressing room at the Liberty
Theatre, New York, 1924.
Adele Astaire Collection, Howard Gotlieb
Archival Research Centre

changed the American musical, carrying with it a new sound, a new verve and
sophistication, and a new spirit, boldly and authentically twentieth-century. As
Fred maintained: "This was no hackneyed ordinary musical comedy. It was slick
and tongue in cheek, a definite departure in concept and design."[3] It was, moreover, the first musical entirely scored by the Gershwin brothers, George and Ira
(writing now under his own name) and the first all-Gershwin show to star the
Astaires.

Musing on the uncanny affinity between Fred and George as artists and inven-
tors, Alexander Woollcott wrote in 1927: "I do not know whether George
Gershwin was born into this world to write rhythms for Fred Astaire's feet or
whether Fred Astaire was born into this world to show how the Gershwin music
should really be danced. But surely they were written in the same key, those
two."[4] The Astaires and the Gershwins seemed predestined, instinctively and
definitively, to draw out the best in one another. *Lady, Be Good!* represented a
remarkable symbiosis of talent, a shared creative idiom that evoked, indeed
defined, the mood and style of the mid-1920s, that articulated the Cowardian
mad jazz patterns and nervous urban energy of this period of unprecedented
modernity.[5] In 2005, the 1926 English Columbia recording of the Astaires singing "Fascinating Rhythm" to George Gershwin's piano accompaniment was
added to the National Recording Registry, which was created by an act of
Congress to preserve sound recordings that are "culturally, historically, or
aesthetically important, and/or that inform or reflect life in the United States."

The following year it was inducted into the Grammy Hall of Fame as a recording "of lasting qualitative or historical significance."

Woollcott described the score as "brisk, inventive, gay, nervous, delightful." But that was not the whole story. There was an additional quality, one reflective of another side to Gershwin's music more generally. In his symphonic works—for example in the Concerto in F or in the middle andantino moderato of *Rhapsody in Blue*—we hear a frontier romanticism alongside the "dizzying polyrhythms"[6] of the modern metropolis; both are identifiably American. Similarly, the score of *Lady, Be Good!*, while "slick and tongue in cheek," has also a tenderness and a yearning, with eloquent shifts from major to minor keys, and seems to issue in equal measure from the two sides apparent in Gershwin's own nature—the one extrovert, the other solitary. William Saroyan observed of the *Rhapsody*: "There is great loneliness and love in it."[7] British musicologist Donald Mitchell, a leading authority on the work of Mahler and Benjamin Britten, discerned the same emotional dichotomy in the music of *Lady, Be Good!* In relation to a 1956 touring production at the Golders Green Hippodrome in North London, he said:

> I doubt if this production of *Lady, Be Good!* was wholly authentic, but it did nothing to obscure and much to reveal Gershwin's specific genius and above all his unmistakeable character, the strangest combination of intense vitality and incurable nostalgia, both exuberantly gregarious and intolerably lonely.[8]

One of the songs that best epitomized this unmistakable character, this strangest combination, was an early casualty of try-outs in Philadelphia, yet on the strength of it the show secured the investment of a very prestigious backer or "angel." The financier and philanthropist Otto H. Kahn, on hearing Gershwin demonstrate part of the score, decided that *Lady, Be Good!* was certain to be a commercial hit and therefore not something he was inclined to bankroll. Kahn's philanthropic interests lay in projects unlikely to yield any financial return, and although he was an early benefactor to Hollywood, he chiefly invested in "high" culture. For many years he served as president and chairman of the Metropolitan Opera Company; he founded the Chicago Grand Opera Company, was chairman of the French Theatre of New York, and was patron of the modernist poet Hart Crane, whose epic poem *The Bridge* was dedicated to him; and in 1916 he headed the Mayor's Honorary Committee of the New York City Shakespeare Tercentenary Celebration and brought Diaghilev's Ballet Russes to America. He was, however, an unexpected champion of jazz as a purposeful and promising art form, declaring it "imperfect, but vigorously alive, novel and distinctive. [It] has a just claim to be taken seriously. It has more right to be ranked as . . . American art than a savorless opera composed with painstaking erudition and technical impeccability after the model of Wagner, Debussy or Strauss."⁹ When Gershwin played "The Man I Love," a song written for Adele to sing in the second act, Kahn deemed it a piece of serious art and worthy of $10,000.

According to Ira Gershwin, Adele sang "The Man I Love" "most acceptably,"¹⁰ but it was felt, inexplicably, that the ballad was "slowing up" the action, so it was dropped before the show reached New York. Kahn cried all the way to the bank. "It was the first time," Ira Gershwin remarked wryly, "he [Kahn] ever made any money from a show."¹¹ The number would also be dropped from two subsequent shows—the original 1927 version of *Strike Up the Band*, which never made it to Broadway, and *Rosalie* in 1928, where it was cut during rehearsals because the star, Marilyn Miller, thought it too melancholy. (Miller was decidedly erring in her judgment of music; later, in the show *Smiles* with the Astaires, she initially refused to sing Vincent Youmans's exquisite "Time on My Hands.") After a visit to New York, Lady Edwina Mountbatten took a copy of the sheet music, autographed by Gershwin, back to England in 1925 and arranged for the Berkeley Square Orchestra to introduce it in London. It became a favorite of other British dance bands. In America, the song's success was assured by its inclusion in the nightclub repertoire of torch singer Helen Morgan, who created the role of Julie LaVerne in Jerome Kern and Oscar Hammerstein's *Show Boat*. Eventually "The Man I Love" was recorded by all the great female jazz vocalists, including Billie Holiday, Lena Horne, Ella Fitzgerald, and Sarah Vaughan.

Otto Kahn remained an admirer of Gershwin. In a speech he gave at a reception following the Carnegie Hall premiere of *An American in Paris* in 1928, he likened Gershwin to Charles Lindbergh as emblematic of the intrepid brilliance of a generation and its "Parsifalesque" outlook on life: "In the rhythm, the melody, the humor, the grace, the rush, and sweep and dynamics of his composition he expresses the genius of young America." He added, however, that as a young American composer, Gershwin lacked a galvanizing legacy of sorrow and needed to experience something of the epic European struggles, suffering, and sacrifices so vital to "the deepening and mellowing and the complete development, energizing and revealment, of an artist's inner being and spiritual powers."¹² Yet what must have attracted Kahn to a song like "The Man I Love" was not its Parsifalesque optimism but its note of intolerable loneliness, the spiritual maturation and soulful stirring implicit in its darker harmony. This darkness perhaps ultimately derived from Gershwin's personal European heritage (as the son of Russian-Jewish immigrants) and his studies in European music, but perhaps more consciously and immediately from his understanding of the angst peculiar to his own century, his own young nation. Artist Isamu Noguchi, who in 1929 sculpted a sleek, broodingly modernist bronze bust of Gershwin, commented a year after the composer's tragically early death: "He was not only a representative of the twenties but through his music a symbol of our youth. His was that rare gift of being able to transfix in such a slender song as 'Oh, Lady Be Good!' the timely, yet timeless image of an era, poignant still."[13]

Contributing an extra dimension to the new sound of *Lady, Be Good!* was Gershwin's innovation of augmenting the pit orchestra, under Paul Lannin's direction, with the duo pianists Phil Ohman and Victor Arden, who recorded hundreds of piano rolls throughout the 1920s. In this he was inspired by Paul Whiteman's effective use of two pianos in his jazz orchestra. He gave Ohman and Arden two-piano arrangements that highlighted the musical connections between the songs, the throughlines in phrasing, and the orchestral interplay. The pair took several solo breaks, with one playing a number straight while the other improvised. Their inventive keyboard style proved so popular that the audience would gather around the pit during the interval and after the final curtain to hear Ohman and Arden's jam sessions, which became, in effect, post-show concerts. Fred was convinced that the two specialty pianos in the pit "had a lot to do with the overall success of *Lady, Be Good!*,"[14] while Gershwin believed "that one reason for the success of this novelty was that the piano is the most telling instrument for music like mine that requires the quickest accent which falls on the full chord."[15]

When Fred and Adele arrived back in New York in the early autumn of 1924, they were greeted at the dock by Alex Aarons and Vinton Freedley, who in January had launched their producing firm with Cosmo Hamilton's farce *The New Poor* at the Playhouse Theatre. Atop a trunk lid, as they waited in customs, the Astaires signed provisional agreements to appear in the new Aarons and Freedley production, still at that stage called *Black-Eyed Susan*. Fred did not think the change of title much of an improvement until he heard Gershwin play the eponymous number, which, in spite of its later identification with Fred, was not performed in the show by either of the Astaires.

In 1952, Fred recorded an impressive version of "Oh, Lady Be Good!" for Norman Granz's Clef label and in collaboration with the jazz sextet of pianist Oscar Peterson, trumpeter Charlie Shavers, tenor saxophonist Flip Phillips, bassist Ray Brown, guitarist Barney Kessel, and drummer Alvin Stoller. British jazz saxophonist and writer Benny Green once stated:

> When [Astaire] assumes that expression of mute appeal and requests, with a slight lilt in his voice: *Oh, sweet and lovely / lady be good, oh lady / be good to me* the listener gets the sense that here is one of those rare occasions when the form and the content, the creator and the interpreter, have fused to produce something not often encountered in popular art, or indeed in anything else—perfection.[16]

But it was comedian Walter Catlett who introduced the number onstage when he sang it to Adele, and not in a romantic vein but in an effort to gain her character's cooperation in committing a complicated deception. Gershwin said of this original version: "Walter was a funny man, and, like a lot of comedians, even his voice was funny—in fact, it was terrible. And what he did to 'Lady, Be Good!' was nobody's business."

Having been away from New York for eighteen months, Fred and Adele were eager to investigate their competition for the coming season and generally reacquaint themselves with the Broadway scene. Among the productions they saw that autumn, in company with George Gershwin, were *What Price Glory?* at the Plymouth; *Kid Boots* with Eddie Cantor at the Selwyn, produced by Ziegfeld and staged by Edward Royce; the Theatre Guild's production of Sidney Howard's *They Knew What They Wanted*, which would be awarded the 1925 Pulitzer Prize for drama; Eugene O'Neill's *Desire under the Elms* at the Greenwich Village Theatre; and the new Dillingham musical at the globe, Jerome Kern's *Stepping Stones*, with Fred and Allene Stone and their daughter Dorothy, who would later dance with Fred in his first stage show without Adele. They also visited the El Fey Club on West Forty-Fifth Street, an often-raided speakeasy run by the legendary hostess Texas Guinan and frequented by "out-of-town buyers, theatrical celebrities, and a sprinkling of the social and underworld elite."[17] Here they saw a young man whom Fred considered "the neatest, fastest Charleston dancer ever"[18]—future screen gangster George Raft. Raft credited Fred with advancing his career by mentioning his name to Martin Poulsen, owner of London's Café de Paris, as a potential star attraction.

The libretto of *Lady, Be Good!*, by Guy Bolton and Fred Thompson, posed no threat to Eugene O'Neill or Sidney Howard—nor, of course, did it aim to. But even by musical-comedy standards, the plot was weak and tortuous, or, in Fred's words, "pretty stupid."[19] The action begins in front of the Trevor home in Beacon Hill, Rhode Island. Siblings Dick and Susie (Fred and Adele) have been evicted from their house by their landlady, wealthy Josephine Vanderwater (Jayne Auburn), because Dick has refused her romantic advances. Josephine's plan is to force a homeless and destitute Dick to marry her. Dick's true love is Shirley Vernon (Kathlene Martyn), but she is poor like him. He considers marrying Josephine in order to support his sister. While camped on the street, Dick and Susie encounter a mysterious hobo, Jack Robinson (Alan Edwards), who is returning from Mexico, where he was rumored to have been murdered. Susie and Jack fall in love. Jack is unaware that he has inherited his wealthy uncle's estate. Meanwhile, a Mexican gangster turns up, who alleges that his sister Juanita (currently in a Mexican prison for biting a man's ear) is the "late" Jack Robinson's widow. He hires "Watty" Watkins (Walter Catlett), lawyer to the Trevors and the Vanderwaters, to retrieve the fortune he claims is owed his sister. Watty will be paid $100,000 for his trouble, but he needs someone to impersonate the Mexican widow. He asks Susie, who eventually agrees to participate in the fraud for half of Watty's fee so that she can save her brother from a loveless marriage. After the inevitable second-act high jinks, revelations, and resolutions, Susie and Jack, Dick and Shirley, Josephine and Watty announce their engagements.

This nonsensical narrative was redeemed by what Fred called "an indefinable magic about the show."[20] George Gershwin had, in the estimation of one British critic, injected "something intangible, almost spiritual" into jazz. His music was perfectly complemented by the wit, irony, playfulness, and pathos of his brother Ira's lyrics. Complementing the slickness of the Gershwins' score were the gleaming art deco sets by Norman Bel Geddes, who was also an industrial designer and known as "the father of streamlining," although earlier that year he had transformed the Century Theatre into a cavernous Gothic cathedral for Max Reinhardt's play *The Miracle*. Bel Geddes, had, too, a well-matched sense of drollery, evident in his opening setting for *Lady, Be Good!* which resembled a bizarre oversized doll's-house street. A similar combination of streamlinedness and whimsy distinguished the comedy playing, not least by Walter Catlett, who had the appearance of "a somber Ed Wynn"[21] and was a gregarious and ribald character offstage.

Then there was the dancing of the Astaires, which had an indefinable magic of its own. In an article in the *New York Times*, the writer and critic Stark Young used the example of the Astaires' performance in *Lady, Be Good!* to illuminate his point that the presence of a generative idea raised dance from a mathematics of movement to the status of Art. The art of the Astaires, he argued, was transcendently whole and expressive in its abstraction and resisted analysis:

> What remains and delights people is the Astaires, and again the Astaires.
>
> And of the Astaires what wins all hearts is a certain pure dance quality of the dancing. The explanations otherwise only serve as illustrations of our futile attempts to force our experiences in every sort of art to make sense in logical or definite explanations. But this dancing remains inexplicable. It is abstract as music is, scarcely imitative at all, quite free and complete in itself. It is agile, clever, tricky, whatever you like to say about it. What really carries us along is more elusive and vital than these. The art of words cannot say it.
>
> Just as Sullivan wrote the comedy of music, this art of the Astaires is the comedy of dance. It alone can express itself.[22]

Integral to this comedy of dance and just as elusive was personality. In his review of *Lady, Be Good!*, Young likened Adele, technically and superficially, to Beatrice Lillie, who had recently made her New York debut in *André Charlot's Revue*, while identifying a fascination uniquely Adele's. Critics and audiences were increasingly fascinated by Fred, whose charmingly awkward persona enhanced, rather than undermined, his insouciant control as a dancer.

Fred and Adele had three duets: "Hang on to Me," an anthem almost to their real-life relationship; "Swiss Miss," which served as their nutty run-around number; and, most famously, "Fascinating Rhythm," which began with a chorus played and sung by Cliff Edwards ("Ukulele Ike," who would later memorably sing "When You Wish upon a Star" as the voice of Jiminy Cricket in Walt Disney's *Pinocchio*). Originally titled "Syncopated City" and referred to by George and Ira's father as "Fashion on the River," the showstopping "Fascinating Rhythm" became, Howard Pollack says, "paradigmatic not only of a certain side of Gershwin's work but of the Jazz Age itself."[23] What is more, it became the archetypal song of the Astaire-Gershwin collaboration. The dance even had George Gershwin's choreographic input, as Fred recounts in his autobiography:

> Adele and I were stuck for an exit step. We had the routine set but needed a climax wow step to get us off. For days I couldn't find one. Neither could dance director Sammy Lee.
>
> George happened to drop by and I asked him to look at the routine. He went to the piano. . . .
>
> We went all through the thing, reaching the last step before the proposed exit and George said, "Now travel—travel with that one."
>
> I stopped to ask what he meant and he jumped up from the piano and demonstrated what he visualized. He wanted us to continue doing the last step, which started center stage, and sustain it as we traveled to the side, continuing until we were out of sight offstage.
>
> The step was a complicated precision rhythm thing in which we kicked out simultaneously as we crossed back and forth in front of each other with arm pulls and heads back. There was a lot going on, and when George suggested traveling, we didn't think it was possible.
>
> It was the perfect answer to our problem, however, this suggestion by hoofer Gershwin, and it turned out to be a knockout applause puller.[24]

This moment of inspiration on the part of "hoofer Gershwin" was recreated six decades later by caricaturist Edward Sorel; in his drawing, George's instructive Terpsichorean attitude is taken from a familiar photograph of Fred in 1936 in which Fred strikes a mock-earnest pose in front of a blackboard as choreographer Hermes Pan supposedly plots his steps in chalk.

Fred and Adele each had a solo number in *Lady, Be Good!* Adele's was an exuberant parody of a Mexican dance, supported by the male chorus and entitled

"Juanita," after the senorita she is called on to impersonate. Fred's was his first full-fledged solo, "The Half of It, Dearie, Blues," and allowed him to experiment as a tap dancer, again with choreographic contributions from Gershwin. Interestingly, Ira borrowed the title of the song from one of the catchphrases of the recently deceased female impersonator Bert Savoy, who was outrageously camp onstage and off, unlike most other drag artistes of the day.

In April 1925, the Astaires capitalized on their Broadway stardom by accepting an offer to dance at the Trocadero nightclub. The proprietors of the Trocadero, Mal Hayward and Frank Garlasco, were keen to emulate the success of the Club Mirador, which was currently featuring the British exhibition dancers Marjorie Moss and Georges Fontana. Moss and Fontana were being hailed as the greatest ballroom dancers since the Castles, allowing the club to impose a $5 cover charge. Fred and Adele's motives in agreeing to perform nightly at 12.45 a.m. during the run of *Lady, Be Good!* in the smoky confines of a nightclub were purely mercenary. They saw it as a means of amassing a small fortune within a short time and using the proceeds to purchase a Rolls-Royce. With nothing to lose, they audaciously asked for $5,000 a week for six weeks, at which Hayward and Garlasco did not flinch, although the record fee was a brief cause célèbre in theatrical circles and a sufficient talking point to guarantee solid business for the first two weeks. While they enjoyed working with Emil Coleman's orchestra, the Trocadero experience was little more than a highly lucrative form of vaudeville, with the Astaires dusting off and adapting some of the specialty routines from their "New Songs and Smart Dances" repertoire and devising new ones. The arduous midnight schedule in the uncongenial nightclub atmosphere was enlivened one night by a Prohibition raid and another by the Astaires' introduction to Adolphe Menjou. By the third week of the engagement, business began to decline and Fred and Adele voluntarily reduced their fee to $3,000 a week for the last two weeks, but not before they had forced the rival Mirador to close. Incidentally, another fashionable Manhattan nightclub of the period was Perroquet de Paris, started by Otto Kahn's eighteen-year-old jazz musician and bandleader son, Roger Wolfe Kahn.

Also in April 1925, Alex Aarons announced that he and Vinton Freedley, in conjunction with Sir Alfred Butt, would present *Lady, Be Good!* in London a year hence. The New York run of 330 performances ended on 12 September 1925. Four nights later, the Astaires' friend and supporter Noël Coward opened with Lillian Braithwaite at Henry Miller's Theatre in the American production of Coward's *The Vortex*, co-directed by the playwright and Basil Dean. This "thrilling, glib and seriously amusing play"[25] earned Coward "the biggest ovation any visiting player has received on Broadway in years."[26] Fred and Adele and their mother spent time socializing with Noël and his mother, Violet, who had accompanied him to New York along with his friend and designer Gladys

Calthrop, before taking *Lady, Be Good!* on the road for an autumn tour of ten major cities.

On 16 January 1926, the three Astaires sailed for Paris aboard the *Majestic*. Their intention was to have six weeks' holiday before rehearsals began in London on 1 March. On 28 January, they met Irving Berlin and his wife, the former Ellin Mackay, with whom they dined and danced at Ciro's. The Berlins, who had married in a civil ceremony three weeks earlier, were on their honeymoon and escaping a barrage of sensationalist newspaper headlines in America, focusing on the fact that Ellin, a Roman Catholic and society heiress, had eloped with Berlin, an orthodox Jew and a Russian immigrant who had grown up on New York's Lower East Side. Years later, when Fred settled in Hollywood, he and Irving worked together on six films and became the most intimate of friends.

After a fortnight of try-outs at the vast Empire Theatre in Liverpool, *Lady, Be Good!* opened in London at the Empire in Leicester Square on 14 April 1926. The English cast replacements included baritone George Vollaire as Jack Robinson (who sang and recorded "So Am I" with Adele), William Kent as Watty Watkins, Sylvia Leslie as Josephine, and Irene Russell as Shirley. Jazz guitarist Buddy Lee took over Ukulele Ike's part. Among the first-night telegrams

Figure 5.2 The Stage

the Astaires received was one addressed to Adele that simply read "LOVE TO YOU AND FREDDY. C. B. D[illingham]."[27]

Once again London welcomed the American "invaders" with a shower of critical superlatives:

> It is high time that musical comedy returned from the hysterical to the historical.
> —*Daily Telegraph*, 15 April 1926

> It is good from time to time there should be musical comedies like *Lady, Be Good!* at the Empire last night with one artist in them like Miss Adele Astaire (and these are very rare indeed) if only to remind us once again how intelligence and vitality are qualities in the world before which all other qualities burn—the Astaires would save any musical comedy— Miss Adele Astaire is, I think, the most attractive thing on any stage.
> —*Evening Standard*, 16 April 1926

> I prophesy a year's run for *Lady, Be Good!* at the Empire. . . . Fred and Adele have only to appear and everybody is blissfully happy. . . . Fred's "Half of it, Dearie, Blues" was one of the biggest things of the night.
> —*Daily Sketch*, 16 April 1926

With *Stop Flirting*, the critics had reached for biblical similes to express their awe at Fred and Adele. On this occasion *The Times* turned to Dickens, making a more prosaic but no less laudatory comparison between the Astaires and Vincent Crummles's "splendid tubs," an attraction for his apprentice dramaturge Nicholas Nickleby to build a piece around: "The two tubs, by which Mr. Crummles intended to indicate two entities that could completely fill the middle of the stage throughout a whole evening, were Mr. Fred and Miss Adele Astaire, and they filled the stage completely whenever they were on it" (15 April 1926).

St. John Ervine summed up the show in four words: "Adele Astaire. That's all!" But he had high praise for Fred as well, calling him "a cool, clever comedian, who can do anything with legs and feet: a genius at his job." Another admirer of Fred's burgeoning talents beyond his dancing was Sir Alfred Butt, who wrote to Fred on opening night: "I do not ever remember anyone who possesses quite so much charm and ability in dancing, added to which you have now developed a natural bent for acting that makes you rival Gerald du Maurier, Ivor Novello, Barrymore and others!"[28]

Gerald du Maurier himself was then appearing with Gladys Cooper in Frederick Lonsdale's *The Last of Mrs. Cheyney* at the St. James's Theatre. The week in which *Lady, Be Good!* opened at the Empire, one could also see in

London O'Casey's *Juno and the Paycock* at the Fortune; comedian Leslie Henson (soon to be part of the next Astaire-Gershwin collaboration) in the British production of *Kid Boots* at the Winter Garden; Tallulah Bankhead in *Scotch Mist* at the St. Martin's; Evelyn Laye in *Betty in Mayfair* at the Shaftesbury; Marie Tempest in *The Cat's Cradle* at the Criterion; Ralph Lynn in Ben Travers's *A Cuckoo in the Nest* at the Aldwych; Edith Evans as the Nurse in *Romeo and Juliet* at the Old Vic; and, in an extended season, Shaw's *Mrs. Warren's Profession*, written in 1893 but banned from public performance on the English stage until 1925.

Fred and Adele had returned to Britain at a critical moment in the nation's history. Two weeks into the London run of *Lady, Be Good!* the Trades Union Congress called a general strike as an act of solidarity with coal miners in the north of England, Wales, and Scotland, whose wages were being reduced and length of shift increased. From their flat in Park Lane, the Astaires had a view over the temporary army barracks and the milk and food depot set up in Hyde Park. Business at the theatre was not greatly affected, despite London transport grinding to a halt. The strike lasted just nine days but revealed bitter class divisions. Like Evelyn Waugh's Charles Ryder, some members of the middle and upper classes regarded it as their patriotic duty to volunteer their labor in what they perceived as a war against Bolshevism. Others thought it a lark to drive buses and lorries, sort the post, and deliver the milk. Very few had any sympathy with or any real conception of the miners' plight, although the king's stance was more conciliatory. George V had reacted angrily to a suggestion by coal-owner Lord Durham that the miners were "a damned lot of revolutionaries" by retorting: "Try living on their wages before you judge them!" Friends of the Astaires, such as Edwina Mountbatten and Lady Diana Cooper, were among the aristocratic volunteers. The strike was called off on 12 May with no guarantee from Stanley Baldwin's government of fair treatment for the miners, who struggled on alone until November and were then compelled back to work for less pay and longer hours.

All this had little impact on the Astaires' busy theatrical and social round. They enjoyed the companionship of friends from America, including Liz and Jimmy Altemus and John Hay "Jock" Whitney, whom they had met in New York when he was studying at Yale and who was now a graduate student at New College, Oxford.[29] They were entertained again by the Prince of Wales and his younger brothers, who remained their most loyal devotees. On 10 August they were invited to 17 Bruton Street, home of the Duke and Duchess of York, to luncheon and to "see the baby," that is, the future Queen Elizabeth II. The night before, the Astaires had been accorded a more formal royal honor when King George and Queen Mary attended the Empire Theatre to see *Lady, Be Good!* A special program was issued to commemorate their visit, twice the size of the regular one and with a cover printed in handsome gold lettering and bearing the royal insignia.

A rather more dubious honor was accorded Adele when the Austrian Expressionist painter Oskar Kokoschka, visiting London, met Adele backstage one evening and asked her to pose for a portrait. She agreed and went twice a week for two months to his studio in Kensington for sittings, but she disliked Kokoschka's lascivious manner and resented his refusal to let her see the work in progress. In a letter to his family in Vienna he referred to Adele as a "Jewish revue star." It was not until years later that Adele finally saw the finished portrait, which depicted her cross-eyed and with her long hair unbobbed, sitting with her legs drawn up on a couch. She is flanked on her right by a piano and open sheet music and on her left by her Aberdeen Scottish terrier "Wassie." Over her right shoulder is a picture of Leda and the Swan. The painting featured in an article about Kokoschka in *Time* of 5 May 1958. Adele was interviewed for the piece and voiced her distaste for the portrait. Three weeks later the following letter was published in *Time* under the heading "She Was Framed":

Sir:
With your permission, I'd like to give my opinion of the Kokoschka picture of my sister. I think it's a hideous mess. As great an artist as this man may be today, he certainly goofed in 1926. My sister is a very pretty girl.
FRED ASTAIRE Beverly Hills

After a run of 326 performances, *Lady, Be Good!* closed in London on Saturday, 22 January 1927. In attendance were the Prince of Wales and, fittingly and poignantly, the Astaires' childhood heroine Adeline Genée. For ten years, from 1897 to 1907, Genée had been the Empire's prima ballerina and, as such, one of the most popular figures of the Edwardian theatre. Fred paid tribute to her in his curtain speech, and she responded with a bow. The Astaires and company were the last performers to tread the boards of the once grand music hall on the north side of Leicester Square. Shortly afterward, it was demolished; Fred and Adele had brought down the house in every sense. The Empire reopened on 8 November 1928 as MGM's flagship cinema, with a screening of *Trelawny of the "Wells,"* a silent film adaptation of Pinero's comedy of 1898, starring Norma Shearer as Rose Trelawny.

The last night of *Lady, Be Good!* in the West End was celebrated and mourned at a party hosted by the Prince of Wales at St. James's Palace, with the revels continuing until four o'clock the next morning. Fred and Adele remained in Britain through the spring as the show made a limited provincial tour, which included a return to the Liverpool Empire and dates at the Glasgow Alhambra and the

Figure 5.3 The Empire Theatre, Leicester Square. *Lady, Be Good!* was its last live stage show before the theatre was demolished in 1927 and replaced by a cinema.
Adele Astaire Collection, Howard Gotlieb Archival Research Centre

Golders Green Hippodrome. They had already signed an agreement with Aarons and Freedley to star in a new Gershwin musical, *Smarty*, to be directed by Edgar MacGregor. The Gershwins had not been idle. While *Lady, Be Good!* was running on Broadway and in London, they had produced scores for three more shows, *Tell Me More*, *Tip-Toes*, and *Oh, Kay!* (featuring the song "Someone to Watch over Me," which was introduced by Gertrude Lawrence). George had premiered his Concerto in F with the New York Symphony at Carnegie Hall on 3 December 1925 and, after the Liverpool opening of *Lady, Be Good!*, had spent a week in Paris, where *An American in Paris* was conceived.

 Smarty had a long and complicated gestation. "We were on the road six weeks," Ira recalled, "and everyone concerned with the show worked day and night, recasting, rewriting, rehearsing, recriminating—of rejoicing, there was none." Fred Thompson and Guy Bolton drafted the original scenario, but the full script was co-written by Thompson and drama critic and Algonquin wit

Figure 5.4 Adele and Fred returning to New York aboard the *RMS Majestic,* June 1927.
Photofest

Robert Benchley. The result was anything but encouraging, and by the time the show debuted at the Shubert Theatre in Philadelphia on 11 October 1927, it was in dire shape. Composer Richard Rodgers, in Philadelphia for the try-outs of his and Lorenz Hart's *Connecticut Yankee,* witnessed the ragged first performance and wrote to his future wife, Dorothy Feiner, "God will have to do miracles if it's to be fixed."[30] Benchley shamefacedly withdrew from the production, exclaiming, "Gosh, how can I criticize other people's shows if I've anything to do with this?" He was replaced by play doctor Paul Gerard Smith, who received final credit as co-author, and for the next few weeks the company were subjected to continuous script alterations. At Ford's Theatre in Washington, Fred remembered "playing one version while rehearsing another."[31] The cast was strengthened by three late changes: Allen Kearns as Adele's romantic interest, aviator Peter Thurston, and Victor Moore[32] and Earl Hampton in the comic roles of two bungling jewel thieves, Herbert and Chester. The Gershwins furiously rewrote the score, compiling around twenty-five numbers of which half were used. "How Long Has This Been Going On?" was cut and replaced by "He Loves and She Loves."

Smarty, re-titled *Funny Face*, finally arrived in New York on 22 November 1927. It was the first show to be presented at Aarons and Freedley's newly built Alvin Theatre, its name coined from the first syllables of "Alex" and "Vinton." The Alvin stood opposite the Guild Theatre on Fifty-Second Street, and in the Rotogravure section of the *New York Times* on Sunday, 18 December 1927, a large picture appeared of Alfred Lunt and Lynn Fontanne greeting their new neighbors, the Astaires. Brooks Atkinson was impressed by the interior, which seemed to have "all the best features of the modern playhouse—even an old English lounge where refreshments may be had. The auditorium is decorated in pastel shades of blue and gray, with ivory and old gold decorations."[33]

Because business in Washington and Wilmington, Delaware, had been poor, with, as Fred put it, "never enough of an audience to give us a reaction,"[34] the company had no way of gauging just how successful the revisions had been. The critical reception of *Funny Face* in New York surprised no one more than its creators and performers. For all its travail, the show was a hit equal to *Lady, Be Good!,* and the Astaires received some of the best notices of their career. The qualities that were consistently extolled in their dancing were speed, intricacy, grace, humor, eccentricity, eloquence, and joie de vivre or effervescence.

> When Harlequin puts on a gray derby hat and Columbine delights in a particularly impudent snub nose, you have the two Astaires. . . . They are a sort of champagne cup of motion, those Astaires. They live, laugh and leap in a world that is all bubbles. They are sleek, long-shanked, blissfully graceful, both of them. Their dance steps flash and quiver with an intricacy which declines to be taken seriously but which is none the less a maker of marvels.
>
> —*New York Sun*, 23 November 1927

> They have not only humor but intelligence; not only spirit but good taste; not only poise but modesty; and they are not only expert eccentric dancers but they never make an ungraceful movement. Twice last evening Fred Astaire took the audience's breath away with his rapid footing and his intelligibility in a brand of clog-dance pantomime. In a particularly refreshing male chorus number to the tune of "High Hat," he gave every indication of proceeding in two directions at once. As a gauche and prevaricating young lady, his sister also dances beautifully, meanwhile making the faces celebrated in the title of the comedy. Within their very individual field the Astaires appear to have things very much their own way.
>
> —*New York Times*, 23 November 1927

The "High Hat" number referred to was one of two antecedents in Fred's stage career to his trademark "Top Hat, White Tie and Tails" routine on screen. In another number without Adele, Fred sang and executed a bravura tap solo to "My One and Only," a performance that the displaced Benchley, writing in *Life*, pronounced "one of the most thrilling dramatic events in town,"[35] and losing nothing in that respect to Max Reinhardt's production of *A Midsummer Night's Dream* at the Century Theatre. Adele sang "He Loves and She Loves" and "'S Wonderful" with Allen Kearns, and brother and sister (playing guardian and ward) united for the title song "Funny Face," "Let's Kiss and Make Up," and "The Babbitt and the Bromide." This last earned Ira Gershwin a place in *The Oxford Book of Comic Verse*. The curious title was taken from Sinclair Lewis's 1922 novel *Babbitt*, which satirized the vacuity and conformity of middle-class American life in the character of middle-aged realtor George F. Babbitt, and from a humorous essay by Gelett Burgess published in *The Smart Set* in 1906 and entitled "Are You a Bromide? Or, The Sulphitic Theory Expounded and Exemplified According to the Most Recent Researches into the Psychology of Boredom." Essentially, a bromide was an utterer of bromidiums—banalities or commonplaces. Thus, the personae assumed by Fred and Adele in the number meet at intervals of ten and twenty years and exchange the same sequence of meaningless patter in a state of complete self-absorption. The Gershwins intended the song to be sung in deadpan unison but instead the Astaires sang alternate lines.

Hello!
How are you?
Howza folks?
What's new?
I'm great!
That's good!
Ha! Ha!
Knock wood!
Well! Well!
What say?
Howya been?
Nice day!
How's tricks?
What's New?
That's fine!
How are you?
Nice weather we are having but it gives me such a pain:
I've taken my umbrella but of course it doesn't rain.
Heigh ho!

That's life!
What's new?
Howza life?
Gotta run!
Oh my!
Ta Ta!
Olive Oil!
Good-bye!

Fred resurrected "The Babbitt and the Bromide" in Vincente Minnelli's *Ziegfeld Follies* of 1946, using it as a vehicle for a rare screen duet with Gene Kelly. He also performed the song with Jack Lemmon in a televised Gershwin tribute in 1972. The original version with Fred and Adele culminated, of course, in the run-around.

Walter Wanger, whose credits as a film producer included *The Sheik* with Rudolph Valentino in 1921, and who was married to Justine Johnstone, star of the Astaires' first Broadway show, invited Fred and Adele to make a screen test for Paramount and tried to interest them in a film version of *Funny Face*. Neither Fred nor Adele was enthused by the results of the test they made, and Wanger failed to secure the rights to the stage show. Paramount did make a film called *Funny Face* in 1957, with Fred and Audrey Hepburn and directed by Stanley Donen, but it bore no relation to the stage version and utilized only four of its songs (five, if one includes the excised "How Long Has This Been Going On?").

Casting a shadow over the triumph of *Funny Face* was a series of tempests in Adele's offstage life. It is possible that she had a failed or unfulfilled love affair with George Gershwin in the mid-1920s. Gershwin, who never married, had his name linked to many women and a reputation for flirtatiousness. Predictably, there has been speculation over the years about his sexuality, but it would seem that only Adele, in an unpublished interview with Helen Rayburn, has claimed categorically that the composer was impotent: "George loved all the girls but absolutely I know he was impotent. . . . He never got terribly involved with any-body. . . . He was a neuter. I would have had George except he wasn't given to women. And he wasn't given to men either. I think that's what caused his brain tumor —something wasn't getting stimulated."[36] Whatever the nature of Adele's involvement with Gershwin and the truth of her claim, what is certain is the volatility of her relationship with William Gaunt, Jr., documented in Ann Astaire's diaries. Gaunt was the twenty-five-year-old son of a Yorkshire wool manufac-turer who had an interest in the Shubert empire. It was through Alex Aarons and as a potential backer of *Funny Face* that he met Adele.

Ann and Fred's opinion of Gaunt was that he was a controlling cad and an adventurer, a conclusion Adele herself reached but only after several fierce quarrels, defiant reconciliations, and public announcements of their engage-ment and of Adele's imminent retirement from the stage. The turbulence of their affair caused Adele, for the first time in her career, to miss a performance and threatened the harmony of her personal and professional relationship with Fred. On the afternoon following the New York premiere, Adele and Gaunt attended a cocktail party. Adele, unused to liquor, became woozy and lost track of time. She arrived for the evening performance after the overture had started and was clearly intoxicated in her first dance number with Fred, who tried to conceal and compensate for her dazed waywardness as best he could. Once they were in the wings, Fred gave Adele a sharp slap on each cheek. He had never struck his sister before and, although she cried, the violent rebuke shocked her into sobriety. In later years, Adele confessed, "I caused my brother a lot of trouble. That upsets me. If he wanted to count back all the times that I've upset him . . . I should just forget it."[37].

Funny Face closed in New York on 23 June 1928. Just two weeks later, on 8 July, Adele was involved in a near-fatal accident while weekending on the Long Island estate of William Bateman Leeds and his wife, Princess Xenia Georgievna Romanov. Adele had accompanied her host aboard his speedboat the *Fan Tail*. When Leeds attempted to start the motor, it backfired and ignited some petrol that had seeped on top of the bilge water next to the keel. He and Adele were suddenly engulfed in flames. Leeds dragged Adele from the boat before pushing it out into the water where within seconds it exploded. Adele was badly burned and spent the rest of the summer in New York Hospital. Newspaper reports of the incident suppressed the fact that William Gaunt had been present that weekend and instead erroneously placed Fred at the scene of the accident. In a strange coincidence, Fred was involved in a car accident the same day while driving back from a party on Long Island with a girlfriend, Mary Atwill, at the wheel. The car turned over on the side of the road, but neither occupant was seriously harmed.

Adele's injuries and hospitalization made it necessary to postpone the London opening of *Funny Face,* and Sir Alfred Butt lost the rights to the assigned theatre, the Winter Garden. The production had, therefore, to remain longer in the prov-inces before being brought in to the West End. It toured to Liverpool, Birmingham, and Cardiff before opening at the Princes Theatre on Shaftesbury Avenue (the present Shaftesbury Theatre) on 8 November 1928.

London by this time had a name, or indeed a diagnosis, for its mania for Fred and Adele—"Astairia."[38] With *Show Boat*, a musical with a full-blooded libretto, running concurrently at Drury Lane, the slender plot of *Funny Face* was unlikely to astonish or move the critics. But the Astaires' dancing provided ample dra-matic substance and nuance. The show had acquired another principal asset in English comedian Leslie Henson, who had headed the cast of Gershwin's

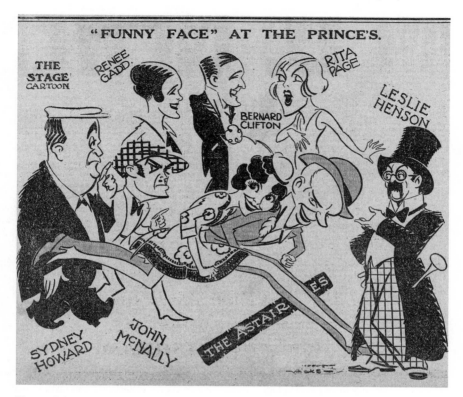

Figure 5.5 *The Stage*

Primrose at the Winter Garden. *The Times* review was predominantly a hymn to Henson's comic genius—to the extraordinary facial and bodily contortions he achieved, which enacted a drama in themselves:

> Mr. Henson alone is well able to make his part greater than the whole. He brings to it impeccable accomplishment and a natural gift of drollery: he sets us storing away memories of this or that gesture or grimace rather than this or that play; and now and then, exploring some poor, outworn theme with the vehemently delighting eye of the artist, he astonishes the audience by his discoveries. . . .
>
> Miss Adele Astaire is a heroine of musical comedy who amusingly mocks her kind, and Mr. Astaire is as agile, as cool, and as brilliant on his feet as ever.
>
> —9 November 1928

Funny Face seemed, *Macbeth*-like, uncannily to court misadventure. The run at the Princes Theatre was interrupted by a gas explosion that occurred in a

Figure 5.6 "The Babbitt and the Bromide". Adele and Fred with Leslie Henson.

disused Post Office "tube" or tunnel under High Holborn shortly before eight o'clock in the morning on 20 December. The explosion killed one workman and injured and gassed seventeen other people. Half a mile of roadway was torn up; the region immediately around the Princes Theatre suffered particularly heavy damage. Opposite the theatre a huge cavity had been blown in the road and gas still floated dangerously about, making the approach to the theatre's entrance impassable and demanding the cancellation of several performances. Photographs were published in the press of the Astaires and Leslie Henson in what looked like a war zone or the aftermath of an earthquake; one showed them seated on the rubble outside the theatre beside a formidable crater, another surveying a hideously twisted lamp-post perched precariously on the ravaged pavement.

Funny Face transferred to the Winter Garden on 28 January 1929 and there finished its London run of 263 performances on 30 June. It would be the last time the Astaires performed together in the city that made them stars and the last show they did with the Gershwins, thereby ending two historic alliances that helped to shape the cultural life of Britain and America between the wars. In fact, the triple alliance between the Astaires, the Gershwins, and London seems the very measure of a specific moment and movement in history, of what playwright S. N. Behrman heard in Gershwin's piano playing, "the rush of the great heady surf of vitality,"[39] of a decade whose modernity is, to us now, at once remote and startlingly fresh.

But it was the future that was preoccupying the Astaires. Among Adele's backstage visitors that night were Prince Aly Khan and the man for whom she would quit the stage, Lord Charles Cavendish, younger son of the ninth Duke of Devonshire. Before they left London, Fred and Adele received a cable from Florenz Ziegfeld: "I have wonderful idea for you co-starring with Marilyn Miller." "This seemed," Fred said, "like the big one we were looking for."[40] Which proved that appearances could be very deceptive.

CHAPTER 6

The Golden Calf

My tears for you make everything hazy
Clouding the skies of blue.
—Walter Donaldson, "You're Driving Me Crazy"

"The kind of flop that even made the audience look bad" was how Fred wryly characterized their next show.[1] If ever a production was inaptly titled it was *Smiles*, as it yielded little in the way of serenity or mirth to those implicated in its brief, tempestuous life and extravagant demise. On paper it seemed a sure-fire hit, an enterprise flawlessly envisioned and replete with blue-chip, gilt-edged stock, including a score by Vincent Youmans and Harold Adamson, but it evolved rapidly into the Broadway equivalent of the Wall Street Crash of October 1929, which had delayed its premiere by effectively bankrupting its producer, Florenz Ziegfeld. Yet, rather like the story of the *Titanic*, it is because of its perceived invincibility, its catalogue of contributory human frailty and error, and its illustrious list of casualties that *Smiles* remains an intriguing debacle.

It was the only time the Astaires ever worked with the man whose name had become a byword for lavish showmanship and musical theatre at its aspirational apex. Their "defection" caused some resentment on the part of Aarons and Freedley, although Fred claimed: "It was all understood and on completely friendly terms, ending our business relationship for the time being."[2] In fact, the London production of *Funny Face* was to be the final collaboration between the Astaires and their "old firm." Alex Aarons, rightly as it transpired, had expressed doubts about the great showman's ability to nurture the Astaires' special talents, particularly as they were to share star billing with Ziegfeld's glamorous protégée and rumored paramour Marilyn Miller. But for Fred and Adele, despite their already established transatlantic prominence, the prospect of appearing for the legendary impresario was one of irresistible promise and prestige.

As Aarons had intimated, Ziegfeld was not an obvious architect for an Astaire vehicle. In any case, a show by Ziegfeld was, unquestionably, a Ziegfeld show.

He had found his calling at the 1893 World's Columbian Exposition in his home-town, Chicago, where he made a star of the Prussian strongman Eugen Sandow and demonstrated his genius for tastefully provocative spectacle; his marketing coup de maître on that occasion lay in recognizing and exploiting the risqué fascination of Sandow's muscular physique to a Victorian female audience. Ziegfeld's star-building feats, and his flair as an arbiter and enticer of popular taste, continued. He was instrumental in launching the careers of celebrated headliners such as Fanny Brice, Eddie Cantor, W. C. Fields, and Will Rogers and in championing the work of songwriters of the calibre of Irving Berlin, George Gershwin, Rodgers and Hart, and Sigmund Romberg. His monument was the *Follies*, a revue series that became an American institution, an unabashed glorification of feminine pulchritude, originally intended to emulate the famed Folies Bergère in Paris. His other, greater contribution to musical theatre history was Kern and Hammerstein's *Show Boat* in 1927, widely lauded as the first American musical play, with its exceptional score and dramatically substantial libretto.

Ziegfeld was an audacious visionary with an unrivaled eye for beauty and design, a master publicist, and perhaps his own most flamboyant creation. What he was unequivocally not was an astute businessman. Kept solvent, albeit erratically, by the success of his productions rather than shrewd financial management, he spared no personal expense in the fulfillment of his sumptuous theatrical vision, the promotion of his pet performers, or the maintenance of a lifestyle commensurate with his godlike self-image. He was also a compulsive gambler, losing small fortunes at Monte Carlo and larger ones on the stock market.

No Broadway producer was immune to the events of Black Tuesday (or the concurrent threat posed by the theatre's new competitor, talking pictures). Their survival rates varied. Like Ziegfeld, the Astaires' old friend Charles Dillingham was wiped out in the Crash and never truly recovered; the gentlemanly impresario suffered a sad, penurious end, existing, until his death in 1934, on charity from former associates, including Fred, who at the start of his Hollywood career gave Dillingham $15,000. Ziegfeld's main rivals, the Shuberts, withstood the deepening economic crisis for two seasons before going into receivership at the end of 1931. They had been notoriously frugal, employing throughout their theatre empire eccentric economy measures such as charging for the paper cups near the water fountains and refusing to supply hot water in the rest rooms. It was they, of course, who in 1918 had craftily kept the Astaires on half salary well beyond the height of the Spanish flu pandemic and regardless of a resurgence in audience attendance. Sound business sense and prudent practice saved Aarons and Freedley for a time, but they eventually lost the Alvin Theatre to the mortgage holders, and after the Gershwins' *Pardon My English*, which they produced at the Majestic Theatre with Jack Buchanan in the lead role, they pursued separate professional interests.

The Astaires, too, lost considerable sums of money. In August 1929 Ann's account was valued at $36,000, while Fred's was worth in excess of $100,000; after the Crash, their combined wealth was less than $27,000. Their earning power, however, had not diminished; the contract they signed with Ziegfeld on 15 December 1929 assured them a weekly salary of $4,000.

Smiles had a projected opening date of 1 March 1930, but it soon became clear that Ziegfeld was having trouble raising the necessary funds. In February he advised Fred and Adele that the show would have to be postponed until the autumn. It was, in the end, two lucrative co-productions that helped subsidize *Smiles*. In association with Arch Selwyn, Ziegfeld had imported C. B. Cochran's London production of Noël Coward's operetta *Bittersweet*, which opened at the Ziegfeld Theatre exactly one week after the stock market plunged. With songs including "I'll See You Again" and "If Love Were All," the show secured Coward's reputation in America and ran for a respectable, if not outstanding, 159 performances. The other timely collaboration was an early Technicolor film version of Ziegfeld's stage hit *Whoopee!*, starring Eddie Cantor. It was released by United Artists in September 1930 with Ziegfeld and Sam Goldwyn as co-producers.

Not only did these two ventures attract backers to *Smiles*, they also supplied part of its literary pedigree. With Marilyn Miller in mind, Ziegfeld purchased from Noël Coward a rudimentary outline for a show. Not fully satisfied with the result, he then commissioned Louis Bromfield, who had won a Pulitzer Prize in 1927 for his novel *Early Autumn*, to develop Coward's initial idea. Marilyn Miller, used to getting her own way with Ziegfeld, insisted that William Anthony McGuire write the definitive draft. McGuire, who was to direct the show, had been the author of *Whoopee!* and of Miller's most recent stage success, *Rosalie*, but he was also a heavy drinker, unpredictable, and unreliable. George S. Kaufman's name was fleetingly attached to the emerging project, and the satirist and short-story writer Ring Lardner was later hired to "fix" the script and furnish additional lyrics, but it was McGuire who finally received sole credit for the book. The title of the show similarly underwent several bewildering permutations, including *Six-Cylinder Love*, *Spinning Wheel*, and *Tom, Dick and Harry*. *Smiles* was ultimately chosen because Miller's string of successes comprised one-word titles derived from the names of her characters—*Sally* (1920), *Sunny* (1925), and *Rosalie* (1928); "Smiles" was the nickname ironically bestowed on the sad-eyed waif she portrayed. But neither its auspicious title nor the notable writers associated with the book's genesis could save the show from disaster.

The story line was incurably weak and, as Fred noted, "rather a throwback to *The Belle of New York*."[3] In a small French town at the end of World War I, four soldiers—an Italian, Englishman, Frenchman, and American—find an orphaned child and take up a collection to send her to America. Ten years later, the grown-up "Smiles" is working as a Salvation Army lass in a Bowery mission.

Her four benefactors have also settled in New York. Bob and Dot Hastings (Fred and Adele's characters), spoilt and bored society types out for a night of fashionable slumming on the Lower East Side, stray into the mission, and on a bet Bob invites Smiles to a Chinese costume ball at their Southampton estate. Bob falls in love with Smiles, who is also being courted by her American guardian, Dick. When Smiles returns to France to seek her roots, Bob and Dick both follow, chasing her back to America, where she chooses to marry Dick.

For all its clichéd improbabilities, Kaufman might, nevertheless, have succeeded where McGuire and Lardner failed. As well as being a proven dramatist in his own right and one of the great humorists of the day, he was Broadway's most versatile and sought-after "play doctor," a ruthless script editor with a thorough command of stagecraft and a known capacity for laboring patiently and under pressure at the tedious tasks crucial to making comedy buoyant and airtight. But with McGuire at the helm, often in absentia and unsteadily at best, rehearsals descended into drunken chaos. *Smiles* went into rehearsal with only half a script; the second act never amounted to more than a vaguely coherent series of musical numbers and improvised scenes.

Miller's main reason for doing the show was that she wanted to dance with Fred. He had choreographed a tap number, "The Wedding Knell," for her and the male chorus of *Sunny*, and, although they had never performed together before, they had crossed early professional paths. In common with the Astaires, Miller was born in the Midwest and was a vaudeville veteran at a very young age, touring with her family's act, The Five Columbians, and evading the Gerrymen (agents of the dreaded Gerry Society). And like Fred and Adele, she made her Broadway debut for the Shuberts—in *The Passing Show of 1914*—and in England was befriended by the Prince of Wales. It was Ziegfeld, of course, who made her a star when she appeared in the *Follies* of 1918 and brought the house down with her impersonation of Ziegfeld's wife Billie Burke, singing "Mine Was a Marriage of Convenience."

Miller's stardom belied the limitations of her Terpsichorean and singing talent and the complications of her private life. By 1930, she had two failed marriages behind her; her first husband, Frank Carter, had died in an automobile accident, while her second, Jack Pickford (whom the Astaires had encountered during the filming of *Fanchon the Cricket* at Delaware Water Gap) was an alcoholic, syphilitic womanizer and drug addict. Miller herself was increasingly dependent on alcohol, and she suffered from a chronic sinus condition. Her extraordinary appeal rested largely on her delicate beauty and her vulnerable, Cinderella-like persona (as captured in her signature song, Jerome Kern's "Look for the Silver Lining"). In an age that emblematized the dark, vampish allure of the flapper, the blonde, blue-eyed Miller projected an enchanting ethereality. She looked, it has been remarked, "like a fairy illustration by Arthur Rackham."[4] In real life she

Figure 6.1 Adele, Fred, and Marilyn Miller, 1930.
Adele Astaire Collection, Howard Gotlieb Archival Research Centre

frequently projected an earthier, less enchanting persona, and during *Smiles* she was at her volatile worst.

William Anthony McGuire was not the only one for whom the rehearsal period passed in an alcoholic haze. Composer Vincent Youmans would turn up drunk to rehearsal, lie down at the back of the stalls, and go to sleep. He seldom played the piano; if any piano-playing was done it was usually by Fred or the teenaged Larry Adler, who had a small part as a street urchin in the Bowery scenes.[5] The year before, Youmans had borrowed $10,000 from Ziegfeld to bring his show *Great Day* into New York, where, in spite of having one of Youmans's best scores ("More Than You Know" and "Without a Song" were two of its hits), it lasted just thirty-six performances. In return for this loan, Youmans had promised to write a score for Ziegfeld, but the relationship between the two men developed acrimoniously, to say the least, and culminated in Ziegfeld taking desperate legal proceedings.

Youmans chose as his lyricist Harold Adamson, a twenty-three-year-old Harvard student whose theatrical experience did not extend beyond summer stock and the Hasty Pudding shows but who, with fellow neophyte Mack

Gordon, devised the perfect lyric to fit the triplet-laden "Time on My Hands," the show's most memorable song. Problems arose when Miller perversely refused to sing the number and demanded it be cut. Out of frustration with her own performance and the stagnating production, she had decided to make the score the focus of her displeasure as well as a convenient scapegoat. Ziegfeld's placatory compromise was to have Paul Gregory (in the part of Miller's guardian and suitor Dick) sing the song *to* Miller, who relented to the extent of singing a single refrain, but only with a new lyric by Ring Lardner, "What Can I Say?," which fitted the melody rather clumsily.

The petty politics and ineptitude that led to its mishandling accounts for the fact that so hauntingly lovely a number, now acknowledged as a standard, did not become popular as a result of *Smiles*. The first recording of "Time on My Hands" was not made until 19 February 1931, six weeks after the show closed—and not in New York but in London, by Ray Noble's New Mayfair Dance Orchestra, with Al Bowlly as vocalist. It became a favorite with the Prince of Wales, who requested dance bands to play it wherever he went. Only then did its popularity filter back to the United States where, in September, Smith Ballew was the first American orchestra leader to record the song.

The song "Blue Bowery" was another unfortunate casualty of Miller's spiteful caprice. Performed by an ensemble player named Harriete Lake, it stopped the show during the try-outs in Boston, but Miller made sure that it was dropped before the New York opening, along with Harriete Lake's other number, "More than Ever," and Lake herself, who, incidentally, moved to Hollywood and changed her name to Ann Sothern.[6]

For Youmans the final straw came when Miller wanted the conductor, his friend Paul Lannin, fired, at which point he threatened to withdraw the music of the entire show. This prompted Ziegfeld to apply to the Superior Court for a special injunction preventing Youmans from any such drastic recourse. When the composer and Lannin arrived at the Colonial Theatre in Boston to collect up their sheet music and abscond back to New York, Ziegfeld, armed with a restraining order, had them bodily removed from the theatre.

The Astaires, meanwhile, had their own legal skirmish with Ziegfeld. Owing to the show's manifold problems, the rehearsal period exceeded its stipulated four weeks, running into six, but the cast had not been paid for the extra two weeks. When the Astaires complained, Ziegfeld countered by accusing them, on McGuire's information, of being persistently late for rehearsal. In her fearlessly outspoken style, Adele told him truthfully that she and Fred had always been on time for rehearsal but that McGuire was routinely to be found on the fire escape making amorous advances to some showgirl or other. It was not until July of the following year that they successfully sued Ziegfeld for their unpaid earnings.

Before the show opened in Boston on 28 October with its unfinished script, even Ziegfeld's patience with the recalcitrant McGuire had been exhausted. He fired him as librettist and brought in Ring Lardner as his replacement. Battling his own demons in the form of alcoholism and tuberculosis, Lardner, as script doctor, made little impression on the now terminally ill patient. After four days in Boston, it was alarmingly apparent that one of the show's few virtues was Larry Adler's harmonica solo in the first scene of the second act. A severely fraught Ziegfeld fumed: "If we don't lift this goddamn book, the whole show is going to be stolen by Larry Adler." "That," replied Lardner, "would be petty larceny."[7]

The critic for the *Boston Evening Transcript* put his finger on one of the show's inherent flaws—that Ziegfeld, Miller, and the Astaires were not a good fit, that they represented two opposing styles, two different eras, of musical theatre. Miller may have been two years younger than Adele and less than a year older than Fred, but she lacked their modernity as well as their stand-alone substance: "She could merely sing, dance, pose and prattle according to her abilities, which do not increase . . . she belongs to an older order of such musical comedy pieces [and needs] a sentimental, prettified, glamorous "vehicle" [which clashes with the requirements of] the light, dry, sophisticated Astaires."[8] The fact was the Astaires were out of place in a traditional Ziegfeld extravaganza, especially one beleaguered by vanity and incompetence. But while the association did them no favors, their professionalism did not falter.

As in his subsequent film career, Fred proved that even in the most forgettable and uninspiring vehicle he could work magic in the form of a thoroughly inspired solo number. Just such a number was "Say, Young Man of Manhattan" (its title appropriated from a recent Paramount picture, which happened to provide Fred's future partner Ginger Rogers with her first role in a feature-length film). The idea for the routine came to Fred at four o'clock one morning. He visualized a long line of chorus boys in top hats and imagined himself shooting them down one by one with his cane, each rifle shot simulated by a loud tap, until his elegantly attired victims resembled the bent and jagged teeth of a giant comb. As a finale he would act as a human machine gun, powered by some unstoppable rhythmic force within and mowing down the already maimed chorus line in a furious salvo of syncopated taps. Leaping out of bed, Fred improvised the effect with an umbrella. Soon he heard his sister's voice issuing querulously from her room down the hall: "Hey, Minnie, what the hell are you doing?"

"I just got an idea for the 'Manhattan' number."

Adele replied sleepily, "Well hang on to it, baby—you're going to need it in this turkey".[9]

The realization of this early-morning brainwave, as choreographed and executed by Fred, was impressive, but it was wasted at the show's outset. All was not lost, however: five years later the basis of this brilliantly imaginative shooting-gallery routine was resurrected and refashioned in Fred's most iconic screen solo, "Top Hat, White Tie and Tails," where, after the number's breezy opening, it served as the blistering climax of a modernistic pantomime in which a solitary Fred interacts with an ominous unseen presence. The darkness and violence that was explored first in "Say, Young Man of Manhattan" (albeit within the palatable bounds of musical comedy), and figures in other film dances such as the despairing, nihilistic tour de force "One for My Baby" (from *The Sky's the Limit*, 1943) are important, and sometimes curiously overlooked, components of Astaire's choreographic language.

Fred wrote in his autobiography: "There's something about a flop show that is hard to describe. You feel a mixture of embarrassment and inadequacy. You want to hide. You imagine as you walk around on the street or any place that everyone is pointing and sneering at you and if they're not, they should be."[10] In Boston one evening after the show, in search of some temporary reprieve from the gloom and shame engulfing the now certain flop in which they were embroiled, Fred and Adele went for a drive along the bank of the Charles River. They were joined by Marilyn Miller and one of the chorus boys. As they crossed the Longfellow Bridge, which connects Boston to Cambridge, Fred asked the driver to stop in the middle. He and Miller got out while the other two waited in the car. As they leant over the railing and looked down upon the river, another car pulled up. Suddenly and unceremoniously Fred was grabbed from behind by one of a pair of burly policemen and shaken "like a dice box."[11] Adele, horrified to see her brother manhandled in this way, raced from the car and threw herself at the policeman, pummeling his chest with her fists while shrieking and cursing at him. The policeman, like a startled dog, dropped his prey. "That's my sister," Fred explained. "You see, we're in a show." The very spot Fred had selected for a moment's quiet contemplation had apparently gained notoriety as a site for suicides, and Fred and Marilyn were naturally mistaken for a college student and his girlfriend carrying out a suicide pact. In William Faulkner's novel *The Sound and the Fury*, published the previous year, the bridge is the setting for the suicide of Harvard freshman Quentin Compson. Having at length convinced the police that in spite of their involvement in *Smiles*, they were not yet suicidal, Fred presented the strong arm of the law with tickets for the show, thus feeling amply revenged for his undignified arrest.

If Ziegfeld appeared to have lost his Midas touch, there was no doubting his bravado. He put his publicity machine into overdrive; if nothing else, the show was going to go down with an almighty bang. The New York premiere he staged on 18 November resembled a Hollywood gala. Thousands of spectators gathered outside the theatre to watch the arrival of an audience that included the Vincent Astors, John Hay Whitneys, William Randolph Hearsts, and William

Vanderbilts. The top ticket price that evening was a record $22.00. But no amount of hype or manufactured stardust could disguise the irredeemably dull and ham-fisted script or the shiftless sense of defeat that had attached itself, leech-like, to the production. The New York critics laid no blame for the catastrophe on the Astaires, whose efforts they extolled as contemporary and the way of the future, untouched by the dead hand of their present incongruous circumstances. "With them dancing is comedy of manners," Brooks Atkinson observed, "very much in the current mode. . . . They give dancing all the mocking grace of improvisation with droll dance inflections and with comic changes of pace. . . . Slender, agile and quick-witted, the Astaires are ideal for the American song-and-dance stage."[12]

Robert Benchley, giving his verdict over a week later in the *New Yorker*, saw the Astaires as a salvational force amid false idols:

> Considered as the Golden Calf brought in on the Ark of the Covenant, [*Smiles*] was a complete bust. Of course, no show with Fred and Adele Astaire in it could really be considered a *complete* bust. There are moments, such as when Fred is shooting down chorus boys with his stick, or, with Adele, is executing the beloved "runaround" to the accompaniment of an uncoordinated French band, when the back of your neck begins to tingle and you realize that you are in the presence

Figure 6.2 Fred and Adele in *Smiles*.
Photofest

of something Pretty Darned Swell. Adele is a fine little comedienne . . . and I don't think that I will plunge the nation into war by stating that Fred is the greatest dancer in the world.[13]

Almost immediately in the wake of opening night, Ziegfeld fell ill. On 27 November he sent Fred a telegram: "Don't worry—I'm feeling better—I'll fix the show! I could have fixed it in the first place, only there were too many cooks. Affectionately, Flo."[14] The trouble was there were too many inebriated cooks and no head chef with the clear vision and sense to avert calamity and effect a positive solution. Ziegfeld, plagued by debt, lawsuits, his relationship with Miller, poor health, and evidently failing judgment, had not a hope of "fixing" *Smiles*. The show limped toward a costly total of sixty-three performances, throughout which Ziegfeld was scarcely to be seen at the theatre. Marilyn Miller, suffering with her sinuses, missed several performances.[15]

Even after the opening, and into December, the score was subject to chops and changes, with the cast struggling to keep pace. One late addition was Walter Donaldson's number "You're Driving Me Crazy," which replaced Youmans's "Hotcha Ma Chotch" as a more suitable duet for Adele and Eddie Foy Jr. (one of several able supporting players in the cast).[16] They were given one afternoon to rehearse the song and, not surprisingly, neither had a firm grasp of the lyrics. As a necessary precaution, Eddie Foy took the cardboard out of his stiff shirt, wrote his and Adele's words on it, and placed the boards in the footlights. At seven o'clock that night, the stagehands came in and swept the stage, assigning the makeshift prompt cards to the dustbin. A little before the curtain went up at 8:30, Foy heard Adele whisper something about the footlights, to which he cheerfully paid no attention, thinking Adele was simply clowning around in her usual fashion. When he discovered too late that the boards were missing, he was forced to extemporize as best he could, singing with interrogative urgency, "You, you're driving me crazy! / What'll I do, oh what'll I do?" Adele, heroically overcoming the urge to corpse, managed to respond with her own cri de coeur, taking a brave if imperfect run at the scansion, "You're going crazy and so am I, / What'll we do, oh what'll we do?" The rest of the duet continued in a vein of frantic invention and barely suppressed hysteria. This farcical episode, and the impromptu lyric it spawned, seems to typify the fiasco that was *Smiles*.

Adele was involved in another episode of musical farce, one that happened offstage but on air. Alexander Woollcott invited her to appear on his weekly CBS radio program *The Town Crier*, a species of arts round-up and literary chat show interspersed with highbrow gossip and plenty of Algonquinesque anecdotage.[17] Woollcott, an ardent admirer of Adele, was to interview her, after which she was to sing "Be Good to Me," one of the numbers she and Fred performed in the show. Adele asked Larry Adler to accompany her on the piano for the occasion. "Take it up half a tone," she said at the studio rehearsal, an innocent and reasonable enough request but one that flummoxed Adler, who played purely by ear and only in one key, C. To play the song in C sharp, thereby using the black notes, was quite beyond his capabilities. "Even the composer wouldn't have recognized what I did,"[18] admitted Adler. After the broadcast Adele was in tears, believing she had let herself and Fred down, which in turn sparked her brother's protective, and in this instance profane, fury. "Don't mess around with Mr. Fred today," Adler was warned by Astaire's valet, Walter; "he'll kill you." The next day, Adler recalls, Fred "left a newspaper in my dressing room, the *Herald-Tribune*. By cutting out letters and re-arranging them, he had manufactured a front-page headline; LARRY ADLER IS A LOUSY CUNT. He never let me forget my disastrous performance and would introduce me to people as 'Adele's great accompanist.'"[19]

Adler, of course, survived to dine out on the story, but he discovered that Fred's perfectionism was a force equally to be reckoned with. The Sunday benefit, a free charity performance often sponsored by the big newspapers, was a Broadway institution and an integral part of promoting a show. For the Broadway player, it was a hallowed obligation. Fred suggested to Adler that they work up their exchange in *Say, Young Man of Manhattan* into a routine that could be used for benefits. Adler assumed one rehearsal would be sufficient preparation of a number with which they were already so familiar, but he hadn't bargained for Fred's exactness and inexhaustible work ethic. They rehearsed the routine for a solid fortnight before Fred pronounced himself satisfied.

For both Astaires, there were distractions from the lugubrious progress of *Smiles*. Partly perhaps to show there were no hard feelings, Alex Aarons had telephoned Fred during rehearsals to ask for choreographic assistance with the show he and Vinton Freedley were about to open, the Gershwins' *Girl Crazy*.[20] Unhappy with their dance director, George Hale, Aarons and Freedley wanted Fred to review each routine and offer what suggestions he could. They felt one in particular needed work: "Embraceable You," which had been written for the aborted Ziegfeld show *East is West* and, therefore, for Marilyn Miller to sing.[21] In *Girl Crazy* the number was staged as a dance duet for Allen Kearns (Adele's romantic interest in *Funny Face*) and nineteen-year-old Ginger Rogers in her first starring role on Broadway.

Rogers was born in Missouri but grew up in Fort Worth, Texas, after her parents divorced and her mother Lela remarried. In 1925 she won the title of Texas State Charleston Champion; her prize was a vaudeville tour that began her career in show business. Lela was a stage mother far better suited to that fearsome epithet than Ann Astaire, but Ginger was devoted to her. By 1930 Ginger had scored a hit as Babs Green in her first Broadway show, *Top Speed*.[22] In terms of personality and her maturing abilities as an actress, she combined the tough, knowing quality of the "Blonde Bombshell" Jean Harlow, whom she physically resembled, with the touching vulnerability of the ingénue—a combination that, on the screen, supremely complemented Fred's own mix of boyishness and urbane knight-errantry.

Fred was able to make several helpful amendments and additions to "Embraceable You," which they rehearsed on the mezzanine, all other space being occupied. And so, in the thick-carpeted foyer of the Alvin Theatre one autumn afternoon in 1930, Fred Astaire and Ginger Rogers danced together for the first time. When both their shows were up and running in New York, Fred invited Ginger to share a midnight supper with him at the Central Park Casino, where they danced to the music of Eddy Duchin's orchestra. Fred's account of their date is characteristically terse, but Ginger is more forthcoming. Already, at that tender age, divorced, and now nursing a secret crush on Lew Ayres, her future husband, she was nonetheless flattered by Fred's attention and excited to be asked out by such a famous Broadway star. At the end of a delightful evening, Ginger reports, Fred bestowed on her a kiss that "would never have passed the Hays Office code!" After that they occasionally went out to a nightclub together or to a movie, but whether their relationship grew beyond a mild flirtation is unclear. When they met again, fatefully, in Hollywood two and a half years later, Ginger says: "Fred looked the same but acted differently. He was not as open, far more formal. I felt I didn't even know him. As if to explain his behavior, he said, "I'm married now.""[23] Martha Nomichson, in her book *Screen Couple Chemistry*, relies entirely on this version of events to play armchair psychologist, inferring from Fred's utterance the "subtext of a sexual history."[24]

At the time of *Smiles*, Fred was infatuated with Marilyn Miller, but with his sister's blunt counsel, he soon realized that she was capable of exploiting his devotion in order to make Ziegfeld and her fiancé Michael Farmer jealous. From the Ritz Hotel in Paris, where she had chosen to recuperate after *Smiles*, Miller told a journalist, "I'll surprise you all. One of these days I'm going to marry Fred Astaire."[25] Adele referred to her as a "publicity hound." In recent months two of Fred's old girlfriends had got married—Liz Altemus to his best friend, Jock Whitney, and Audrey Coates to Marshall Field—but Fred himself gave no indication of being any closer to settling down. His work came first. Adele, on the other hand, was tiring of the rigors of life on the stage, and at thirty-four, her thoughts turned to retirement. Influencing her state of mind was the fact that the young nobleman she had met in London, Lord Charles Cavendish, had lately arrived in New York and was plainly smitten with her. They began to see a great deal of one another, which was duly noted in the gossip columns.

"Charlie" had been sent by his family to undertake an apprenticeship with J. P. Morgan & Co. For the Duke and Duchess of Devonshire, one of the advantages of having their charmingly wayward son in the United States was the Prohibition laws, but Charlie's first order of business was to make contact with a bootlegger and to have his suits adjusted to accommodate a discreet flask. He had some aptitude for finance and, to begin with at least, applied himself to his work, but he applied himself far more assiduously to the delights and temptations of New York's social whirl.

As well as being impressed by his title, Adele genuinely liked Charlie and convinced herself she was in love with him. Her most serious beaux had all been wealthy men unconnected to the precarious world of theatre, and, if she were to marry, it would be not only for love but also for security: "I decided I wanted somebody who had something in his background that I wouldn't have to worry about." One night at 21, then a popular speakeasy, she found herself saying to Charlie, "You know, you and I get along so well. We ought to hitch up."

"You're right," he said.

Early the next morning Charlie telephoned Adele: "You proposed to me last night and I accepted. If you don't marry me, I'll sue you for breach of promise."[26]

Charlie's industrious carousing eventually lost him his job with J. P. Morgan; he returned to England two weeks after the opening of *Smiles*, which he had attended. He and Adele maintained an almost daily correspondence, but before their engagement could be officially announced or their wedding planned, there were two obstacles to surmount: the Duchess of Devonshire's formidable disapproval of the match and Adele's intense guilt at the thought of abandoning her brother and breaking up their life-long partnership. Nor was Adele eager to end her career on a flop.

During her absence from the show, Miller had undergone an operation to relieve pressure on her sinuses. When her return signaled no increase in ticket sales, Ziegfeld decided to close the show on 10 January, seven weeks after its premiere. Fred, who was ill and running a high temperature, played the final performance against his physician's advice. As a result, he was confined to bed for a week. He felt the failure of *Smiles* keenly and personally. But such is the extraordinary nature of show business, whose only certainty is constant flux, that the most ignominious flop can be followed by the most glorious triumph. Among those who caught the show before it closed were lyricist Howard Dietz and composer Arthur Schwartz, currently enjoying the tremendous success of their third revue together, *Three's a Crowd*. Dietz and Schwartz were both graduates of that rich breeding ground of great songwriters, Columbia University.[27] Their first revue, *The Little Show* in April 1929, was conceived as an intimate alternative, even an antidote, to the Ziegfeld-style spectacular. The show they were now working on, and pitched backstage to Fred, was to be acclaimed the greatest of all revues, a Broadway watershed. If *Smiles* belonged to an older order of musical theatre, this new venture was miraculously in step with, indeed ahead of, the times. It was also to be Adele's swan song.

CHAPTER 7

Frater, Ave atque Vale

Yesterday, my heart sang a blue song
But today, hear it hum a cheery new song.
—Howard Dietz and Arthur Schwartz, "New Sun in the Sky"

At MGM in 1953, producer Arthur Freed and director Vincente Minnelli cre-ated one of the greatest movie musicals of all time, *The Band Wagon*, an engag-ingly fresh and grown-up version of the hackneyed "let's-put-on-a-show" scenario. It starred Fred Astaire in a mature, multi-dimensional role with vaguely autobiographical resonance. Early in the film, fading Hollywood star Tony Hunter (Astaire) stands bemusedly and somewhat rebelliously amid the gaudy nocturnal clamor of an unrecognizable Forty-Second Street. Confronted by a strip of penny arcades, honky-tonk dives, poker joints, and bargain basements, he laments the passing of the Broadway of his halcyon youth, along with its "carriage trade." Suddenly pointing to a theatre across the way, he remarks: "The New Amsterdam—I had one of my biggest successes there, ran a year and a half." This is one of several self-referential allusions in Betty Comden and Adolph Green's witty screenplay to Astaire's own life. The big success was Dietz and Schwartz's *The Band Wagon,* which ran for 260 performances at the New Amsterdam.[1] The film uses many of Dietz and Schwartz's songs from the 1931 revue (both as featured numbers and incidental music) but otherwise bears no resemblance to the stage show to which it pays oblique homage at the outset.

The Band Wagon was, if you like, the anti-*Smiles*. The formula of its success lay not only in its considerable creative ingredients but also in its coherency and clarity of vision and a tautness and rigor in its construction, as well as a vital sense of discipline and delight in its execution. Dietz and Schwartz insisted that the show have the same consistency as a good book musical and, to that end, Dietz had only one co-writer on the sketches—George S. Kaufman, the man who, given the chance, might have rescued *Smiles*. Dietz usually came up with an original idea, wrote a first draft, and sent it to Kaufman to make it work.

Howard Dietz was himself an experienced wordsmith. He studied journalism at Columbia, began his career as a copywriter, was a regular contributor to "The Conning Tower," Franklin P. Adams's famous column for the *New York Tribune*, and became publicist and head of advertising at Samuel Goldwyn Productions and later at MGM. It was he who devised MGM's Leo the Lion mascot and its Latin motto, "Ars Gratia Artis." He is also credited with importing the parlor game charades from France to New York. Arthur Schwartz was likewise an uncommonly erudite songwriter. He had earned a Doctor of Jurisprudence from Columbia, taught English in the New York Public School system, and practiced law for four years before being lured to Broadway. He was once dubbed "the Professor Einstein of Tin Pan Alley."[2] Schwartz was another self-taught pianist and helped defray the costs of his college education by playing the piano in neighborhood movie houses.

A strong cast was assembled for *The Band Wagon*: apart from the Astaires, the principals were Austrian-born dancer Tilly Losch, who began her career with the Vienna State Opera Ballet, while studying modern dance, and who worked with Max Reinhardt at the Salzburg Festival; the acerbically droll Helen Broderick, later a member of the Astaire-Rogers "repertory company" at RKO; and Frank Morgan, who would achieve lasting fame as the carnival huckster and fraudulent Wizard in MGM's 1939 film *The Wizard of Oz*.

In Hassard Short they had a truly innovative director and lighting designer. *The Band Wagon* was one of the first Broadway shows to eliminate footlights in favor of lighting from the front of the balcony.[3] In Max Gordon they had a producer who had both an eye for detail and a reassuring grasp of the overall design, a leader who inspired confidence and affection while demanding strict attention to the task in hand. Adele says that she and Fred "adored Max Gordon. He always had a funny thing to say, and always had a cigar in his mouth. He'd say, 'Listen, you kids better do this and you'd better do that, do you hear.' I'd say, 'Don't get the whip out, Max. ' Max knew a lot about the theatre. He was wonderful; he knew what was right and what was wrong."[4]

In 1934 he was immortalized in Cole Porter's song "Anything Goes":

> When
> Rockefeller still can hoard en-
> Ough money to let Max Gordon
> Produce his shows,
> Anything goes.

Dominating the world of revue in this period were four major series: the *Ziegfeld Follies*, of course; the Shuberts' *Passing Shows*; the jazz-paced *George White's Scandals*; and *Earl Carroll's Vanities*. All, in varying degrees, were governed by a central aesthetic of lavish spectacle and ornamental femininity. And all, to a greater or lesser extent, exploited, rather than challenged or elevated, popular taste. The *Vanities*, for example, relied on nudity and burlesque-style humor. There were more intimate alternatives, such as Rodgers and Hart's *Garrick Gaieties*, first produced by the Theatre Guild in 1925, and Irving Berlin's *Music Box Revues* (1921–25), whose de facto theme song was "Say It with Music." In these the emphasis was on the music, which, as a consequence, was the main drawcard. Dietz and Schwartz's *The Little Show*, an unequivocal response to the big revues, also boasted a superior score, which included "I Guess I'll Have to Change My Plan" (a number subsequently danced by Jack Buchanan and Fred Astaire in the film of *The Band Wagon* and, for one night only at the London Palladium, by Buchanan and Laurence Olivier.) But what further set it apart was its wit, the precedence it accorded sophisticated satire over spectacle.

From its very opening it was clear that *The Band Wagon* was sui generis, that it pointedly shunned visual opulence in favor of a lean and ultramodern aesthetic, that it was out to break the rules and to have fun in the process. As the audience filed into the auditorium, they found the curtain already up, while onstage the company were gradually taking their seats in a virtual mirror image of the arriving patrons. "Ushers" onstage wore uniforms identical to the genuine article in the aisles below. As the house lights dimmed, the company sang "As Others See Us (It Better Be Good)." Although Derrida had not yet coined the term, the number was essentially a "deconstruction" of formulaic revue, a mad and merciless kaleidoscope of the genre's set pieces. There was an insanely pointless blackout, a senseless and saccharine melody sung by ingénue and juvenile, a ludicrous torch song, the eccentric dancer, the "apache," the acrobatic chorus, and the back-talk comedians—a miniature edition, in other words, of the conventional revue. At the end of this series of brisk burlesques, the wildly gesticulating chorus went stamping off shouting, "If you haven't got rhythm, / If you haven't got rhythm, / If you haven't got rhythm, / Then you haven't got rhythm!"

For a show to make so daring a statement of self-awareness and sardonic intent, it needed also to deliver the goods, to come bearing gifts of its own. Kaufman, Dietz, and Schwartz were not the sort of creative team lazily to content themselves with debunking, however cleverly, the clichés of their craft without offering something original and meaningful in their place. They avoided the pitfalls of pretentiousness and mere topicality; they did not, for instance, travesty a current hit play or film. "Part of [the show's] originality," Ethan Mordden affirms, "lay in a wish to start all its fun from scratch."[5] One novelty in its presentation was to preface the songs—after the manner of the music halls— with a few lines of amusing and unexpected patter. Alongside savage satire and bold exposé there was intelligent ribaldry, melodic sophistication, and from the performers a Thespic credibility worthy of the "legitimate" theatre. *The Band Wagon* managed not only to deconstruct but also to civilize the art of stage revue.

There was something else that made *The Band Wagon* stand out and made it, literally, revolutionary. It was, thanks to Short and scenic designer Albert R. Johnson, the show that introduced the *double* revolve or turntable. The revolve had been introduced to Broadway in the previous decade and most notably employed in the Shuberts' *A Wonderful Night*, a sly facsimile of Reinhardt's *Die Fledermaus*, and in Herman Shumlin's production of Reinhardt's *Grand Hotel*. While the ordinary revolve allowed for rapid, more seamless scene changes, and left set designers less at the mercy of stagehands, the double revolving stage added an extra rhythm to the proceedings and created striking stage pictures as it turned in two directions concentrically and at various speeds. The production numbers, Mordden enthuses, "seemed a very physics of dance, amazing the performers taking hold of them, scattering then reordering them in patterns that now favored and now challenged the décor."[6] As for the décor, it was from circular mass constructions on the inner revolving stage, rather than from backdrops, that the majority of *The Band Wagon*'s stunning effects radiated.

With this scenic innovation in mind, the show's intended title had been *The Spinning Wheel*, which Fred objected to on the grounds that it had been a working title for *Smiles* and was, therefore, full of negative connotations. On their way to Philadelphia for the tryout, Max Gordon remarked to Fred: "I'm not concerned about the actors or the material in this show, but if the revolving stage gets fouled up on opening night, we're dead." Frank Morgan, in his second-act monologue "P.S.," mused metatheatrically: "Any minute it may turn a little too far, and eighteen somewhat surprised stagehands will have to go into an impromptu ballet."

But the turntable behaved impeccably on opening night and at every performance throughout the run. *The Band Wagon* had its first tryout at the Garrick Theatre in Philadelphia on 12 May 1931 and garnered rave reviews. As we know from Moss Hart's vivid characterization of his mentor and collaborator in *Act One*, opening nights were an agony for Kaufman, who spent them brooding at the back of the stalls and pacing the carpet at a tremendous clip. He suggested to Dietz and Schwartz: "It might be a good idea to leave the play in Philadelphia and take the notices to New York." Nevertheless, when the show arrived at the New Amsterdam on 3 June, it was hailed as the dawn of a new era in the artistry of the American revue and even harbinger of the perfect state. Brooks Atkinson led the accolades:

> After the appearance of *The Band Wagon* which was staged at the New Amsterdam last evening, it will be difficult for the old-time musical

show to hold up its head. George S. Kaufman and Howard Dietz have put the stigmata on stupid display by creating a thoroughly modern revue. . . . Everything fits the rapid modern pattern of a sardonic stage revue. . . . In fact, *The Band Wagon* brings the revue stage up to date. After this the suffocating magnificence of formula showmanship will seem more lethal than ever.[7]

Dietz recalled that, in view of Adele's impending marriage and her decision to leave the show in Chicago the following spring (during the post-Broadway tour), "a new balance in the parts was created and it was planned that *The Band Wagon* should be more of Fred's show." Of the musical numbers, Fred and Adele appeared together in four; Adele had a duet with Frank Morgan and Fred with Tilly Losch; and Fred had one solo.

The first Astaire duet was "Sweet Music," in which, against type, Fred played the part of an irresponsible and irrepressible brother to Adele's scolding and pragmatic sister. It was a number designed more than anything to showcase Fred's coordination and musicianship, much like the celebrated "golfing" number he performed on film seven years later, "Since They Turned Loch Lomond into Swing." Here he played the accordion (sneaking in a delightful riff on a familiar phrase from Gershwin's *Rhapsody in Blue*) and danced with the cumbersome instrument strapped to his body.

In "Hoops" Fred and Adele played a pair of knowing and mischievous Parisian children, Louis and Marie, who chatter blithely about the adulterous behavior of their elders while trundling their hoops in the Parc Monceau. The set consisted of a centrally thrusting and rather phantasmagoric mass of vegetation ringed by a low white picket fence. There, as the stage revolves, they merrily pester the passing parade: a nurse with a baby carriage, a trysting couple, a gendarme, two nuns, and a stout and scholarly gentleman. With the turntable spinning them around the central plot of greenery, the Astaires parodied their own trademark run-around, guiding their hoops in ever-widening circles until they reached the stage left wings. So popular was this impudent number that Brooks Costume Company, at 260 West Forty-First Street, was swamped for orders of duplicates of the Astaires' chic infant wear for New Year's Eve costume parties.[8]

"New Sun in the Sky" was an exultant expression of new-found bliss, sung and danced by Fred alone as he put the finishing touches to his evening dress in front of a mirror, prefiguring his early film solos "A Needle in a Haystack" and "Top Hat, White Tie and Tails." For their second duet and the show's penulti-mate number, Adele joined her brother and the male and female chorus, in top hat, white tie, and tails, to perform "White Heat" against a set of gleaming silver and black Art Deco beauty, dominated by the semblance of a gigantic wireless coil or, conceivably, a top hat.

Figure 7.1 Fred and Adele in "Hoops".
New York Public Library, Vandamm Theatrical Photographs

Figure 7.2 Fred and Adele and chorus in "White Heat".
New York Public Library, Vandamm Theatrical Photographs

Figure 7.3 "I Love Louisa" with, l to r: Tilly Losch, Fred, Adele, Frank Morgan, and Helen Broderick.
New York Public Library, Vandamm Theatrical Photographs

As an ingenious finale to the first act, the double revolve metamorphosed into a Bavarian carousel, as the company cavorted and lustily bellowed an energetic parody on the "stein" song, led by Fred as a mock Student Prince with a thick German accent. The music Schwartz originally thought would suit the carousel number was the sentimental "High and Low," but Dietz felt it lacked the requisite character. Rushing from his apartment to his MGM job one day, Dietz scribbled some words on a pad of paper, plumped the notepad on the piano, and left. Schwartz went to the piano and read: "I love Louisa, Louisa loves me. When we rode on the merry-go-round, I kissed Louisa."[9]

The most enduring number in *The Band Wagon* score was conceived very late one night at Dietz's house. Wanting to write a song with a meaning beyond the romantic, Dietz went from book to book in his library, searching for ideas for a title. Eventually he lighted on *Dancers in the Dark*, by first-time novelist Dorothy Speare, published in 1922 and detailing the life of the young "excitement-eaters" of the Jazz Age.[10] "That's it!" Dietz exclaimed. Schwartz, who was with him, got his meaning immediately: "You mean, in a sense, all of us are dancing in the dark?" He went home and straight to his piano. The melody he played in the early hours of the morning was one he felt he had known all his life. Having no manuscript paper to hand, he kept playing it over and over so as not to forget it. "Dancing in the Dark" is a romantic melody, certainly, but it has an existential urgency and a dramatic sensibility unusual in a popular song and within the framework of revue.

For the film *The Band Wagon*, Fred crafted one of his most beautiful duets to "Dancing in the Dark," which he performs with Cyd Charisse, both of them costumed in cool white against a simple, moonlit, and unashamedly synthetic Central Park setting. It is an extraordinary dance of emotional discovery, richly textured in its somatic phrasing and intricately responsive to Conrad Salinger's voluptuous but delicately modulated orchestration. For this reason it is often erroneously assumed that Fred performed "Dancing in the Dark" onstage, but neither of the Astaires had anything to do with the number. The song was introduced by John Barker and danced sinuously by Tilly Losch and the Albertina Rasch Girls on a stage lined with slanted mirrors that reflected shifting patterns of varicolored lights. Brooks Atkinson spoke of this particular set's "macabre splendor."[11]

Agnes de Mille is sometimes called the inventor of the dream ballet because of "Laurey Makes Up Her Mind," the "landmark" fifteen-minute dance sequence she devised as a finale to the first act of Rodgers and Hammerstein's *Oklahoma!* in 1943. George Balanchine's biographer, Bernard Taper, has stated categorically that "Peter's Dream" from *Babes in Arms* in 1937 was "the first dream ballet to be seen on Broadway."[12] In fact, as Mordden demonstrates, "the earliest Dream Ballet . . . in the musical's history" was "The Beggar Waltz" in *The Band Wagon*.[13] This romantic pas de deux, imaginatively choreographed by Rasch for Fred and Tilly Losch, put the revolving stage to use as "an instrument of narrative beauty";[14] and with it a new dimension to Fred's dancing began to evolve.[15]

The story of the dance opens with a beggar (Fred) on the steps of the Vienna State Opera. The company's star ballerina, on entering the stage door, sees the beggar and drops a few coins in his outstretched hand. The mendicant falls asleep, and the stage revolves to reveal the sumptuous interior of the opera house and the lustrous substance of his dream. He has exchanged his rags for a costume of rich cloth and is center stage in a *Coppélia*-like spectacle, partnered by the prima ballerina, whom he worships, and dancing to Schwartz's ballet music with its soaring crescendos dissolving into a lilting waltz. As the fantasy ends, the set again revolves, returning to the opera house exterior. The beggar awakes, and the ballerina re-emerges from the stage door. Meeting his gaze, she pauses and tosses him her small purse. As she departs, he sinks back forlornly onto the steps. The number was an indication of Fred's ripening powers as a great dance dramatist. As the eponymous beggar, his body adroitly and affectingly portrayed supplication, exclusion, and dejection; as the imagined premier danseur, it assumed impressive and jubilant command of the stage.

Figure 7.4 Tilly Losch and Fred in
"The Beggar Waltz".
New York Public Library, Vandamm
Theatrical Photographs

In 1935 Clifford Whitely presented a revue called *Stop Press!* at London's Adelphi Theatre. The show, directed by Hassard Short, comprised selections from *The Band Wagon*, Dietz and Schwartz's book musical *Revenge with Music* (1934), and Irving Berlin and Moss Hart's hit revue *As Thousands Cheer* (1933). "The Beggar Waltz," renamed "The Beggar's Dream," was one of the selections and was danced by Robert Helpmann and Florence Chumbecos, who had been in the chorus of *The Band Wagon* and replaced Tilly Losch on the post-Broadway tour. Albertina Rasch was not credited in the London program as choreographer. Helpmann, always an Astaire fan, was currently being paid 3 pounds a week as principal dancer at the Vic-Wells Ballet; the revue was for him a lucrative and illuminating interlude. It was the first time he had encountered American modern dance techniques, which fascinated him and which he later incorporated in his own ballets, *Miracle in the Gorbals* and *Adam Zero*. When *Stop Press!* went on tour, Helpmann returned, like a prodigal son, to the Vic-Wells and took the lead in Ninette de Valois's newest creation, *The Rake's Progress*.

The cost of transplanting or reconstructing the elaborate turntable scenics precluded the possibility of a London transfer for *The Band Wagon*, although Alfred Butt had cabled Fred on 17 July 1931: "If I can secure English rights of *Bandwagon* [*sic*] would you agree play in it under my management next autumn or earlier if you are free?'

Fred was given greater opportunity than usual to shine in the non-musical segments of the show. The revue format, of course, allowed him to play a range of characters in a variety of sketches rather than the kind of brotherly juvenile role he had assumed in book musicals up to that point. He seized the opportunity with both hands, and he was seen, almost for the first time, not merely as Adele's straight man but as a comedian in his own right and, what is more, a very capable actor, whose best asset was his intrinsic corporeal fluency.

In "The Pride of the Claghornes," a sketch lampooning the mores of the Good Old South—all mint juleps and Negro spirituals—a comically bewigged Fred played Simpson Carter, the dimwitted fiancé of Adele's Breeze Claghorne. As Col. Jefferson Claghorne (Frank Morgan) toasts the newly betrothed pair, Carter's parents arrive with the shocking revelation that Breeze is a virgin and has thus dishonored the hallowed tradition of the deflowered Southern Belle. The colonel sends his daughter away from the plantation, blaming the backward Carter for shaming her, and bemoaning the younger generation's lack of respect for the fine old ways of the South.

The *Herald Tribune* designated Fred's lazy, hick southerner "one of the grand comic characterizations of the year, providing not only humor and satire, but also racy portraiture."[16] His drawling, impassive reading of the phrase "a mighty fine baudy o' wauter" seldom failed to bring down the house and was remembered with "a mellow glow" by at least one commentator over twenty years later. But it was his silent comedy that most impressed Robert Garland of the *World Telegram*: "Within a few short minutes, he presents a complete characterization

Figure 7.5 "The Pride of the Claghornes" with, l to r: Helen Broderick, Adele, Frank Morgan, and Fred.
New York Public Library, Vandamm Theatrical Photographs

with scarcely any words at all. What I'm getting at is that Mr. Astaire brings something of the poor old legitimate theatre into the New Amsterdam."[17]

Fred featured in two other sketches, "For Good Old Nectar" and "Pour le Bain." The first of these was another parodic inversion of custom and expectation, aimed in this instance at campus life. Instead of rooting for the varsity football star, an alumni cheering section loudly spur on the history champion, zealously quoting "match" statistics and hoisting him on their shoulders in triumph. "Pour le Bain" was a comment on the absurdity of certain modern marketing and display techniques, with a possible nod to Marcel Duchamp's "Fountain" of 1917 (a "ready-made" sculpture in the form of a standard porcelain urinal). The timid Mrs. Prescott of Westchester (Helen Broderick) enters the Eclipse Tile and Marble emporium to discover the last word in cultured salesmanship and plumbing fixtures exhibited as works of art. Fred, clad in a bathing suit, struck elegant poses as a *demonstrator* of various bathroom appliances, simulating a kind of performance art. Having satisfied her interest in handbasins and bathtubs, Mrs. Prescott intimates to the salesman that no mention of another type of fixture has passed between them. Whereupon the cultivated salesman, quoting Keats's "Ode on a Grecian Urn," says, "Heard melodies are sweet, but those unheard / Are sweeter." Blackout.

On entering the Lambs Theatre Club the day after the show opened, Fred was greeted by one of his fellow members with the exclamation: "Boy, I hear you're an actor!" He had proved his consummate versatility and his effectiveness both as an ensemble player and as primus inter pares. The critics were united in admiration for his precision as a satirist and his depth as a dancing tragedian. In the *Herald Tribune* he was proclaimed "the individual triumph of the show,"[18] and in the *New Yorker* "one of the most valuable pieces of theatrical property in the business."[19] There was even an earnest suggestion that Fred was now a plausible contender for Shakespeare's Prince of Denmark, an opinion once echoed by John Gielgud, who played the role over 500 times in six productions. Director Max Reinhardt and actress Helen Hayes wanted Fred to play Puck in separately planned productions of *A Midsummer Night's Dream*, but to no avail.[20] Having heard Astaire recite a few lines of Shakespearean verse in a radio play he did for the *Screen Guild Theatre* in 1939,[21] I am less certain of his aptitude for the Bard, although, had he wanted to (which is highly unlikely), he could probably have given fascinating interpretations in dance of Hamlet and Puck, according to his modern and distinctive style.

While Fred had, in the words of the *New York Tribune*, "kicked over the bushel" and acquired new respect as an individual artist, Adele was by no means forgotten or outshone. She may have fallen out of love with the stage and longed for rest, but she was still at the peak of her powers. "The brilliance of [Fred's] work," wrote Richard Watts Jr., "should not cause any one to suspect that his sister has been left in the background. . . . Miss Astaire, who combines the finest qualities of the professional and amateur, is so far as I am concerned, not only the finest of the girl comics, but is also the only actress who manages to combine a major gift for hilarity with a very definite personal allure."[22] Ashton Stevens concurred: "Heaven doesn't send every generation an Adele Astaire. . . . She's one of God's few women who can be both funny and bewitching."[23]

Like the show itself, both Astaires were praised for their modernity, for being effortlessly ahead of their own time, thus further underlining one of the major problems with *Smiles*—its inability to accommodate or keep pace with that modernity. Here, by contrast, Fred and Adele were eminently well served by the freshest of material most deftly turned, material that did not require its audience to check their brains with their hats. Fittingly, through the show, the Astaires became part of sound-recording history, for *The Band Wagon* was technologically groundbreaking in more ways than one. On 5 October 1931, together with Dietz and Schwartz, they joined the Leo Reisman Orchestra in a bold experiment by the RCA Victor Company, a long-play version of selections from the show (seventeen years before Columbia introduced the first microgroove LP). This revolutionary disc was designed for playback at 33⅓ revolutions per minute and pressed on a twelve-inch disc, with a duration of ten minutes playing time per side, compared with the four-minute limit of the conventional 78 rpm disc.

The Band Wagon was not only one of the earliest commercially available 33⅓ rpm records (or "Program Transcriptions" as they were known)[24] but also the very first American "original cast recording."[25] After a forty-second overture, Leo Reisman introduces Fred and Adele and Dietz and Schwartz, each of whom voices a self-consciously cheery "Hello." Reisman then continues:

> Due to this record playing twenty minutes, we are able to present, for the first time, a rather comprehensive musical review of *The Band Wagon* score. The music of the first act will be played on this side of the record, with Fred and Adele singing their songs. And, then, you may turn me over on my back and follow the second act, during which you will hear Arthur Schwartz, the composer, at the piano playing "White Heat."

One of the moving highlights of this historic recording is being able to hear the music of "The Beggar Waltz" in its entirety. The recording is available today on CD, but the original vinyl discs are scarce. Program Transcriptions required a special turntable, which was, for the vast majority of people at the height of the Great Depression, a quite unaffordable luxury.

On 17 December 1931, Fred and Adele made their first radio appearance together on NBC's *Fleischmann's Yeast Hour*, a pioneering musical variety program hosted by crooner and bandleader Rudy Vallée. Vallée began with an

Astaire medley— numbers from *The Band Wagon* and other Astaire successes. Fred and Adele sang "Hang on to Me" from *Lady, Be Good!* and "My One and Only" from *Funny Face* and concluded with a special Astaire version of the 1931 hit "Goodnight, Sweetheart," which Vallée had helped to popularize in the states.[26] The curtain had to be held for Fred and Adele that evening and a police escort provided to get them to the theatre on time.

When news of Adele's engagement was officially announced in the autumn, or rather leaked to the press, it made headlines on both sides of the Atlantic:

Maybe She'll Really Wed This Time
                    —*New York Daily Mirror*, 23 October 1931

Miss Adele Astaire to Wed Peer's Son
                    —*New York Times*, 23 October

Song Comes True: Duke's Son "Hitches His Wagon to a Star." Girl of the Twinkling Feet
                    —*Scarborough Mercury*, 23 October

It Will Be Lady Cavendish Soon for Fred's Sis
                    —*New York Review*, 24 October

Duke's Son Vanishes AFTER News of His Engagement. The Shy Lover
                    —*News Chronicle*, London, 24 October

Dancer's Romance with Duke's Son
                    —*Sunday Mail*, Glasgow, 25 October

"Marry Man Younger Than Yourself"; Adele Astaire Following Own Advice
                    —*Havana Post*, Cuba, 11 November

As planned, Adele left the show in Chicago. The last dance she and her brother performed onstage was, perhaps appropriately, "White Heat." That night the orchestra played "Auld Lang Syne" and, at a small party backstage, the cast presented Adele with a stylish fitted traveling case. At midnight she boarded the sleeper car to New York. In keeping with his emotionally terse prose style, Fred devotes just three short sentences of his autobiography to the momentous occasion of Adele's departure: "She retired from theatrical life on the evening of 5 March, 1932, at the Illinois Theatre, Chicago. It was not a sad affair. There were a few tears but we soon laughed our way out of it."[27] Others were more demonstratively plaintive in their valedictory utterances. Ashton Stevens declared it a day "to wear a black gardenia [because] Heaven doesn't send every generation an Adele Astaire."[28] Ann Astaire, who had nurtured so devotedly this already legendary Broadway pairing, recorded in her diary: "I am sad to think of this ending of a great partnership."

While Fred was soon to face the trauma of carving out a solo career, it was Adele who was the more traumatized by their actual parting. She remembered weeping "all the way to New York. My pillow was soaked! I kept wondering if I was doing the right thing. Mama wasn't so sure. I had to tell myself that I was. I felt as if something was guiding me—and I went along." Her sorrow and near grief at being separated from the brother whom she loved more than anything in the world was compounded by guilt at having deserted him professionally. In spite of the notices Fred had received for his "individual triumph" in *The Band Wagon*, neither his sister nor his mother seemed at all confident of his ability to cope personally or artistically without them at his side.

On Saturday, 12 March, Ann and Adele set sail for London aboard RMS *Majestic* in preparation for Adele's wedding, which would take place without Fred in attendance. Making the voyage with them were Winston Churchill and his eldest daughter, Diana. Churchill, who had been consigned to the political wilderness and hit hard by the Crash, was returning home from what was supposed to have been a profitable forty-lecture tour of the United States. On his second night in New York, however, he had been knocked down by a car while crossing Fifth Avenue on foot. He sustained painful and debilitating injuries and spent eight days in Lenox Hill Hospital, just around the corner from the Astaires' apartment at 875 Park Avenue. The lecture tour had thus to be reduced by half the number of engagements and limited to the Northeast and the Midwest. Churchill and Adele had met several times in London over the years and were delighted to renew their acquaintance. A menu survives from the *Majestic*'s restaurant, dated 13 March 1932, on the back of which is written: "I hear you play Backgammon, and I hereby send you my challenge for an early battle. WC."[29]

While Adele and the future British prime minister engaged in fierce combat over the backgammon table, Ann worried about Fred "battling with an understudy" (Vera Marsh had taken over Adele's role in *The Band Wagon*). But her anxiety was not confined to her son's career prospects. On their first night at sea, she wrote in her diary: "I hate leaving Freddy to work alone. However I understand that Mrs. Ph. Potter is occupying his mind and heart much of the time. I wish he would not marry her—she is divorced and has a boy three years old!! Poor Freddy—surely he will avoid this."

The lady in question was indeed occupying Fred's mind and heart. Significantly, the succinct, almost passing mention of Adele's retirement in

Fred's autobiography occurs in a chapter entitled "Phyllis" and is reflective of the fact that he was, in the spring of 1932, not so much sanguine as distracted. For the first time in his career his private life was taking precedence over work.

Fred met Mrs. Potter one Sunday afternoon in the late summer of 1931 at a "golf luncheon" given by Virginia Graham Fair Vanderbilt on her Long Island estate in Manhasset, a party "destined," he said, "to become the outstanding event of my life."[30] He found himself seated at a table with Dorothy Fell and her close friend since childhood, twenty-three-year-old Phyllis Livingston Potter, and any thought he had of playing golf that afternoon vanished.

> I was fascinated by Phyllis. Her exceptional, fragile beauty and gentle charm held me rather spellbound. I loved the way she could pronounce her r's. Another thing that captivated me was the fact that she did not mention ever having seen me on the stage. I knew she had not been to *Band Wagon*, but she couldn't remember anything I had done before that either.[31]

Details of Phyllis's family background—other than the fact that she was of patrician stock—and the circumstances of her upbringing are rather vague. It is difficult to form a complete account of her early childhood and her parents' marriage, but certain facts have been overlooked or inaccurately recounted by most Astaire biographers. She was born Phyllis Livingston Baker in May 1908, the second child of Dr. Harold Woods Baker, a prominent Boston gynecologist, and his wife, Caroline E. Livingston, a descendant of Robert Livingston, the first chancellor of New York and a member of the Committee of Five that drafted the Declaration of Independence. She had an older sister Kathleen and, what is not commonly known, a younger brother Harold Jr. It is usually reported that at the age of ten, after her father's death and her mother's remarriage, Phyllis went to live with her aunt and uncle in New York. In truth, Phyllis's parents had divorced after Caroline, who had been a nurse during World War I, left her husband to marry a blind soldier named Frank H. Pratt and went to live in Europe. Harold also remarried and until 1933 was surgeon for out-patients at the Free Hospital for Women in Boston and for several years instructor in gynecology at Harvard's Graduate School of Medicine.[32]

When their parents' marriage broke down, Phyllis and Kathleen became wards of their mother's sister Maud Livingston and her husband Henry Worthington Bull, an extremely wealthy couple who had no children of their own. Henry Bull was a senior partner at the brokerage firm Harriman & Co. The Bulls had homes on East Sixty-Second Street in Manhattan, in Islip, Long Island, and in Aiken, South Carolina. Phyllis was educated at the Brearley School in New York and at Fermata in Aiken. She made her society debut in 1926 and the

Figure 7.6 Phyllis Potter and Fred at Belmont Park, May 1932.

following year, aged just nineteen, married Eliphalet Nott Potter III (nicknamed "Bo"), a young Wall Street broker. The marriage was unhappy and short-lived, but it produced a son, christened Eliphalet Nott Potter IV and known as "Peter." By the time she met Fred, Phyllis was separated from her husband and again living with her aunt and uncle.

Fred knew Henry Bull in his capacity as president of Belmont's Turf and Field Club and had seen his niece at Belmont Park, although he had not been introduced to her. At the end of the luncheon he asked if could call her, and she agreed. Clearly there was a mutual attraction, but Phyllis, who was naturally reserved, had also to be cautious in her position—her divorce was not finalized until March 1932, and Peter's custody was an ongoing and acrimonious point of dispute between the estranged couple. Soon Fred was invited to tea to meet Peter and, after some persuasion, Phyllis came to see *The Band Wagon*. She went backstage afterward with a group of friends and, on being prompted for her opinion, pronounced Fred's performance "vewy good," which he considered "the most valued praise of all time."[33] A few nights later she came again, but this time, to Fred's utter anguish, with an inebriated suitor in tow. It was the start of a testing two-year pursuit on Fred's part.

Hermes Pan, Fred's friend and collaborator from the start of his film career, described Phyllis as "probably the most misunderstood lady in Hollywood. She used to frighten everybody because they thought she was so aloof and snooty—and she wasn't. She was a little, slight thing, but she could scare the life out these big producers and directors, just by her attitude and with one word; you could see them squirm."[34]

But with people in whose company she felt relaxed, she was fun and down to earth. Pan was not the only one to see a different side to Phyllis from her intimidating formality. Dorothy Fell's erstwhile sister-in-law, Josephine ("Fifi") Schiff, remembered Phyllis as having "a marvelous giggle and a little devil look. We used to call her 'the pocket Venus.' She was shy with strangers, but very loving with friends."[35]

One of Fred and Phyllis's closest Hollywood friends was David Niven, of whom Fifi Schiff said, "there was nobody more fun, and *he* certainly wouldn't have been around if she was stuffy."[36]

She also recalls that Phyllis was a lenient, affectionate, and "hands-on" mother.

Phyllis was entirely untheatrical and shared with Fred an abhorrence of large gatherings and a passion for privacy. Surprisingly, she also shared with him a pixyish sense of humor and a taste for offbeat antics. Schiff tells a story about Phyllis and Dorothy Fell that is both bizarre and revealing:

> One day they went to a costumer, got themselves made up as ragged old ladies, with grey wigs, and then did an old-lady make-up, carried baskets, went to a florist, bought all his wilted violets, went to the entrance of the Colony Restaurant where most of their friends lunched every day. They stood outside and, as anyone approached, they begged them to buy their violets. The only person that gave them a dollar was a very elegant and social man, William Rhinelander Stewart. But no one recognized them the whole time they were there.[37]

On another occasion, the two girls donned wild wigs, long hair almost down to their knees, in which they paraded down Fifth Avenue, dressed otherwise perfectly normally.

Adele revealed that her brother had once confided in her his desire and determination to get married because "he didn't want to wake up with the morning papers" and because he knew that many people believed him to be homosexual.[38]

He was often, she said, the object of some male's infatuation and even received propositioning letters. But until he met Phyllis, he had not given any real indication that he was actively seeking a wife. As a teenager, he tended to fall for older women who bore his adoration with kindly tolerance. Later on, like his friend the Prince of Wales, his more serious romantic entanglements were with women who were already married. There were casual liaisons with girls, such as the young Ginger Rogers, who were available but whom he (or his mother) would not have considered suitable for marriage.

Such was Fred's sincerity of purpose in his quest for Phyllis's hand that it was not long before he made his intentions known to the two most important women in his life thus far. While Ann disapproved of Phyllis in the particular and was generally alarmed at the very idea of Fred marrying anybody, she fondly imagined he would in time yield to maternal counsel. Adele was equally perturbed but she could discern the intensity of Fred's feelings for Phyllis and knew he would not easily be dissuaded. On New Year's Eve 1931, Fred and Adele attended a party at the Mayfair Club, a swanky social club for the theatrical aristocracy. The next day, Adele wrote to her fiancé Charlie: "Fred was at another table with his beautiful Mrs. Potter (he has 'it' badly)."

One of the unpublished extracts from Fred's autobiography reads: "If any fellow thinks it over I imagine he will realize that all the important decisions and crises in his life have been influenced by women. . . . [Influencing] every turn and phase of my life there have been three remarkable ladies—each utterly different from the other: my adorable wife Phyllis, Adele, my mother."[39]

The members of this formidable feminine triumvirate, who between them steered the course of Fred's life, were divided not by their differences but by their similarities of purpose and temperament, their strength of will and their possessive love for Fred. Maintaining a fragile peace between them, and assuring each of her singular importance in his life, was to be for Fred a twenty-year balancing act.

When the *Majestic* docked at Plymouth, reporters swarmed onto the ship in search of Adele, whereupon Churchill leapt into the role of protector, concealing Adele in the ship's lounge behind the decorative palm trees and informing the reporters that she and her mother had already disembarked. At their destination of Southampton, however, they were not so fortunate. The press were lying in wait, and Ann and Adele were followed from the ship to the train station. In London they were met by Lord Charles, who whisked them away in a taxi, only to be pursued by the journalists. Finally they agreed to make a brief statement, and Adele showed off her unusual engagement ring, a platinum ring shaped like a Russian coronet set with baguette diamonds.

Adele faced the initial introduction to her future mother-in-law with a mixture of trepidation and subdued bravado, aware that the Duchess opposed the marriage. Although she received Adele graciously, Evelyn Cavendish had not softened in her attitude and had decided that the wedding ceremony should be an intimate family affair, with no London fanfare and attracting the least possible publicity. She instructed Ann Astaire to write to the archbishop of Canterbury, Cosmo Lang, asking permission for the ceremony to be held in the private chapel at Chatsworth. There had never been a wedding in the chapel, and a special dispensation was required. A draft of Ann's concise petition has survived:

> Mrs Astaire would be very grateful if His Grace would grant a special licence to enable her daughter to be married to Lord Charles Cavendish in the private chapel at Chatsworth as she has every wish that this marriage should take place.

The license was duly granted, but the wedding had to be postponed by a fortnight because the bridegroom, who had been in ill health for several weeks as a result of excessive drinking, was now suffering with appendicitis and needed to be hospitalized. The two-week delay, reported in the papers back home, elicited a caustic cablegram from Florenz Ziegfeld, still smarting from having to compensate the Astaires for extra rehearsal time: "Are you going to charge for the delay?"

While she had adopted a demure persona for her first meeting with the Duchess, Adele reverted to type at a large family gathering on 21 April, which included Charlie's maternal grandmother; the Marchioness of Landsdowne; his father's brother, Lord Richard Cavendish; and various cousins. Among those assembled was Lady Mary Cecil, the wife of Charlie's older brother Edward, the Marquess of Hartington. "Moucher," as she was called, remembered Adele's colorful entrance on that occasion:

> The family was all gathered in the library standing like stone pillars in front of the fireplace waiting for Adele to be announced. When she was introduced, the heavy doors at the end of the library opened and there stood this tiny girl, beautifully dressed. We waited for her to approach, but instead of walking toward us, she suddenly began turning cartwheels and ended up in front of us. Everyone loved it.[40]

Unlike his wife, the dull, dutiful Duke of Devonshire was beguiled by Adele and had given the marriage his tacit approval. But, as he was an implacable anti-papist, he was appalled to discover that Adele was Catholic and insisted she be baptized in the Church of England before the marriage could be consecrated. So, at eleven o'clock on the morning of 9 May 1932, the vicar of Edensor, W. H. Foster-Pegg, baptized Adele before she dressed for the wedding.

The small seventeenth-century chapel, with its ceiling painted by Louis Laguerre, was decorated with daffodils and acacia; two myrtle trees stood in the sanctuary; and the marble altar was flanked by scarlet camellias and vases of arum lilies. Adele wore a gown designed by Mainbocher, beige satin with touches of orange at the waist, a set of blue fox furs and a beige beret, a sapphire and diamond brooch (a gift from Lord Hartington), and a diamond bracelet from

Charlie. She carried a bunch of orange carnations grown in the gardens at Chatsworth. The papers stated that her mother gave the bride away; in fact Charlie's brother-in-law, Henry Hunlocke, escorted Adele. Foster-Pegg officiated, and Lord Hartington acted as best man. The three bridesmaids (one of whom, Lady Elizabeth Cavendish, was to be the close companion of future poet laureate John Betjeman) and two pageboys were Charlie's nieces and nephews. Twenty choristers, boys and men from the village church, were in attendance. The first hymn was "Praise the Lord, ye Heavens Adore Him; the psalm "I Will Lift Mine Eyes" was sung; and the hymn "O Perfect Love" concluded the simple service.

After a private luncheon, Adele and Charlie drove to Liverpool and from there sailed to Ireland and their new home, Lismore Castle in County Waterford. Under the laws of primogeniture, the property was an unorthodox gift for the Duke to bestow on Charlie, but he was especially fond of his errant younger son. The original castle had been erected by King John in 1185 on the site of Lismore Abbey, overlooking the Blackwater River. Four years later it was demolished by the Irish and rebuilt as an episcopal residence for the local bishop. In 1589 the lease was granted to Sir Walter Raleigh, who sold the property, during his imprisonment for high treason in 1602, to Richard Boyle, later the first Earl of Cork. Boyle enlarged and embellished the castle, making it his principal seat, where in 1627 his son Robert Boyle, the "father of modern chemistry" and discoverer of Boyle's law, was born. Lismore was heavily involved in the Cromwellian wars, and in 1645 a force of Catholic confederacy commanded by Lord Castlehaven sacked the town and castle. In 1753 it passed to the Cavendish family when Lady Charlotte Boyle, the only surviving daughter and heiress of the fourth Earl of Cork, married William Cavendish, the fourth Duke of Devonshire.

It was the sixth Duke, known as the "Bachelor Duke," who was responsible for the castle's present imposing appearance; in the mid-nineteenth century, he had rebuilt it in the Gothic style from the plans of the visionary Joseph Paxton, who had been head gardener at Chatsworth and had designed London's Crystal Palace. For all its splendor and its 200 rooms, Adele claimed the castle had only one bath and joked that while other Cavendishes had married heiresses who came with magnificent dowries, she gave the family a second bathroom at Lismore. She probably exaggerated the dearth of facilities, but she did have several modern bathrooms installed in the castle at her own expense. It amused Adele to think that after its illustrious history of princes, bishops, aristocratic adventurers and trail-blazing scientists, Lismore Castle should end up in the custodianship of a "hoofer" from Omaha, Nebraska.

Partly needing to take stock and put some distance between herself and Fred's ardent persistence, Phyllis had gone to Europe with her aunt and uncle. She was sure of her feelings for Fred but not convinced that their lives could be made compatible or that marriage to a man in so notoriously peripatetic a profession was in the best interests of her son. As soon as *The Band Wagon* closed Fred followed her, intending also to visit his sister and new brother-in-law at Lismore. He traveled with his valet, Walter Williams, and arrived in London on 26 May. His mother met him at Waterloo Station, and the next day the small party left Paddington for Ireland. Walter created something of a sensation in Lismore, being the first black man its inhabitants had ever seen; he was stared at and frequently touched but enjoyed his moment of celebrity.

Adele relished having her brother almost entirely to herself. They spent their afternoons tramping over the castle grounds, including the ancient yew walk where Edmund Spenser is believed to have written *The Faerie Queene* in Raleigh's time. During these walks, Fred unburdened himself to Adele about his love for Phyllis and the torment he was suffering. Adele alternated between sympathy and reproach, astonishing Fred by expressing the same disapproval as their mother. After five days, Fred and Ann returned to London, where Phyllis was already staying. Ann's diary at this point plainly documents her dislike of Phyllis and the growing tension between the two women, while her consistent misspelling of Phyllis's name cannot but seem psychologically eloquent.

> Fri. 3 June, 1932
> Fred and Phillis. We all had tea at the Carlton.
>   Fred and I dined alone—Fred telling me about his <u>love</u> for Phillis (he was rather depressed)—why?

> Sat. 4
> Fred worried me—He seemed unreasonable in wanting to get married before his next show opened.

> Sun. 5 June, 1932
> Fred assured me that he would not be foolish about marrying before he could support his wife <u>properly</u>. Of course I feel relieved, to feel that he will have time to get thoroughly acquainted before the step.

> Thurs. 23 June, 1932
> I went to Sandown Races with Fred, Jack Leach and Phillis. I felt like "<u>3</u> a crowd." Phillis was disagreeable (Ann Astaire's diaries in Mugar Memorial Library, Boston University).

Fred's increasing acceptance as an actor and comedian, coinciding as it did with Adele's retirement, placed him at an interesting, if daunting, professional crossroads. At the age of thirty-three, he could himself contemplate forsaking the rigors of dancing and conceivably embrace the challenges of straight acting, a possibility made more tangible by a handful of offers in that direction. Producer and director Guthrie McClintic, the husband of Katharine Cornell, asked if he would be "interested in playing delightful comedy part in enchanting new play I plan to direct at Belasco Theatre early in August."[41] Producers A. L. Jones and Morris Green wanted him for the part of Tony Pell in *Under Glass*, a comedy by Eva K. Flint and George Bradshaw.[42] There were, as well, tempting musical offers that would similarly stretch his dramatic talents. On 9 April 1932, Ziegfeld cabled Fred to ask whether he would consider appearing in an all-star revival of *Show Boat*, which would also include Helen Broderick.[43] The offer that held most appeal, however, came from Dwight Wiman and Tom Weatherly—the lead role in a musical play called *Gay Divorce* with a score by Cole Porter. Fred harbored a few reservations about the script, believing it needed revision before he could commit to it, but he had left New York with the offer pending.

In London, spending as much time as he could with Phyllis and thinking only of being able to secure his future with her, Fred's professional focus and diligence seemed to have deserted him. He received a cablegram asking whether he was still interested in doing the Porter show and, if so, whether he would return to New York immediately to discuss plans. Fred was reluctant to leave. It was Phyllis who gently and shrewdly sealed his personal and professional fate:

"I think you should go back and investigate your future career. After all, if we are going to be married you'll have to work—won't you?"

The next day Fred was aboard RMS *Berengaria* bound for New York.

CHAPTER 8

By Myself

For who else would qualify
After you, who?
—Cole Porter, "After You, Who?"

When *Gay Divorce* opened at the Ethel Barrymore Theatre on 29 November 1932, the critics were underwhelmed. The book, adapted by Samuel Hoffenstein and Kenneth Webb from an unproduced play by Dwight Taylor, was attacked for its lethargy, for its inanity, and more for its outmoded prurient naughtiness than its scandalous subject matter: collusive divorce and the comically inverted mechanics of staged adultery. Its central character, Guy Holden, an American writer of cheap romantic novels, is holidaying in London, where he falls in love with a young woman named Mimi, who disappears after their one and only meeting. Unbeknown to Guy, Mimi is anxiously trying to obtain a divorce from her fusty geologist husband, Octavius Pratt. When the pair fortuitously reunite at a seaside hotel that caters for assignations illicit and conspiratorial, Mimi mistakes Guy for the professional co-respondent hired by her lawyer to "compromise" her.

The stage play was, of course, afforded greater license, as regards suggestive dialogue, daring costuming, and its blithe treatment of genuine adultery than the subsequent film version of 1934, which was subject to the stringent Production Code (also known as the Hays Code).[1] For example, the first-act "curtain," a climax of confusion between the would-be divorcée and the unwitting co-respondent, went a line and an action further than its screen equivalent:

MIMI: Here! (*She hands him the key of her room.*) Come to my room at ten o'clock.
(*She crosses to hotel entrance. He follows.*)
And bring your own pajamas!
(*He is so startled by her action that he sits on steps suddenly, drops the key and as curtain is descending he reaches for it.*)

Figure 8.1 Fred (Guy Holden), Erik Rhodes (Tonetti), and Claire Luce (Mimi) in *Gay Divorce.*
Photofest

The *Boston Transcript* described the "intimate musical play," as it was billed, as "a prologue and a first act with hardly more body and style and little more diversion than a parlor entertainment gone dirty."[2] Brooks Atkinson branded it "flat and mirthless entertainment beneath a highly polished exterior. . . . Before the evening is over it employs most of the hotel and bedroom fiddle-faddle that went out with risqué farces."[3] And John Anderson in the *New York Evening Journal* said it was "weighted to death by a somnolent tale . . . and unfolded with approximately the care and interest a high wind takes in unfolding a newspaper on a draughty corner."[4]

To such complaints, Fred responded in a rare public statement and with eloquent chagrin:

> *Gay Divorce* wasn't written by Ibsen and I don't quite understand why so many reviewers insisted upon criticizing it as though it were meant to be a lofty essay into the field of ethics or esthetics. It's nothing of the sort. It's just plain romping around for the amusement of the people who pay to see it. Critics, it seems to me, too often refuse to approach a play in the spirit in which it is offered; they don't view shows with

sufficient detachment. It's no great indictment of a reviewer's critical capacity to find that after he has razzed a show the audiences shriek with laughter at it. The audiences may be wrong, but I think that when by and large a drama or musical show gives a lot of people a lot of pleasure there must be something in it even if the critics have patronizingly passed it by as being only so-so stuff.[5]

His irritation at the critics' condemnation of the plot's contrivances and inconsequentiality is not simply indicative of his habitual mistrust of "arty" aspiration. What is fascinating about this measured outburst is the fact that it is simultaneously a denial of artistic intent ("just plain romping around") and a refutation of the charge that light musical fare is meaningless and something to be "passed by."

The show's dramaturgical shortcomings were compounded by the boorish behavior of the first-night audience, drawn largely from the Social Register, whose "brandied roarings" earned them censure and satirization as coutured roughnecks, "barbarians in evening dress."[6] Some arrived late, others ran up and down the aisles talking over the dialogue onstage, and every number was greeted by a rowdy ovation. Fred was given credit for surmounting this misguided fervor and the uninspired plot, but it was his new "sisterless" status that garnered most attention in the press, where he was treated with pitying condescension as an artistic amputee:

An Astaire still dances; but unmistakably without the comedic flair and zest that Miss Adele used to instill. . . . Not for the general good is he now sisterless.

—*Boston Transcript*, 8 November

Fred Astaire stops every now and then to look offstage towards the wings as if he were hoping his titled sister, Adele, would come out and rescue him.

Some of us cannot help feeling that the joyousness of the Astaire team is missing now that the team has parted.

—*New York Times*, 30 November

One thing is certain, after viewing last night's performance we have come to the conclusion that two Astaires are better than one.

Tellingly, even in Walter Winchell's generally positive review, Fred was referred to as "the personable and talented brother of Lady Cavendish,"[7] his identity as an individual performer having been subsumed by his sister's recent matrimonial ennoblement. In his autobiography Fred recalled, in almost masochistic detail, the critics' persistent, no doubt galling, refrain of lamentation at Adele's absence. But he added: "I was not upset because they missed my sister. I'd have been disappointed if they hadn't, but at any rate my job was cut out for me and the show had to be put over."[8]

What he had chiefly to conquer was an entrenched preconception that he was the lesser half of a unified creative entity. The critics seemed unable or unwilling to accept him as a lone star. With characteristic caprice, they also seemed to have forgotten his performance the year before in *The Band Wagon*, in which he had triumphed beyond expectation, winning unanimous acclaim for his dramatic and comedic abilities, one critic going so far as to declare: "The American theatre could produce a far worse Hamlet."[9]

They now decided that Fred, left entirely to his own devices, was not Prince Hamlet nor was meant to be, that he had perhaps fulfilled his theatrical destiny as an attendant lord to his sister's sovereign talent. Nor did they discern in him the stuff of which romantic heroes are made or the histrionic capacity to carry a show:

> Fred Astaire, when his miraculous feet are quiet, gives a curious impression of unemployment.
> —Harold Lockridge, *New York Sun*

> As an actor and as a singer, Astaire does not approach the perfection he achieves with his feet. In *Gay Divorce*, it must be recorded he has perhaps taken on too much of a task.
> —Mark Barron, *Syndicated columnist*

> As the signs go, he misses—and the audience misses—the stimulation and the flair of his more comedic sister. As actor, he remains more sympathetic than expert, earnest and sometimes amusing with awkward good intentions.

> His acting is a little shame-faced, a bit uncertain. He has not yet become sufficiently accustomed to himself as an actor to be completely at home when not relying upon his feet to give him nonchalance.
> —*Brooklyn Eagle*, 4 December

> I am not sure they have done right by Fred Astaire in making him a conventional hero of romance. He is by natural selection a Frank Craven of the musicals.[10] His wit and charm are mostly in his feet.

Cut him off at the ankles and he is just another boy on the stage doing his earnest best.

—*Daily News*, 4 December

Yet the evidence of "Night and Day"—the number that ultimately defined the show and ensured it a respectable Broadway run—should have served to establish Fred's credibility as a romantic leading man. "The Beggar Waltz" in *The Band Wagon* could be seen as the familiar Astaire dance-drama in embryo; it was a pas de deux of real pathos, and a substantial test of his acting skills. But the dance that definitively signaled the fulfillment of his potential as a romantic actor was the exquisitely choreographed "Night and Day," a number that told a richly layered story in itself and significantly advanced the main plot. And it preceded by more than a decade the dances Agnes de Mille created for Rodgers and Hammerstein's *Oklahoma!*, which are often cited by musical theatre historians as groundbreaking in their integration into the plot and their revelation of character and psyche.

Fred and Adele's real-life relationship had necessarily precluded duets of an overtly romantic nature, especially after they became famous as brother and sister. Now, with a new leading lady in the extremely nubile Claire Luce, that prohibition was lifted. In their shows together, Fred and Adele were usually involved in separate romantic sub-plots with other characters, but even then Fred had seldom been called on to communicate great depth of emotion or to project physical passion. Love scenes discomfited him. Luce later recalled having to urge him in rehearsal to take hold of her: "Come on, Fred, I'm not your sister, you know."[11] But in "Night and Day" Fred exploited the medium of dance in a way that rendered conventional expressions of romantic love and sexual desire superfluous, indeed pallid by comparison.

Luce, who had started out as a cigarette girl in a nightclub, was a lissome, long-legged dancer who transmitted a quality of voluptuous languor and mild exoticism. In a jungle number designed by Albertina Rasch (choreographer of *The Band Wagon*) for the *Ziegfeld Follies* of 1927, she rode a live ostrich, adorned with a rhinestone collar, onto the stage of the New Amsterdam, slid off its back, and performed a dance using two large feathered fans.[12] With her style in mind, Fred applied himself purposefully to the creation of "an entirely new dancing approach."[13] The result was an acknowledged masterpiece, a highly dramatic, highly expressive dance, splendidly evocative of the ardency of Cole Porter's lyrics and the insistent, insinuating pulse of his music. The exotic, aching rhythms of Porter were something of a departure for Fred and distinct from Gershwin's fascinating, syncopated rhythms suffused with New World energy and speed, as Ethan Mordden explains:

Gershwin has drive; Porter has *pulse*. He is seductive, sinuous. What made "Night and Day" one of the biggest international song hits of its

Figure 8.2 Fred and Claire Luce in "Night and Day".
Photofest

era was its sex appeal—the sensual effect of the urgently repeated notes in the verse and the title phrase, of the descending chromatic lines spanning nearly an octave, of the flashy breakout on "oh, such a hungry yearning," of all this ambivalent wondering with a solid beat pumping through it.[14]

Fred did not immediately recognize the song's potential as the show's savior and as a classic of the Great American Songbook; he was more concerned with the daunting vocal challenges it posed, with its forty-eight-bar chorus, unusual harmonic changes, and octave-and-a-fourth range, deriving little comfort from Porter's assertion that it had been written specifically for his voice. Yet, as we can hear from his first recording of "Night and Day" with the Leo Reisman Orchestra in 1932.[15] Fred's interpretation not only truly captures the ballad's leitmotif of longing, it also perfectly illustrates his effectiveness as a singer. The limitations of his vocal range impose on his style a conversational intimacy and, in contrast to the godlike effortlessness of his dancing, a very human and appealing note of strain, which, in the case of "Night and Day," underscores the "hungry yearning." Above all, he brings to any song he sings a sincerity and an actor's dramatic intuition. The London critic J. T. Grein ascribed to Fred "the art of the *diseur*—the art of electrifying his audience by singing a song with a mere semblance of a voice. It is a case of diction triumphing over melody. The melody—and one of the tunes is really charming—is a mere vehicle; the text as uttered, feelingly, passionately, aye, witchingly, is the driving force."[16]

Fred's choreography for "Night and Day" is preserved, in adapted form, in the RKO film *The Gay Divorcée*. Miraculously, the stage version of the dance was also captured on film and is contained in the only known footage of Fred onstage. This was shot by actor and eccentric dancer Fred Stone at the Shubert Theatre in 1933. By then, Stone's daughter Dorothy had taken over the part of Mimi from Claire Luce. What is extraordinary about watching this silent footage, apart from the heightened and haunting dreamlike quality of the dance, is the way one can almost hear the music by means of seeing the dancers' movements. Integral to Fred's genius as a dancer was his exceptional musicality, which enabled him to translate vision into hearing, to let his audience *see* the music, as though he were melody and rhythm incarnate.

The show's second most popular duet (also partially reintroduced in the 1934 film), the last dance before the finale, entailed the show-stopping stunt of dancing over a table. It was a difficult and hazardous trick, which, often in rehearsal and occasionally in performance, resulted in falls. The audience responded to these mishaps with the same glee and suspense that a juggler elicits. One such fall, however, had calamitous consequences for Claire Luce:

> Fred fell plop on top of me, and I could feel my knee snap and my hip go, and I could hardly get up. Fred quickly helped me up, gave the signal to the orchestra leader, and we did it all over again. It was near the end of the play and I got through it. . . . I was in the hospital for ten weeks with my foot up in traction and told I mustn't dance again. Against all advice of all physicians, I went through the season with him in London and it got worse and worse and worse. I didn't want to face it; I even did a revue after that with "Cocky," C. B. Cochran, and danced my head off because I knew it was the last thing I was ever going to do. And that was the end of my dancing career.[17]

With Adele's retirement, Fred's confidence as a comedian also, of necessity, developed. Having played something of the straight man throughout their partnership, he now had to depend more fully on his own comic assets. While he lacked his sister's instinct for devilment and her passion for perilous clowning, he did have a subtle streak of mischief that began to declare itself in a flair for extemporization; although, with Fred, we may be sure there was an element of careful reckoning, of calculation, to his spontaneity. One night, a few months into the run, he felt that a particular scene was lagging, not "getting over." The scene involved the description of a luncheon party in which Guy Holden tells his lawyer friend Teddy Egbert (G. P. Huntley) how he met his mystery woman. The scripted exchange is as follows:

> GUY: Well, she was sitting next to me. I was lifting a forkful of overdone chop to my mouth when suddenly I became aware of her . . .
> EGBERT: They always cook those blasted chops too much.
> GUY: As a rule yes . . . oddly enough, she too was lifting a forkful of chop—rare, I thought—when I spoke to her.

But this night Fred, casting a furtive eye at Huntley, said, without warning: "I was lifting a forkful of overdone ravioli to my mouth."

"How would ravioli go without garlic?" the astonished Huntley improvised without missing a beat. And much to their joint amazement, the line brought the house down.

At every subsequent performance over a number of weeks, Fred lifted a forkful of something different to his mouth—bear, venison, bologna, quail, corned beef—well done, overdone, rare, medium—testing Huntley's vigilance and resourcefulness. Then one night, on an impish impulse, he suddenly reverted to the original line. Stunned, Huntley groped about in the recesses of his mind for the original rejoinder. It wasn't there, and all he could think of to say was Teddy's usual parting phrase "Cheerie Bean."

"Sure, pork and beans—my favorite dish," Fred ad-libbed.

"Half-baked, as you were," replied Huntley, recovering his wits and rescuing the laugh.

After that, Huntley held daily conferences in his dressing room, soliciting suggestions from other cast members as to how to outwit Fred. Menus and chefs were consulted about all manner of food combinations so that the call board came to resemble a cookbook, covered as it was with every conceivable kind of recipe.

Another example of Fred's puckish line in improvisation occurred late in the run; on making his entrance in the Seaside Hotel scene one night, he produced a yo-yo. It was a fresh and delightfully amusing touch, suiting the currency and playfulness of his character.

In an ironic mergence of events, *Gay Divorce*, Fred's first solo venture after the amicable dissolution of his partnership with Adele, coincided with his determined real-life pursuit of a society divorcée. This irony did not escape the speculative attention of the press; rumors of Fred's impending marriage to Phyllis Potter grew rife, and sometimes fanciful in inference. On 21 December 1932, Walter Winchell reported: "Fred Astaire bought an 'engagement ring' last week . . . For Phyllis Potter? . . . or a 'Gay Divorcée'?" Society columnist "Madame

Flutterbye" (the nom de plume of Molly Thayer), without naming Fred's "fian-cée," construed the complications impeding their nuptials as a question of social position and propriety: "Her parents are inclined to disapprove of the marriage until Fred ceases to be 'a dancing man.' So after the run of *Gay Divorce*, Fred's present starring vehicle, is over, he will supposedly quit the stage and take up directing or producing plays. . . . His recent admittance to the Racquet and Tennis Club has undoubtedly helped to smooth out matters with his future papa-in-law."[18]

By the time the show opened, the couple had been inseparable for over a year but were, in fact, no closer to setting a date for their marriage or even formal-izing their engagement. The rapid disintegration of her first marriage and the unresolved issue of Peter's custody demanded constant circumspection and a certain dilatoriness on Phyllis's part, but these were by no means the only obstacles in Fred's way, or the most implacable. In a further irony, it was not Phyllis's family who were inclined to disapprove of the match; the fiercest oppo-sition came from Ann Astaire. Ann could reasonably be expected to have reser-vations about her son's involvement with a divorcée and the mother of a small child. In truth, however, even a woman free of these encumbrances, and consid-ered to be a more suitable choice of wife, would have incurred Ann's resistance. For Ann—and Adele—any eligible contender for Fred's affections threatened the intimacy and primacy of their tightly guarded family unit. Phyllis's close friend Fifi Fell remarked in retrospect: "I don't know whether they actively objected or not, but Mrs Astaire and Delly both worshipped him so, that anyone that he was considering marrying would have naturally had . . . there would have been a reticent feeling about that. Fred and Adele and their mother had been so close."[19]

It was not long before the stress of trying to appease his mother and win her approval of Phyllis, added to the trauma of embarking on a solo career, began to exact a physical toll on Fred. After the third night's performance he became ill and went straight to bed. Ann records in her diary that she "doctored him into a 'sweat bath' and next day he was better in body but still depressed about the critics and business." (Ann Astaire's diary in Mugar Memorial Library, Boston University) Typically in her diary, Ann appears not to appreciate how her intransigent attitude toward Phyllis and the war of attrition being waged on the issue of Fred's marriage were contributing to his despondency. Her entry for New Year's Day 1933 indicates her loving concern for her son as well as her emotional dependence on him; it also furnishes a glimpse of Fred's efforts to demonstrate to his mother her continuing importance in his life: "Fred and I walked to church and back. Then we had tea together at home—I loved it—and he seemed to, dear Fred. I wish more than anything for him to get some really great offer for a play or movie contract. He is so ambitious and deserves it.

The 'half' success of the show is disappointing to him but not discouraging thank <u>dear</u> God!."[20]

In a letter to Adele, written in the early part of 1933, Fred confided his increasing frustration and near despair at his impossible situation.[21] Although acutely aware of his sister's own negative feelings toward Phyllis, he clearly feels able to unburden his most private self to her and to enlist her sympathy, knowing that Adele would recognize from first-hand experience their mother's peculiar obduracy. The letter provides a rare insight into Fred's complex relationship with his mother and presents a vivid psychological portrait of a man under siege. In its frank disclosure of the nature and extent of Ann's opposition, and Fred's procrastination, it offers a much fuller and more faithful account of the circumstances delaying the marriage than is found in Fred's autobiography and most secondary sources. It is worth, therefore, quoting at length:

> Gosh I wish I could get married Delly—it would be so much easier—when one gets to this stage it's just no use waiting that's all. If I don't marry her in the next two months she's going to have to go abroad with the family for seven months and I <u>don't</u> want to be left alone that long. She begs me to do <u>it</u> now and I feel so damn stupid not to be doing it. After all we've been inseparable for a whole year and a half and there is no doubt about whether or not we are suited to each other. She will not see anybody else and I don't want to either.
>
> Mother is so difficult at times—she'll have a fit I suppose if I get married to anybody within the next ten years. I don't know what she expects me to do—keep a couple of tarts or play with myself.
>
> She dislikes that little Phyl and I know she has no reason to at all. Phyl has been sweet to her—sent flowers at Xmas and done many things but you know how terribly hard Mother is to penetrate sometimes. I'm so tired of sneaking in at night—having all my telephone conversations listened to etc. I also know that Mother would be much better off if I married and she had her own life to plan.
>
> Damn it—it's all so difficult and unfair Delly, and <u>I don't want to lose this girl</u>. If she gets away for a long time anything can happen. All the girls that I've liked in the past have gone off and married—one can't expect them to wait forever—not that I want any of those in the past' cause I never asked any girl to marry me until <u>this one</u> and I mean it.
>
> I think it's unfair to take so much of her time and stall along with no definite plans—after all I've asked her and she has accepted and now there's no use in being miserable. She is just what I want and that's that.

Say a little prayer for me babe—that things will turn out right and Mother will come round. She's the only one worry I have[22]

Fred's own prayers were answered surprisingly quickly. Soon after that cri de coeur, he sent another, very different letter to Adele, jubilant that at last an armistice had been negotiated between Ann and Phyllis:

Mother has been simply wonderful and a complete understanding seems to have been reached between us and honestly it's such a relief.

Bless her heart Delly—we had a long talk and things seem to be completely thrashed out.

My plans are as follows—at the completion of the run of the show here—and it looks as though we'll run well into May or so—I shall take a trip to Paris and "tie it on" with Phyl!

We've decided that it is impossible to get married in New York while the show is running on account of the publicity etc. involved so Phyl is going to sail with her aunt about the middle of April and wait for me to come over which I hope will be about 1st June. . . .

I am so happy about it Delly 'cause I simply couldn't stand it any longer as it was and neither could Phyl. Mother has been a different person these last few days since the arrangements have been made and I know the whole thing is going to be much better for her and everyone in general.

Gosh I'm so happy Delly—Mother worried me so much and since her talk with Phyl she is so different. Up to now she simply didn't know her that's all. I suppose you are still skeptical you wise old gal but you can take it from me—I know what I want and by gosh I'm going to get it.[23]

In the light of Fred's determination and assurances, Ann probably yielded to the inevitable, but she did so graciously. The truce that ensued was always a slightly uneasy one. Ironically, Ann and Adele believed Phyllis to be jealous and possessive where Fred was concerned, and, in Adele's view, Phyllis's behavior toward her mother-in-law was less than conciliatory: "I got to like her very much. She made him so happy. I disliked it because she kept him from doing so many things, that's what I didn't like. . . . She was very jealous. . . . Fred won't admit that but he knows it very well. But he did tell me one thing that when she was dying she said, 'I've never been very nice to Granny, have I?' Mother tried, but she was very hurt very often by her. Phyllis was possessive in a way that I didn't like."[24]

Fred's carefully formulated plans for "tying it on" with Phyllis did not come precisely to pass; in the midst of Phyllis's custody battle with Bo Potter, another complication arose in the form of an exciting career opportunity for Fred. One day he happened to encounter Mervyn LeRoy, a contemporary from his vaudeville days and now a film director at Warner Bros. LeRoy expressed his enthusiasm for *Gay Divorce* and his conviction that it would make an ideal vehicle for the screen. According to Fred, however, the proposal was summarily quashed by LeRoy's boss, Jack Warner, who barked, "Who am I going to put in it—Cagney?" Meanwhile, a more imaginative and up-and-coming movie mogul had his eye on Fred. On 13 January 1933, David Selznick, head of production at the financially ailing RKO Studios, sent this memorandum to director Mark Sandrich and producer Louis Brock:

> I am tremendously enthused about the suggestion New York has made of using Fred Astaire. If he photographs (I have ordered a test), he may prove to be a really sensational bet. . . . Astaire is one of the great artists of the day: a magnificent performer, a man conceded to be perhaps, next to Leslie Howard, the most charming in the American theatre, and unquestionably the outstanding young leader of American musical comedy. He would be, in my opinion, good enough to use in the lead of a million-dollar picture—provided only that he photographs, which I hope is the case. I trust you and Mr. Sandrich will keep confidential the fact that we are considering and negotiating with him, since I am certain that as soon as it becomes generally known that he is at last considering pictures, there will be a wild scramble on the part of all studios to test him.

Despite Selznick's certainty to the contrary, there was no danger of a wild scramble or a bidding war for Fred's services. It was more as a compliant pawn than a hot property that Fred eventually entered the motion picture stakes. A screen test was duly arranged in New York by RKO's East Coast story editor, Kay Brown. The results were far from dazzling. The infamous and frequently misquoted verdict attributed to an anonymous studio official—"Can't act. Slightly bald. Also dances"—I tend to regard as apocryphal, although I am sure the legend evolved from and, accurately reflects, a genuine indifference about Fred's movie promise.[25] At any rate, Selznick himself felt "in spite of his enormous ears and bad chin line, that his charm is so tremendous that it comes through even in this wretched test, and I would be perfectly willing to go ahead with him for the lead in the Brock musical." His endorsement of Fred was one of the last executive decisions Selznick made at RKO; a week later, he left the studio, following a dispute with the new corporate president, Merlin Aylesworth, over creative control. He joined his father-in-law, Louis B. Mayer, at MGM and established a second prestige production unit, parallel with that of Irving Thalberg. As a consequence, Fred made his screen debut in the MGM picture *Dancing Lady*, having been "lent" by RKO, with whom he had signed a contract. He made just a cameo appearance playing himself in his Broadway incarnation, but was auspiciously introduced by Clark Gable and partnered (albeit awkwardly) by Joan Crawford. He was then returned to RKO, where he was paired, in a supporting character part, with Ginger Rogers in *Flying Down to Rio*.

On 11 July Phyllis testified before Justice Selah B. Strong in the Brooklyn Supreme Court that she had not accepted Fred's proposal of marriage and would not do so at the risk of her child's welfare.

> Q. Quite recently a certain gentleman whose name I do not wish to mention, has proposed marriage to you?
> A. Yes, he has.
> Q. Do you regard him in every way as acceptable?
> A. I do, yes.
> Q. Have you given him your consent to a marriage?
> A. I have not given him any consent, no.
> Q. Why are you withholding your consent or decision on this offer of marriage? . . .
> A. Because I was afraid of interfering with my child's welfare, looking after my child or being able to give him all my time, and in the best interests of him, I did not want to do anything that would hurt him.
> Q. And until you are satisfied that any such remarriage would be to the best interests of the child, it is not your intention to remarry.
> A. That is true.

On 12 July the court granted her plea for extended custody, with the right to take her son abroad for up to six months in any year. That evening in Justice Strong's chambers Phyllis and Fred were married. Henry Bull gave the bride away, and Phyllis's attorneys, Fanny E. Holtzmann and her brother Jacob L. Holtzmann, acted as witnesses. Just before the ceremony, Fred dashed to the corner jewelry store to buy a ring, the Marriage Bureau was telephoned, and a messenger hurried over to the courthouse with a license. The headline in the New York Evening Journal ran: "Astaire Weds $30,000,000 Heiress with $5 Ring."

The couple spent the next day cruising up the Hudson River on Mrs. Payne Whitney's yacht Captiva, and on 14 July they boarded a Ford Trimotor aircraft (nicknamed "The Tin Goose") bound for the West Coast. On the eve of their departure, Fred wrote to his mother, who had been in Ireland with Adele since early June. The letter reads partly as a declaration of independence and partly as a petition for forgiveness:

> Sweet Ma, our wedding day was <u>very</u> lovely and in a rush as you probably know by now. . . .
>
> Mother we are divinely happy—the things I've always seen in Phyllis have come <u>out</u> strongly in these past few weeks and we <u>are right</u> for each other, Mother dear!!!
>
> I have many things to tell you—longing for you—I feel you are <u>nearer</u> to me than ever though it may not always be that we can be under the same roof.

What transpired in the course of the next three months it is not my present purpose to record; suffice it to say that one of the most celebrated careers in film history was tentatively launched. At the end of this Californian adventure, with two appearances to his new film credit but little faith in his film future, Fred sailed for England with his wife and stepson to honor his contract to star in the London production of *Gay Divorce*. He did not know it, but this would be his last stage appearance.

The relocation to London meant that Fred and Phyllis could enjoy a postponed honeymoon of sorts, although rehearsals were to start immediately. On arrival, the new family moved into the Carlton Hotel, but Phyllis soon found a small Mayfair townhouse at 3 John Street (now Chesterfield Hill),[26] not far from Berkeley Square, which they leased for the length of the run. On 8 October, while settling back into London life and the routine of rehearsals, Fred was telephoned from Lismore by his brother-in-law with the tragic news that Adele had lost a baby girl in premature birth. Ann, who had set sail for Ireland the day before in order to be with Adele for the birth, received the news in a cablegram at sea. It was a heartbreaking disappointment for the close-knit family, and especially for Adele, who, in spite of self-doubts about her maternal aptitude, had come to want the child more than anything. Ill and confined to bed, her sense of desolation and despair was profound.

After its British premiere tryout at the Theatre Royal, Birmingham, on 23 October, *Gay Divorce* opened in London at the Palace Theatre on 2 November. Rejoining Fred from the original New York cast were Luce, Erik Rhodes as the gigolo Tonetti, and Eric Blore as the hotel waiter. The other principals, Huntley, Luella Gear (Hortense), and Betty Starbuck (Barbara Wray), were replaced by Claud Allister, Olive Blakeney (the character having been renamed Gertrude Howard), and Joan Gardner. It was a seamless opening but for one faltering moment in the final dance—the show-stopping but treacherous over-the-table trick. Twenty-six years later, Fred remembered the incident with barely diminished anguish:

> We didn't fall but we bobbled on top of the table as we went over, causing an uncertainty to the finishing step which followed. When the number ended there was a hand but it suddenly stopped dead and we could not do an encore. The audience seemed puzzled. I felt terrible about it because usually there were unlimited encores to that dance. Minnie sure had something to moan about there. Everything else had gone so well with "Cores" and "Mores." I felt sick.[27]

He felt compelled in his curtain speech to apologize for the lapse, to the blank incomprehension of many in the audience who, not having Fred's perspective of the crisis, had failed to notice any break in the continuity of the number.

Phyllis, fraught with nerves, spent the evening in her husband's dressing room, emerging just long enough to catch from the wings the imperfect over-the-table trick. The British press naturally took a keen interest in Fred's new bride, and, when she was able to be glimpsed that night, she was admired for her charming voice and manners, her delicate beauty, and her simple gown of white crepe with diamond shoulder clasps.

The first-night audience was an illustrious one and included Prince George, Lord Charles Cavendish, Viscount Castlereagh, the Duchess of Marlborough, Sir Alfred and Lady Butt, Lady Diana Cooper, Sir Arthur and Lady Colefax, Gladys Cooper, Charles B. Cochran, Noël Coward, Evelyn Laye, Somerset Maugham, and Gordon Selfridge (founder of the famous department store in Oxford Street). The most notable absentee was, of course, Adele, who was still too weak to travel. She did, however, send her brother a large bowl of forget-me-nots, and two weeks into the run, on 16 November, attended the show herself, creating a frisson throughout the theatre. During the interval she was greeted with affectionate applause, which she acknowledged with a little bow and a wave to the gallery.

For Adele it was an intensely moving experience: "It was quite thrilling to see my brother up there on stage and I cried. And everybody in the theatre knew I was there. They all knew his sister was out front and they were all watching my face when he danced with Claire. Tears came down my face and I started to cry."[28]

She was delighted to see Fred finally receiving the individual recognition she believed their partnership had denied him: "I feel when I left him he had a chance to show what he could really do because he always stood back for me. He always stood back while I got the laughs; I was the clown. I wasn't a good dancer.

He was a much better dancer, but I got away with it. . . . I had what they call 'personality.'"[29]

But there must also have been mixed emotions. While Adele always maintained that she did not regret her retirement and, in fact, could not wait to escape the drudgery of dancing and rehearsal, it was brought powerfully home to her, at that darkest hour of her personal life, exactly what she had relinquished—the unique excitement of live performance, the awesome responsibility of one "whose business it is, as Homer says, 'To shake the regions of the gods with laughter.'"[30]

That evening the Astaires were reunited for the first time in eighteen months, and the following Sunday they enjoyed a celebratory supper at Quaglino's in Bury Street. To mark the occasion, Fred presented Adele with a bracelet of small medallions, inscribed with the names of their shows together. He had sufficient courage to put "Flop!" on three of them.

A fortnight later Adele saw the show a second time. She had recently received a leather-bound diary as a gift from her friend Dorothy Hale and began her chronicle on 29 November, after seeing Fred: "Saw my divine brother again in his play—he is so wonderful. There is no one like him—if only he hadn't married that woman, I think I'd be completely happy."[31] As this entry reveals, Adele was still far from reconciled to Fred's marriage and looked on Phyllis with the resentment and mistrust reserved for a usurping rival. Undoubtedly her hostility toward Phyllis was aggravated by her present grief and deepening sense of isolation.

The critical response to the show in London was markedly different from that in New York. It was not so much that the story was received any more favorably on Shaftesbury Avenue than it had been on Broadway; W. A. Darlington of the *Daily Telegraph* said it "plumbed depths of imbecility not often sounded even in this kind of show,"[32] while the *Stage* found the plot "sordid" and objected to Porter's use of the word "bitch" in the song "Mister and Missus Fitch."[33] Rather, the English critics were quick to apprehend in Fred's transcendent performance the emergence of a distinct theatrical personality, not a clever juvenile bereft of his older sibling's iridescence but a charismatic leading man ripening into a nuanced actor and equipped with formidable star quality of his own. Without question London's critics and audiences missed Adele and mourned her retirement, but, unlike their New York counterparts, they did not let their sorrow at the end of this glorious union prejudice their acceptance of Fred as an artist in his own right (although the *Bystander* did detect "an unconscious lonesomeness in his work").[34] Just as, a decade earlier, London's approbation had secured the Astaires unprecedented transatlantic celebrity, it was now pivotal both in establishing Fred as a discrete and viable dramatic prospect and in the evolution of a unique stage and screen persona.

London did not *discover* Astaire the actor-dancer but did perceive hitherto untapped depths to his acting within and outside the dance. Since *Stop Flirting*, the city's dance and theatre commentators had been impressed with Fred's unusual corporeal expressiveness, his employment of the whole body as a prime narrative instrument. In *Gay Divorce* they identified a strengthening or maturing of his storytelling powers, which they deemed revelatory. What they felt they were witnessing was a master dramatist, one who could articulate through his movements ecstasy or despair, who could make aphorisms with his ankles, and who could render incarnate the wit of a Noël Coward or a Gertrude Lawrence and the ethereal enchantment of Shakespeare's Ariel or Oberon.

Grein, essaying an explanation of "the uncanny eloquence of his feet," said: "There is something in those feet that means more than a *tour de force*. Those nimble, graceful, volatile feet are voluble in their evolutions. They convey something; they accentuate, as it were, the dialogue, render it more apt and telling."[35] Ivor Brown marveled at Fred's illuminating, transforming physical wit, a strange alchemy combining fluidity and volatility: "A spider in a whirlwind would not move spare limbs more rapidly than he; but it is not the tricks of his agility which illumine the play, but a kind of furious, fantastic grace, the poetry of mischief, Harlequin's art."[36]

Most incisively, a review in London's *Illustrated Sporting and Dramatic News* isolated two key components of Fred's silent eloquence, which we particularly associate with the cinematic Astaire—the hypnotic and protean exposition of character achieved apparently without artifice or self-consciousness: "The limbs of Fred Astaire are, like W. S. Gilbert's lover's professions, 'eloquent everywhere.' What in the private is an ugly jerk, in Captain Astaire is a mood index, for he cannot kick a footstool without expressing character. . . . He can suggest instant changes of mood and all seems so unpremeditated that you feel you have stolen unawares on a dancer who thinks he is alone."[37] This is reminiscent of the painter J. B. Yeats's description of Isadora Duncan dancing onstage:

> I saw her (from her own box) dancing in the biggest theatre, and on the biggest stage in N. York—a figure dancing all alone on this immense stage—and there again you felt the charm of the self-contained woman. Several people said: Is it not like watching a kitten playing for itself? We watched as if we were each of us hidden in ambush.[38]

There is one discovery for which London must take entire credit and that had vital implications for Fred's continuing solo career. It was a discovery Adele also made when she saw her brother across the footlights for the first time: "I'd never seen him from out front before. It was also the first time I realized that Fred had sex appeal. Fred! Where did he get it? He's so un-conceited looking." "Night and

Day" was the apotheosis of Fred's idiosyncratic masculinity, a commanding gentleness, which translated so well to the screen. But where New York saw "an earnest and appealing underdog,"[39] London saw "a Puck revealing a great stage-lover, a comedian, a man of the world, commanding all the secrets of caressing, unostentatiously, but full of graceful insinuation."[40]

In several reviews Fred was depicted as a sophisticated and seductive incarnation of Peter Pan, a debonair and chivalrous urchin roaming a cosmopolitan Neverland:

> Fred Astaire sings "After You, Who?" and every right-minded female knows she'd do all she could to comfort him, given half the chance.
> —*Bystander,* 22 November

> Mr. Astaire has, ingrained in him, a charm that makes most females in the audience want to mother him.
> —*Tatler,* 29 November

> He suggests the wistful little-boy-lost, irresistible to a Barrie-reared English audience.
> —*Time and Tide,*

The best and wittiest summation of Fred's new-found appeal to a mass maternal instinct was made by James Agate, whom Alistair Cooke called "the irascible, dogmatic, opinionated but brilliant journalist, and I believe the best critic of acting we have had this century." In reply to the question asked by his colleague Dwight Taylor, "What is Mr. Fred Astaire's secret?,"[41] he announced:

> Mr. Astaire's secret is that of the late Rudolf Valentino and of Mr. Maurice Chevalier, happily still with us—sex. But sex so bejewelled and be-glamoured and be-pixied that the weaker vessels who fall for it can pretend that it isn't sex at all but a sublimated, Barriesque projection of the Little Fellow with the Knuckles in his Eyes. You would have thought by the look of the first-night foyer that it was Mothering Thursday, since every woman in the place was urgent to take to her chinchilla'd bosom this waif with the sad eyes and twinkling feet. It was a great night, for on it Mr. Astaire was born again to the London stage, a star danced, and the mother which is in very woman cried.[42]

What London had singularly discovered in the post-Adele Fred was a magnetism based paradoxically on vulnerability, a personality, at once knowing and guileless, that irresistibly combined ardent gallantry, restrained yearning, self-deprecation, and self-confidence. Mordden is quite wrong when he says that *Gay Divorce* "created a new persona for [Fred] as a sardonically romantic bon vivant."[43] This suggests an impenetrable nonchalance, but what Fred conveyed was far more winning—a potent fragility or, rather, tenderness.

Gay Divorce—and, more important, London's receptiveness to Fred as lead-ing man—was a crucial factor in his subsequent attainment of celluloid immor-tality. Guy Holden, an American in London, seems quintessentially to anticipate the Astaire screen persona of the 1930s. He is, recognizably yet atypically, the boy next door, an engaging amalgam of midwestern candor and continental carelessness. Outfitted by Savile Row and Jermyn Street, this twentieth-century paladin is elegantly armored in gray trousers, brown coat, and brown shoes, and in his pocket is a handkerchief of the new henna red shade. He also sports anar-chic sartorial insignia such as a necktie around his waist. In short, he is the very embodiment of brash refinement. Nanette Kutner's profile of Fred, "Young Man from Omaha," written in November 1932, serves equally well as a description of the modernity and Anglo-Americanism of Guy Holden:

> When he dances, through his mad rhythms and perfect lines comes a trace of dignity. His dances are cartoons of dignity; they typify the young man about town. He is modern. He is Gershwin's music orches-trated in taps. He is Twentieth Century. He is fast, his movements, his talk, the nervous quick motions of his head. He is this generation. He is Leslie Howard breaking into a clog.

This new transatlantic hero, this democratic aristocrat, is most purely epito-mized in the dance soliloquy "A Needle in a Haystack" in the film *The Gay Divorcée*, a number that replaced rather than replicated the correspondingly located "After You, Who?" from the stage show. Here we find Guy Holden in the sitting room of his London flat, changing from a dressing gown into street wear and, in the process, tap-dancing on the hearth, vaulting a sofa, executing a breath-taking series of cabrioles, and leaping aloft a chair before offhandedly donning his hat and making his exit. This superb sequence is remarkable for several rea-sons, all of them revolutionary in terms of the history of the movie musical: its simple interior setting; its psychological significance; its succinct exposition of character; and its sublime transfiguration of the everyday.

What I wish to focus on, however, is its subtle but meaningful arrangement of juxtapositions, which exemplify what Len Platt, in his analysis of the decline of West End musical comedy, defines as "a changed world order with America positioned not just as the leading economic power, but also as the new home of modernity and innovation."[44] The first juxtaposition of the old and new world orders occurs in the interaction between Guy Holden, rakish, omnipotent emblem of proto-Cool, and his imperturbable middle-aged English valet. Patiently and impassively the valet catches, in swift succession, Guy's cravat, dressing gown (which Guy backhands to him), and discarded choice of necktie before proffering, with an air of ceremonial solemnity, a looking glass and tie bar.

The second juxtaposition can be observed as Guy, in his shirtsleeves, leans contemplatively against the mantelpiece on which is placed a Roman bust, a young Augustus, under whose watchful imperial gaze Guy begins spontaneously to rap out rhythms with his hands and feet. His clownish Chaplinesque waddle across the hearth amusingly undercuts the sculpture's Roman *gravitas* and *dignitas*. This particular juxtaposition also indicates that Astaire's Guy Holden is a reinvention of Roman *urbanitas*, an indefinable metropolitan sophistication that becomes visible only in relation to those who lack it and that the neoteric poet Catullus elevated to the status of a guiding aesthetic and a moral principle.

As the dance progresses, Guy's restless, mercurial form is juxtaposed with another Roman statue, appropriately of Mercury, the god with winged heels and, among other things, patron of invention, wit, persuasion, and chance. At the end of the sequence, the valet tosses hat and umbrella to Guy, who is poised contrapposto atop a chair. The bowler and tightly furled umbrella—supreme symbols of stolid Englishness—are contrasted with the rakish angle at which Guy sets his hat and his insouciant parting salute.

Fred reprised his "American in London" in other films of the 1930s; Jerry Travers in *Top Hat* and Jerry Halliday in *A Damsel in Distress* are, in essence, variations on Guy Holden. The character symbolizes all that London discovered in Astaire, the actor-dancer, and urged on the rest of the world. Guy Holden encapsulates the very quality that so endeared Fred and Adele to a disenchanted postwar London and on which Fred's iconic screen image is founded—a sense of delight and "a willingness of the heart."

CHAPTER 9

After the Dance

How I hate this goodbye—
Funny thing, so do I.
—George and Ira Gershwin, "So Am I"

In 1953, two of Adele's most ardent literary admirers, P. G. Wodehouse and Guy Bolton, wrote this potted version of the Astaires' after story; it is genuinely elegiac but also typically Wodehousean in its whimsy:

> Adele closed her career with a triumphant performance in *The Band Wagon* by George S. Kaufman, Howard Dietz and Arthur Schwartz. She then married the Duke of Devonshire's second son and retired to Lismore Castle in Ireland, leaving a gap that can never be filled. Fred struggled on without her for a while, but finally threw his hand in and disappeared. There is a rumour that he turned up in Hollywood. It was the best the poor chap could hope for after losing his brilliant sister.[1]

As we know, "rumors" of Fred's migration to Hollywood were not ill-founded; in 1937 he even "turned up" as the hero of a Wodehouse screenplay (*A Damsel in Distress*). During the London run of *Gay Divorce*, and having almost forgotten that his film career hung in the balance, he received a cablegram from Pandro S. Berman, RKO's twenty-eight-year-old acting head of production: "*Flying Down to Rio* colossal success stop offering seven year contract stop make sure film rights *Gay Divorce* stop representative with negotiation rights on the way to you." Shortly afterward, Berman himself traveled to London to see the show and judge its screen-worthiness. He purchased the film rights for $20,000, a lowly sum even in 1934, and a rare deal was negotiated that ensured Fred a percentage of the film's profits and complete autonomy over how his dances would be presented. From a letter he wrote to Adele on the cusp of his great Hollywood experiment in 1933, it is clear that if Fred imagined he had any sort of future in Hollywood, it was as an irregular commuter from Broadway or the West End; he cites the examples of Leslie Howard and Herbert Marshall in his eagerness to "do the picture in Hollywood and scram away to England." But when *Gay Divorce* closed at the Palace Theatre on 17 April 1934, Fred and Phyllis, on returning to the States, moved permanently to the West Coast, and Fred never again appeared in a fully mounted stage show.

At the insistence of the Hays Office, and in an instructive piece of moral sophistry, the project was primly re-titled *The Gay Divorcée*, on the basis that while a party to a divorce might legitimately be described as gay, divorce itself was a grave business. The script underwent several revisions because, as Joseph I. Breen of the Association of Motion Picture Producers informed Merian C. Cooper (Berman's predecessor), "from the printed page, we get the notion that it is based upon the attempt to secure a divorce by collusion. Also, a number of the lines of the play are a bit too broad to be acceptable either from the standpoint of our Production Code, or from political censorship" (RKO/UCLA). This slightly bowdlerized Broadway borrowing was the first vehicle to star Fred Astaire and Ginger Rogers. The rest, as they say, is history.

In Ginger Rogers, Fred acquired his most popular and effective screen partner, one who, in her own way, was every bit as complementary as Adele—temperamentally and aesthetically. Rogers became an accomplished straight actress, winning an Academy Award for her performance in *Kitty Foyle* in 1940, but she never acted more impressively or affectingly than in her dances with Fred or in simply being serenaded by him. Fred, however, still bore the psychological wounds of his struggle to emerge from under his sister's luminous shadow, and having only just proved his worth as a solo artist, he resented being so swiftly and irrevocably teamed with another performer. This he communicated unambiguously in a letter to his agent, Leland Hayward, dated Friday, 9 February 1934, and typed entirely in capitals with his familiar underlinings (Hayward was also Rogers's agent):

WHAT'S ALL THIS TALK ABOUT ME BEING TEAMED WITH GINGER ROGERS? I WILL <u>NOT</u> HAVE IT LELAND—I DID NOT GO INTO PICTURES TO BE <u>TEAMED</u> WITH HER OR ANYONE ELSE, AND IF THAT IS THE PROGRAM IN MIND FOR ME I WILL NOT STAND FOR IT. I DON'T MIND DOING ANOTHER PICTURE WITH HER BUT AS FOR THIS <u>TEAM</u> IDEA IT'S <u>OUT</u>! I'VE JUST MANAGED TO LIVE DOWN ONE PARTNERSHIP AND I DON'T WANT TO BE BOTHERED WITH ANY MORE. I'D

RATHER NOT MAKE ANY MORE PICTURES FOR RADIO IF I
HAVE TO BE TEAMED UP WITH ONE OF THOSE MOVIE
"QUEENS."[2]

Fortunately, cooler, more calculating heads prevailed, and Pandro Berman, in
an equally emphatic cable wired to Hayward on 26 February, made explicit that
such decisions did not rest with Fred and that, his Broadway laurels
notwithstanding, his value as a piece of motion-picture "property" was yet to be
determined:

TELL ASTAIRE HOLD HIS WATER WITH REGARD TO
TEAMING STOP HE IS NOT YET READY TO BE STAR IN HIS
OWN RIGHT AND IF WE WANT BOLSTER HIM WITH GOOD
SUPPORT FOR NEXT FEW PICTURES THINK HE SHOULD
THANK US STOP GINGER ROGERS SEEMS TO GO RATHER
WELL WITH HIM AND THERE IS NO NEED ASSUME WE WILL
BE MAKING PERMANENT TEAM OF THIS PAIR EXCEPT IF
WE CAN ALL CLEAN UP LOT OF MONEY BY KEEPING THEM
TOGETHER WOULD BE FOOLISH NOT TO.

But if the studio's strategic efforts to prolong and capitalize on the winning
formula of Astaire and Rogers rankled, there was no doubt that the new medium
suited Fred's individual genius and his perfectionism. He particularly relished
having the ability to hone his performance away from the scrutiny of a live audience and to commit only the best of multiple takes to celluloid. Well before his
Hollywood prospects were assured, he began to formulate an ambitious and pioneering vision of how dance should be filmed. In an interview he gave from his
dressing room at the Shubert Theatre, he said: "I feel that no one has ever really
done anything original in the way of dancing on the screen. It's always the same
old thing. I hope to create something entirely new. There ought to be a photo-
graphic medium of developing and putting across rhythm on the screen." Yet his
expectations did not always match his ambitions. Initially he was reluctant to do
a film version of *Gay Divorce* because, as he explained to story editor Kay Brown,
"So much of it is held up by "hoofing," which of course cannot be done as advan-
tageously on the screen"[3]. To Berman he also voiced his belief that using "Night
and Day" in the picture would be "a great mistake"[4]. Within a few years, however,
and with "Night and Day" as the catalyst, he had revolutionized the movie dance
musical.

Fred was fortunate in having at his disposal the resourcefulness of a first-rate
film unit at RKO, directors of the calibre of Mark Sandrich and George

Stevens, and an "in-house" choreographic editor in Hermes Pan, with whom he discovered an astonishing creative rapport. He had also at his command an apparently instinctive understanding of how the camera should serve the dance and how the dance could exploit the camera.

> I have always tried to run a dance straight in the movies, keeping the full figure of the dancer, or dancers, in view and retaining the flow of the movement intact. . . . Keeping the whole body always in action before the camera, there are certain obvious advantages that the screen has over the stage. You can concentrate your action on the dancer; the audience can follow intricate steps that were all but lost behind the footlights, and each person in the audience sees the dance from the same perspective. . . . In consequence, I think that the audience . . . get a larger, clearer and better-focused view, and so, derive a larger emotional response.[5]

Fred's insistence on keeping the full figure of the dancer always in view of the camera, his removal of meaningless inserts and editing effects, and his limited or judicious use of cuts preserved the choreographic integrity of the dance, focusing attention on the dancer's body and investing the story he told with a compelling fluidity and coherence. These innovative principles, which made such an impact on the Hollywood musical, raising it to unprecedented heights of narrative sophistication, are seldom adhered to today; instead the camera has reasserted its dominance over the dancer, with distracting, and often destructive, results.

While Fred was engineering this revolution and, in the process, attaining worldwide celebrity, what of Adele, who had triumphantly closed her career at its pinnacle? For a time she enjoyed playing the part of the chatelaine of Lismore Castle, but after the death of her baby girl and Fred's marriage and re-settlement in California, she became periodically depressed, feeling dismally sequestered, and sometimes accusing her brother of neglect. Fred usually responded sensitively and with good humor, perceiving that such accusations were born of intense frustration, and he did his earnest best to reassure his sister and mother of their secure place in his affections. Occasionally his own frustration at the competing pressures on him rose to the surface:

> It worries me to have you get hurt feelings all the time. I have so much to do and so many sides to satisfy that I sometimes wonder how I do as well as I'm doing. . . .
>
> You must remember, babe, that if you had not left the stage, perhaps we would still be at it as the same old team, wondering all the time what

would happen when we busted up as I had been doing for several years. Let us be thankful for that which we have received—and realize that we are both doing o.k. in our respective ways—very o.k. I'd call it.

Our little close-coupled trio held a very unique position in the world—I cannot think of another situation like it in any family. Three very sensitive people suddenly separated (not really, but only from the point of living under one roof) and all trying to make things work out—and we're not doing so badly.[6]

It was not merely that her bucolic existence began to pall or that she missed getting out before the footlights; Adele knew that her sweet, amiably irresponsible husband was on a downward spiral of alcoholism. For much of their married life, Charles Cavendish was back and forth to German spas for "cure" treatments, as well as in and out of London nursing homes and hospitals, endeavoring at his wife's behest to curb his addiction. Adele believed it was a problem endemic to Charlie's generation of young English aristocrats and partly blamed Rosa Lewis, the legendary proprietress of the Cavendish Hotel, for encouraging Charlie's drinking from the time he was an undergraduate at Cambridge. The Cavendish, on the corner of Jermyn and Duke streets, had a reputation for raffishness and worse, and became something of an indulgent haven for young noblemen, like Charlie, out of reach of the university proctors and their "bulldogs." "Rosa Lewis loved Charlie," Adele said. "She would always be there with a whisky for him. She liked me in the beginning, but she didn't like me later on because I would stop him drinking."

Tragically, in October 1935 Adele gave birth prematurely to stillborn twin boys who were buried close by her daughter in the graveyard of St. Carthage's Cathedral in Lismore. Three months later in Los Angeles, Phyllis Astaire gave birth to a healthy baby boy, who was named Fred Jr. Although this happy event served to deepen Adele's sense of loss and failure, she and Charlie made a special trip to California to see her new nephew. While in Hollywood she agreed to do a series of screen tests for Fred's original champion, David O. Selznick, who by now had formed his own studio, Selznick International Pictures, and was considering Adele for a dramatic role in *Dark Victory*—the part of Ann King, the best friend and secretary of Bette Davis's terminally ill Judith Traherne. While flattered by Selznick's offer, and envisaging the revival of her career as a means of bringing purpose to her life, Adele did not take long to decline the role, which was eventually played by Dublin-born actress Geraldine Fitzgerald. As with her aborted film venture in Britain a year later (again at Selznick's instigation), three forces conspired to dissuade her: her own disappointment, and indeed horror, at how she looked on screen; her fear of embarrassing her brother; and the need to care for her ailing husband.

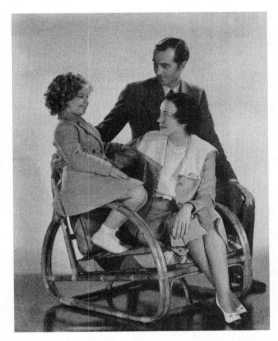

Figure 9.1 Adele and Lord Charles Cavendish with Shirley Temple, Hollywood, 1937.
Adele Astaire Collection, Howard Gotlieb Archival Research Centre

Adele and Charlie arrived back in London in the midst of the Abdication Crisis, which Adele dubbed "Simpsonitus." A British resident of the United States wrote to Geoffrey Dawson, editor of *The Times*: "The doings of the King, as reported in the American Press, have in the course of a few months transformed Great Britain, as envisaged by the average American, from a sober and dignified realm into a dizzy Balkan musical comedy attuned to the rhythm of jazz."[7] In spite of her close friendship with Edward when he was Prince of Wales, this was a view that Adele, as a transplanted American, closely echoed. For all her madcap ways and the raciness of her language, she was staunchly conservative in her political and moral outlook. She denounced the king's behavior, which she witnessed at firsthand, as a deplorable dereliction of duty. Her diary entries make plain, in her distinctive style, her abhorrence of the situation and her passionate conviction that the king was "screwy":

> The King is selfish and slipshod in his very responsible position. . . . As an American, I resent the old traditions being done away with, and in their place, this cheap and undignified display of modern ruling. Most of the old regime are being sacked. . . . A very rowdy weekend was held

at Himley Hall, Lord Dudley's place, and the chosen orgy consisted of
Eric Dudley, Foxie Gwynne (American), Pat Jersey (recently estranged
from her husband), the King and Mrs. Simpson—my authentic reports
of this party are terrific—it seems odd that a King could do such a
thing—but then I'm American and narrow-minded about such things—
especially where ruling royalty is concerned.

The King is a selfish bastard and forgets that his life is for his country,
not to carry on an indiscreet life with the American "adventuress." . . .
He shoves her in the most holy of places—and expects people to
accept her.

It's too much! . . . The world is in a frenzy and he wants to marry that
whore. . . . If he does abdicate, which is more than possible, he ought to
be put in a padded cell.[8]

On the day his reign officially ended, 11 December 1936, Edward made a
BBC broadcast from Windsor Castle in which he famously spoke of his inability
to "carry out the heavy burden of responsibility and to discharge my duties as
King as I would wish to do without the help and support of the woman I love."
Adele derided this "calculated" appeal and supposed romantic gesture as "cheap,
would-be dramatic and nauseating."

On 11 July 1937, at the age of thirty-eight, George Gershwin died following
surgery for a malignant brain tumor. For Fred, in particular, it was an enormous
personal tragedy. A week later he wrote to Adele:

I did not see him—it was too late—nobody was allowed to see him the
last few days. Ira told me the last word he spoke was my name. In trying
to make himself understood it came out and then he collapsed and
never was able to function again. It's all so cruel—poor George. . . . It is
difficult for me to work with all of the songs in the new picture
[*A Damsel in Distress*] without constantly thinking of him.[9]

On 8 September a memorial concert was held at the Hollywood Bowl and
broadcast live by CBS Radio. With an audible catch in his throat and even greater
feeling than he had sung it before or since, Fred performed "They Can't Take
That Away from Me" from *Shall We Dance*, the song for which Gershwin received
a posthumous Academy Award nomination.

On 6 May 1938, Charlie's father, the ninth Duke of Devonshire, died at
Chatsworth. To cope with his grief Charlie drank yet more heavily. He seemed
determined on a course of self-destruction, aided and abetted by a corrupt man-
servant who covertly supplied him with liquor. He experienced periods of

disorientation, and his personality began to change; he became truculent and at times verbally abusive. On the first anniversary of the Duke's death, Adele suffered a miscarriage and was bedridden for nearly a month. She was forty-two years old, and her life was at its lowest ebb. Her last hope of curing her husband's alcoholism by producing a healthy heir was gone. War with Germany was looming, but ironically it was this global catastrophe that, in many ways, proved Adele's salvation.

With Charlie incapable of active service, the Devonshires funded the purchase of two fighter planes for the Royal Air Force, dubbed "Cavendish" and "Adele Astaire." Adele initiated a farming project at Lismore but was anxious to take a more active part in the war effort and to escape the oppressive atmosphere of the castle. In June 1940 she wrote in her diary: "I realize how small and frivolous and utterly unimportant my life has been (especially in the past seven years) compared to the greatness and history-making period of the past eight months of this world war—it's staggering how everything is pale and transparent by comparison."

In late 1942, on one of her frequent visits to London, Adele was introduced to Colonel Kingman Douglass, who was stationed there as chief of U.S. Air Force Intelligence. Douglass had been a decorated flyer in World War I and had been involved in the creation of the Office of Strategic Services, the forerunner to the Central Intelligence Agency. In civilian life he was an investment banker in Chicago and married with three sons. Adele recalled, "I pretended not to take much notice of him, but then he started calling me up and we got to know each other better and better."[10]

It was Douglass who suggested to Adele that she might work at the newly opened "Rainbow Corner," the American Red Cross Club near Piccadilly Circus, on the corner of Shaftesbury Avenue and Denman Street. Leaving her mother at Lismore to nurse Charlie, now a permanent invalid, and run the estate, Adele worked seven days a week at the club until the war in Europe ended. She helped at the information desk, danced with the GIs, and sometimes went shopping for them. Her main duty, however, was as an amanuensis, writing letters home for the soldiers, often signing these missives "Adele Astaire, Fred's sister." She found her years at Rainbow Corner the most fulfilling and stimulating since her retirement from the stage.

In March 1942, Fred and Phyllis's second child was born, a girl named after her mother but known by her middle name, Ava (pronounced Ah-va).

Just before Christmas 1943, Charlie began having convulsions and suffering delirium. The convulsions damaged his heart, and alcohol poisoning was diagnosed. All the while Ann Astaire cared for him and sent Adele reports of his condition. Virtually forsaken by his own family, Charlie related to Ann as a surrogate mother. She was at his bedside when he died on 23 March 1944 at the age

Figure 9.2 Adele writing letters home for American servicemen at Rainbow Corner, London, 1944.
Adele Astaire Collection, Howard Gotlieb Archival Research Centre

of thirty-eight. Adele was in London at the time but was granted compassionate leave to return home. She confided her feelings to her diary:

> [Charlie] admittedly has been a source of great worry and anxiety to me most of our married life—but always a loyal and devoted husband. His weakness for drink is not to be blamed on him—he had a tortured soul and has never been meant for this hard cruel world. . . . Our stormy life together was so momentary that every worry I had about him is washed away and only great love and devotion and undying faith in him will live with me forever.[11]

Charlie was buried beside his infant children at St. Carthage's. None of the Devonshires attended his funeral.

That summer, Fred arrived in London to begin his USO tour of Europe. There is extant Pathé News footage of Fred and Adele at the opening of London's Stage Door Canteen on 31 August. Fred acted as master of ceremonies for the event and, at the end of the evening, was joined onstage by his sister in her Red Cross

Uniform. Despite pleas from the audience for them to dance together, Fred insisted that they could not do so impromptu. His six-week tour, performing for the personnel of the First Army Division, took him to France, Belgium, and Holland, and included an appearance before 5000 troops at the Palace of Versailles.

When Irving Berlin took over the score of *Annie Get Your Gun* after Jerome Kern's sudden death in 1945, he wanted Adele to play Annie Oakley. Like Wodehouse's Billie Dore, it was a role that would probably have suited her splendidly, but after some consideration, Adele chose instead to get married—to Kingman Douglass, now divorced from his wife in Chicago. She and her new husband would divide their time between four homes: The Dorchester in New York; Lismore Castle; "Mount Gordon" in Middleburg, Virginia (an attempt by Kingman to recreate the atmosphere of Lismore); and Round Hill in Jamaica. The house in Jamaica was part of a new development in which Noël Coward had also purchased a property. To mark the opening of the development, Coward hosted a Beach Bonfire Barbecue at which Adele was photographed dancing, with wild and gleeful abandon, with a group of Fire Dancers; the picture appeared on the cover of the *West Indian Review* of 16 January 1954. On the reverse of the

Figure 9.3   Fred at Valognes in Normandy, 3 September 1944. Adele Astaire Collection, Howard Gotlieb Archival Research Centre

Figure 9.4   Adele with fire dancers, Round Hill, Jamaica, 1954.
Adele Astaire Collection, Howard Gotlieb Archival Research Centre

print in Adele's possession, she had written "Rather voodoo-ish—wild drums. When I have to get up and dance . . .".

At Round Hill Adele entertained a glittering list of friends and relations, including Jackie and John Kennedy.

On the completion of *Blue Skies* in 1946 it was announced that Fred was retiring from films. At forty-seven, he questioned whether he had the physical and creative stamina to sustain such a demanding career. With Phyllis's encouragement, he established the first Fred Astaire Dance Studio, on New York's Park Avenue, whose grand ballroom was named after Adele. The chain of schools that followed proved a costly and troublesome venture, and a decade later Fred sold his proprietary interest. His retirement, however, was short-lived. In 1948 he took over from an injured Gene Kelly the lead in MGM's *Easter Parade*. The following year he received a special Academy Award "for his unique artistry and his contributions to the technique of motion pictures."

Up until this point Fred had considered himself singularly blessed, in both his professional and private life, but in 1954 his world fell apart. His beloved wife, a heavy smoker, died of lung cancer at the age of just forty-six. Fred

Figure 9.5   Adele with John F. Kennedy at Round Hill, Jamaica, c.1953.
Adele Astaire Collection, Howard Gotlieb Archival Research Centre

had begun rehearsals at Twentieth Century Fox for an adaptation of Jean Webster's *Daddy Long Legs* with Leslie Caron, but the idea of completing the picture was inconceivable to him in his distraught state. He offered to pay out of his own pocket all the production expenses so far incurred. Eventually, however, he was persuaded that work was the best antidote to his grief, and filming continued.

Fred cherished the companionship of his young daughter, who resembled her mother in many ways, and his career continued to flourish. Beginning in 1958, he produced four groundbreaking television specials, partnered by an exciting young dancer named Barrie Chase, and the following year he made his debut as a dramatic actor, playing a nuclear physicist in Stanley Kramer's *On the Beach*. But the loss of Phyllis was one from which he never recovered. Adele later remembered: "He used to take me to her grave with all the flowers that she loved, the camellias that she planted, and put them on the grave and burst out crying."[12]

In 1959 Fred penned his autobiography, in longhand and without the aid of a ghostwriter. *Steps in Time* (a title suggested by Noël Coward) is written in an elegant, and engaging, if less than penetrating, style. As an ex cathedra statement of artistic motivation by the world's most celebrated dancer, the last line of the book is ludicrously reductive: "I just dance."[13]

In what must have seemed to Adele a terrible instance of déjà vu, her second husband was steadily becoming alcoholic, although not to the fatal extent that Charles Cavendish had been. In New York in 1968 he was seriously injured when struck by a bus that had mounted the curb, and only a few months later he was involved, as a passenger, in a motor accident that left him with a collapsed lung. In 1971 he died from a brain hemorrhage. Adele moved permanently to Arizona, where she had bought a house earlier that year, and settled into a relatively quiet life. She shared with Fred a passion for television soap operas, and the two would spend hours on the telephone discussing the characters and story lines of their favorite shows.

Age did not wither Adele's infinite capacity to shock and torment. But even she knew not to trespass too far on her brother's intensely private nature. She recalled that when staying at his house she would not think of going near his bedroom unless the door was open. And when she accompanied him to church of a Sunday morning she would find Fred, at the "kiss of peace," suddenly on his knees beside her, apparently deep in prayer, and bidding her to follow his lead as a measure to avoid the social discomfort the moment held for him.

In 1975 Ann Astaire, who in recent years had grudgingly relinquished some of her fierce independence and been living with her son, was ninety-six. This reluctant stage mother with the grace and bearing of a duchess to the manner born, a gentle but most potent force in her children's lives, died in her sleep on 25 July. A few days later, Adele, who was at Lismore for the summer, declared in a very serious tone to some guests, "Now Fred and I are orphans."

With Phyllis and Ann both gone, Adele could at least look forward to spending more time with her brother, free of rivals—or so she thought. In 1980, having been a widower for twenty-six years, Fred married jockey Robyn Smith, more than four decades his junior. If the union surprised his children and many of his friends and fans, it seems to have traumatized Adele. Her close friend Sybil Connelly was convinced the marriage "contributed enormously to her death." In a reconciliatory gesture, Fred spent the first Christmas of his new marriage alone with his sister in Arizona.

Early in the New Year Adele suffered a major stroke and lapsed into a coma. She never regained consciousness and died on 25 January in her eighty-fifth year. Fred received the news while on location in Saratoga Springs, New York, for his last film role in *Ghost Story*. So tremendous was his grief that he could not bear to be alone and asked his co-star, Douglas Fairbanks Jr., to move into the adjoining hotel bedroom so that he could leave the door open at night. Having also to cope with the coldest winter in fifty years, he became ill, and at director John Irvin's request, Fred's daughter Ava flew to New York and stayed with her father until filming was completed.

Some of Adele's ashes were buried next to her mother's grave in Chatsworth, California. The rest were taken to Ireland by Ava and scattered around the graves of Charlie and the children, and over the castle wall at Lismore. A small portion Ava kept to scatter over the garlic patch in her own garden near Schull in West Cork, because of her aunt's fondness for garlic.

Just eight weeks after Adele's death, in a fulsome ceremony at the International Ballroom of the Beverly Hilton Hotel, the American Film Institute bestowed on Fred its Lifetime Achievement Award. In his clearly heartfelt and unscripted acceptance speech, Fred said: "My sister Adele was mostly responsible for my being in show business. She was the whole show, she really was. In all the vaudeville acts we had and the musical comedies we did together, Delly was the one that was the shining light and I was just there pushing away."

Fred's final years were not especially happy ones. For one endowed with such graceful agility all his life, the inevitable impingements of old age were deeply disheartening. Largely the result of the grueling nature and unusual longevity of his dancing career, he suffered from painful arthritis and an inner-ear problem that affected his balance. Eating, which had never held much appeal for him, became a chore. He died of pneumonia on 22 June 1987 at the age of eighty-eight. The national and international press coverage of his death was of the sort normally reserved for the passing of a president of the United States. But one of the finest and most moving tributes paid to Fred was more low-key; it came from his son-in-law, Richard McKenzie: "Fred might have wished for a private image different from his public one but he couldn't quite pull it off. The adjectives applied to him were true. He was a good fellow—never a guy. F. A. bowed out at the right time. But I shall miss him terribly. Me and the world."[14]

In November 1972 Fred and Adele were inducted into the Theatre Hall of Fame (created the year before) "in recognition of their outstanding contribution to the American Theatre." A decade later, the Astaire Awards (subsequently renamed the Fred and Adele Astaire Awards) were established by the Anglo-American Contemporary Dance Foundation "to honour Fred Astaire and his sister Adele and to award the achievement of an outstanding dancer or dancers and an outstanding choreographer in each Broadway season".[15]

In their later years Fred and Adele were seen by a privileged few dancing together at the Lambs Club Spring Gambol held in Fred's honor in 1962 and at the Hollywood premiere of *That's Entertainment!* in 1974. In the years since their deaths there have been occasional tribute shows and revivals of their musical comedies; *Lady, Be Good!*, for example, was successfully staged by Ian Talbot at the Open Air Theatre in London's Regent Park in 1992 and again in 2007.

Those who were lucky enough to see the Astaires onstage dancing to George Gershwin's music are now very scarce. The shows, and the Astaires' peculiar fascination and magic, properly belong, as I observed at the start, to a vanished world, which in no small part they helped to define. But if there is an enduring image of Fred and Adele, a perfect summation of their public and private relationship, of the resilient and redemptive spirit they evoked, it is brother and sister huddled together under an umbrella and singing, in an artlessly elevated expression of mischief and hope, the Gershwins' "Hang On to Me":

Fred:
> That's right! Hold tight!
> We're on our way!

Adele:
> Uphill until . . .

Both:
> We lose the shadows.
> If you'll hang on to me

Figure 9.6 Fred and Adele in "Hang on to Me", *Lady, Be Good!*.

While I hang on to you
We'll dance into the sunshine out of the rain
Forever and a day,
We'll make December May;
That's all I have to say.

Chronologies

1. (a) The Shows

Year	Show	Theatre	Opening night	No. of performances (New York or London)	Producer	Director	Librettist	Composer/ lyricist	Roles played by Astaires	Musical numbers performed by Astaires
1917	Over the Top	Shubert, New Haven	20 Nov.		Lee & J.J. Shubert	Joseph Herbert	Philip Bartholomae, Harold Atteridge	Sigmund Romberg, Herman Timberg (music); Charles J. Manning, Matthew C. Woodward, Philip Bartholomae (lyrics)	Various, including: F: M. Auguste / The Announcer; A: Adele	"Frocks and Frills" (F & A, Vivian Oakland); "Where is the Language to Tell?" (F & A); "The Justine Johnstone Rag" (F & A, Vivian & Dagmar Oakland, Betty Pierce, Ted Lorraine)
		44th Street Roof, New York	28 Nov.	78						
1918		Chestnut Street Opera House, Philadelphia	Jan.							

Show	Theater/Location	Date	No.	Producer	Director	Book/Lyrics	Music	Cast	Songs
	Garrick, Washington, D.C.								
	Belasco, Washington, D.C.	16 Feb.							
	Philadelphia								
The Passing Show of 1918	Globe, Atlantic City	Mid-July		Lee & J.J. Shubert	J.C. Huffman	Harold Atteridge	Sigmund Romberg, Jean Schwartz (music); Harold Atteridge (lyrics)	F: Mr. Chicadee / Chanticleer / A Waiter / Fred; A: Miss Dansant / Miss Robin / Mrs. Reizenweber / Adele	"I Can't Make My Feet Behave" (A, Bouquet of Winter Garden Steppers); "Squab Farm" (F & A, Nest of Milk Fed Squabs); "Bring on the Girls" (A, Emily Miles, Helen Carrington, Some Beautiful Girls); "Twit, Twit, Twit" (F & A, a flock of Dancing Birds); "Quick Service" (F & A)
	Winter Garden, New York	25 July	125						
	Shubert, Boston	Dec.							

(Continued)

Year	Show	Theatre	Opening night	No. of performances (New York or London)	Producer	Director	Librettist	Composer/ lyricist	Roles played by Astaires	Musical numbers performed by Astaires
1919		Chestnut Street Opera House, Philadelphia	14 Feb.							
		Shubert Colonial, Cleveland	8 April							
		Detroit Opera House, Detroit	24 April							
		Palace, Chicago	May							
		Alvin, Pittsburgh	June							
	Apple Blossoms	Baltimore	Sept.		Charles B. Dillingham	Fred G. Latham & Edward Royce	William Le Baron (based on the novel *Un Mariage sous Louis XV*, by Alexandre Dumas)	Fritz Kreisler, Victor Jacobi (music); William Le Baron (lyrics)	Johnny and Molly	"A Girl, a Man, a Night, a Dance" (F & A, Florence Shirley); "On the Banks of the Bronx" (F & A, Rena Parker, Percival Knight); "Tambourin Chinois" (F & A)

Year	Theater	Date	
	Globe, New York	7 Oct.	256
1920	Colonial, Chicago	30 Aug.	
	Forrest, Philadelphia	Dec.	
1921	Shubert Majestic, Providence	25 Jan.	
	Worcester, Worcester, Mass.		
	Colonial, Boston		
	Ford's, Baltimore		
	Washington, D.C.	14 Feb.	
	Saxon, Toledo	10 April	
	Elmira, N.Y.	April	

(*Continued*)

1. (a) The Shows (continued)

Year	Show	Theatre	Opening night	No. of performances (New York or London)	Producer	Director	Librettist	Composer/ lyricist	Roles played by Astaires	Musical numbers performed by Astaires
		Court Square, Springfield, Massachusetts	April							
	The Love Letter	Forrest, Philadelphia	4 Sept.		Charles B. Dillingham	Edward Royce	William Le Baron (based on the play The Phantom Rival, by Ferenc Molnár)	Victor Jacobi (music); William Le Baron (lyrics)	Richard Kolnar and Aline Moray	"I'll Say I Love You" (F & A, Ensemble); "Upside Down" (F & A); "Dreaming" (F & A, ENSEMBLE)
		Globe, New York	4 Oct.	31						
		Lyceum, Rochester	Nov.							
		Tremont, Boston	Dec.							

1922	For Goodness Sake	New Haven	Alex A. Aarons	Priestly Morrison	Fred Jackson	William Daly, Paul Lannin (music); Arthur Jackson (lyrics); additional numbers by George & Ira ("Arthur Francis") Gershwin	Teddy Lawrence and Suzanne Hayden	"All to Myself" (F & A, Ensemble); "When You're in Rome" (F, Marjorie Gateson, Charles Judels, Ensemble); "Oh Gee! Oh Gosh!" (F & A); "The French Pastry Walk" (F, Charles Judels, Vinton Freedley, Ensemble); "The Whichness of the Whatness" (F & A)
		Hartford						
		Lyric, New York	20 Feb.	103				
		Chicago						
		Bridgeport						

(Continued)

1. (a) The Shows (continued)

Year	Show	Theatre	Opening night	No. of performances (New York or London)	Producer	Director	Librettist	Composer/ lyricist	Roles played by Astaires	Musical numbers performed by Astaires
	The Bunch and Judy	Forrest, Philadelphia	6 Nov.		Charles B. Dillingham	Fred G. Latham	Anne Caldwell, Hugh Ford	Jerome Kern (music); Anne Caldwell (lyrics); one number by Ivor Novello and Dion Titheradge	Gerald Lane and Judy Jordan	"Pale Venetian Moon" (F & A); "Peach Girl" (F & A); "Morning Glory" (A, Ensemble); "Every Day in Every Way" (F & A); "Times Square" (F & A, Ray Dooley, Patricia Clark, Johnny Dooley); "Clansman March and Fling" (A, Philip Tonge, Ensemble); "How Do You Do, Katinka?" (F & A)
		Globe, New York	28 Nov.	65						
		Baltimore								

Year	Title	Theatre	Date	No.	Producer	Director	Author	Music/Lyrics	Cast	Songs
1923	*Stop Flirting: A Musical Farce* (London version of *For Goodness Sake*)	Royal Court, Liverpool	30 April		Alfred Butt in conjunction with B. A. Meyer with Alex A. Aarons	Felix Edwardes	Fred Jackson	William Daly, Paul Lannin (music); Arthur Jackson (lyrics); additional numbers by George & Ira ("Arthur Francis") Gershwin	Teddy Lawrence and Suzanne Hayden	"All to Myself" (F & A, Chorus); "Stairway to Paradise" (F & A, Marjorie Gordon (later Helen Gilliland, Dorothy Waring), Jack Melford, Mimi Crawford, Henry Kendall (later E. Louis Bradfield, Denis Cowles); "Oh Gee! Oh Gosh! (F & A); "It's Great to Be in Love" (A, Mimi Crawford, Marjorie Gordon); "The Whichness of the Whatness" and "The Oom-Pah Trot" (F & A)
		Shaftesbury, London	30 May	418						
		Queen's, London	30 July							
		Strand, London	22 Oct.							
		Prince of Wales, Birmingham	31 Dec.							

(Continued)

1. (a) The Shows (continued)

Year	Show	Theatre	Opening night	No. of performances (New York or London)	Producer	Director	Librettist	Composer/ lyricist	Roles played by Astaires	Musical numbers performed by Astaires
1924		Grand, Hull	28 Jan.							
		King's, Glasgow	4 Feb.							
		Royal Lyceum, Edinburgh	18 Feb.							
		Strand, London	29 Mar.							
	Lady, Be Good!	Forrest, Philadelphia	17 Nov.		Alex A. Aarons, Vinton Freedley	Felix Edwardes	Guy Bolton, Fred Thompson	George & Ira Gershwin	Dick & Susie Trevor	"Hang on to Me" (F & A); "Fascinating Rhythm" (F & A, Cliff Edwards); "So Am I" (A, Alan Edwards); "The Half of It, Dearie, Blues" (F. Kathlene Martyn); "Juanita" (A, Male Chorus); "Swiss Miss" (F & A)
		Liberty, New York	1 Dec.	330						
		Shubert, Newark, N. J.	14 Sept.							

Year	Show	Theatre	Date	Producer	Director	Book	Music/Lyrics	Cast	Songs
		National, Washington, D.C.							
		Cleveland	6 Oct.						
		Ford's, Baltimore	Oct.						
		Apollo, Atlantic City	Oct.						
		Forrest, Philadelphia	10 Nov.						
		Nixon, Pittsburgh							
1926	*Lady, Be Good!*	Empire, Liverpool	29 Mar.	Alfred Butt with Alex A. Aarons and Vinton Freedley	Felix Edwardes	Guy Bolton, Fred Thompson	George & Ira Gershwin; lyrics of additional numbers by Desmond Carter, Lou Paley	Dick & Susie Trevor	"Hang on to Me" (F & A); "Fascinating Rhythm" (F & A, Buddy Lee); "So Am I" (A. George Vollaire); "I'd Rather Charleston" (F & A); "The Half of It, Dearie, Blues" (F, Irene Russell); "Juanita" (A, Male Chorus); "Swiss Miss" (F & A)

(*Continued*)

1. (a) The Shows (continued)

Year	Show	Theatre	Opening night	No. of performances (New York or London)	Producer	Director	Librettist	Composer/ lyricist	Roles played by Astaires	Musical numbers performed by Astaires
		Empire, London	14 April	326						
		Empire, Liverpool	14 Feb.							
1927		Alhambra, Glasgow	7 Mar.							
		Hippodrome, Golders Green	28 Mar.							
	Funny Face	Shubert, Philadelphia	11 Oct.		Alex A. Aarons, Vinton Freedley	Edgar MacGregor	Fred Thompson, Paul Gerard Smith	George & Ira Gershwin	Jimmy Reeve and Frankie Wynne	"Funny Face" (F & A); "High Hat" (F, Chorus Men); "He Loves and She Loves" (A, Allen Kearns; "Let's Kiss and Make Up" (F & A, Ensemble); "'S Wonderful" (A, Allen Kearns); "My One and Only" (F, Gertrude McDonald, Betty Compton, Chorus Ladies); "The Babbitt and the Bromide" (F & A)

		Ford's, Washington, D.C.								
		Nixon's Apollo, Atlantic City	7 Nov.							
		Wilmington	14 Nov.							
		Alvin, New York	22 Nov.	250						
1928	*Funny Face*	Empire, Liverpool	24 Sept.		Alfred Butt and Lee Ephraim with Alex A. Aarons and Vinton Freedley	Felix Edwardes	Fred Thompson, Paul Gerard Smith	George & Ira Gershwin	Jimmy Reeve and Frankie Wynne	"Funny Face" (F & A); "High Hat" (F, Chorus Men); "He Loves and She Loves" (A, Bernard Clifton); "Let's Kiss and Make Up" (F & A, Ensemble); "'S Wonderful" (A, Bernard Clifton); "My One and Only" (F, Renée Gadd [later Eileen Hatton], Rita Page, Chorus Ladies); "The Babbitt and the Bromide" (F & A)

(Continued)

1. (a) **The Shows** (continued)

Year	Show	Theatre	Opening night	No. of performances (New York or London)	Producer	Director	Librettist	Composer/ lyricist	Roles played by Astaires	Musical numbers performed by Astaires
		Royal, Birmingham	8 Oct.							
		Empire, Cardiff	22 Oct.							
		Princes, London	8 Nov.	263						
1929		Winter Garden, London	28 Jan.							
1930	Smiles	Colonial, Boston	28 Oct.		Florenz Ziegfeld	William Anthony McGuire	William Anthony McGuire	Vincent Youmans (music); Clifford Grey, Harold Adamson (lyrics); additional lyrics by Ring Lardner; one number by Walter Donaldson added in December	Bob & Dot Hastings	"Say, Young Man of Manhattan" (F, Male Chorus); "Hotcha Ma Chotch" (A, Eddie Foy Jr., cut after opening and replaced with "You're Driving Me Crazy"); "Be Good to Me" (F & A); "Anyway We Had Fun" (F, Marilyn Miller, added after opening); "If I Were You, Love" (F & A); "I'm Glad I Waited" (F, Marilyn Miller)

Year	Title	Venue	Date	No.	Producer	Director	Book	Music / Lyrics	Cast	Songs
		Ziegfeld, New York	18 Nov.	63						"Sweet Music" (F & A); "Hoops" (F & A); "New Sun in the Sky" (F); "Miserable Without You" (A, Frank Morgan); "I Love Louisa" (F & A, The Company); "The Beggar Waltz" (F, Tilly Losch, Ensemble); "White Heat" (F & A)
1931	The Band Wagon	Garrick, Philadelphia	12 May		Max Gordon	Hassard Short	George S. Kaufman, Howard Dietz	Arthur Schwartz (music); Howard Dietz (lyrics)	Various, including: F: Simpson Carter / The Demonstrator; A: Breeze / Ivy Meredith	
		New Amsterdam, New York	3 June	260						
1932		Illinois, Chicago								

(Continued)

1. (a) The Shows (continued)

Year	Show	Theatre	Opening night	No. of performances (New York or London)	Producer	Director	Librettist	Composer/ lyricist	Roles played by Astaires	Musical numbers performed by Astaires
	Gay Divorce	Wilbur, Boston	7 Nov.		Dwight Deere Wiman, Tom Weatherly	Howard Lindsay	Dwight Taylor (based on an unproduced play by J. Hartley Manners); musical adaptation by Kenneth Webb and Samuel Hoffenstein	Cole Porter	Guy Holden	"After You, Who?" (F); "Night and Day" (F, Claire Luce); "I've Got You on My Mind" (F, Claire Luce); "You're in Love" (F, Claire Luce, Erik Rhodes)
		Shubert, New Haven	21 Nov.							
		Ethel Barrymore, New York	29 Nov.	248						

1933								
Gay Divorce	Shubert, New York	16 Jan.						"After You, Who?" (F); "Night and Day" (F, Claire Luce); "I've Got You on My Mind" (F, Claire Luce); "You're in Love" (F, Claire Luce, Erik Rhodes)
	Royal, Birmingham	23 Oct.	Lee Ephraim	Felix Edwardes	Dwight Taylor	Cole Porter	Guy Holden	
	Palace, London	2 Nov.	180					

1. (b) Charity Performances

Year	Event	Venue	Date	Notes
1920	Actors' Equity Association Benefit	Metropolitan Opera House, New York	9 May	
1923	Air League Royal Ball	Royal Albert Hall, London	17 July	A special one-night-only performance. It was announced: "Adele and Fred Astaire will give special exhibition dances and introduce their new Tango at midnight."
1924	Theatrical Garden Party	Royal Hospital Gardens, Chelsea	24 June	An annual event in aid of the Actors' Orphanage at Langley, Bucks. F & A ran the "*Stop Flirting* Ballroom'.
1924	Meggie Albanesi Scholarship Fund	St. Martin's Theatre, London	10 July	A matinée to raise funds for a RADA scholarship in memory of the actress Meggie Albanesi who died, aged 24, on 9 December 1923.
1925	The Lambs Annual Public Spring Gambol	Metropolitan Opera House, New York	26 April	Fred part of a large dancing number staged with Pat Rooney, Carl Randall, Harland Dixon, Hal Skelley, Hal Sherman, and Wallace Ford.
1926	Theatrical Garden Party	Royal Hospital Gardens, Chelsea	22 June	F & A ran the Strawberries and Cream.
1929	Theatrical Garden Party	Royal Hospital Gardens, Chelsea	11 June	F & A ran "Eve's Garden."
1930	New York American Christmas and Relief Fund		29 Dec.	A benefit appearance by F & A and Marilyn Miller.

Year	Event	Venue	Date	Description
1932	Benefit for the Actor's Dinner Club	Casino Theatre, New York	9 Oct.	A benefit at which Fred appeared ninth in the programme, after Laurette Taylor.
1932	Benefit for the Dancer's Club and Unemployed Dancers	Mecca Temple, New York	Dec.	Fred and Claire Luce in a bill that also included Bill Robinson.
1933	Benefit for the Actors' League Fund and Stage Relief Fund	WMCA Theatre, New York	1 Feb.	Fred appeared in a musical sketch, "Yellow Curls—The Depression Gaieties."
1933	Benefit	Metropolitan Opera House, New York	26 March	Produced by the Citizens' Committee in Aid of Stage Relief and billed as "A Benefit for the Benefit of Actors who have played Benefits for the Benefit of Others." Fred and Claire Luce performed "Night and Day."
1933	King George's Pension Fund for Actors and Actresses Command Performance	Theatre Royal, Drury Lane, London	11 Dec.	An annual performance in aid of King George's Pension Fund, in the presence of King George V and Queen Mary. Fred and Claire Luce "in a duet and dance from *Gay Divorce*."

2. Other notable events in theatre, 1917–1933

Year	Event	Premiere
1917	(Feb.) The Morosco Theatre opens on Broadway.	(Feb.) *Oh Boy!* (music by Jerome Kern)
	(April) The Bijou Theatre opens on Broadway.	(March) *Our Betters* (Somerset Maugham)
	(Jun.) First Pulitzer Prize for drama awarded to Jesse Lynch Williams for *Why Marry?*	(Aug.) *Leave It to Jane*
	(July) Herbert Beerbohm Tree dies	(music by Jerome Kern)
1918	(12 Feb.) Broadway theatres closed to save coal for the war effort.	(Feb.) *Oh, Lady! Lady!!* (music by Jerome Kern)
	(Feb.) Vernon Castle dies.	(Aug.) *Yip Yip Yaphank*
	(Feb.) Sir George Alexander dies.	(music by Irving Berlin)
	(July) Arthur Laurents born.	(Sept.) *Someone in the House* (George S.
	(Aug.) Alan Jay Lerner born.	Kaufman)
	(Oct.) Jerome Robbins born.	(Sept.) *The Soldier's Tale*
	(Nov.) A standard Actors' Equity contract is established.	(Stravinsky)
	(Nov.) Walter Hampden hailed as the greatest American Hamlet since Edwin Booth.	
	(Dec.) Edmond Rostand dies.	
	(Dec.) The Theatre Guild formed to present "the best of European and US drama."	
1919	(Jan.) Sir Charles Wyndham dies.	(May) *La, La, Lucille* (music by George Gershwin)
	(Jun.) Pulitzer Prize for drama awarded to Eugene O'Neill for *Beyond the Horizon.*	(Aug.) *Exiles* (James Joyce)
	(Jun.) Diaghilev's Ballet Russes premieres *La Boutique fantasque* at the Alhambra Theatre, London.	
	(Jun.) Uta Hagen born.	
	(Aug.) Actors' Equity calls the first strike in the history of the American theatre.	
	(Nov.) The musical *Irene* begins its record-breaking run of 670 performances at the Vanderbilt Theatre, New York.	
	Richard Rodgers and Oscar Hammerstein II collaborate for the first time, writing three songs for the annual Varsity Show at Columbia University.	

2. Other notable events in theatre, 1917–1933 (continued)

Year	Event	Premiere
1920	(Jan.) Ruth Draper makes her professional debut in monologues at London's Aeolian Hall.	(April) *The Skin Game* (John Galsworthy)
	(Jun.) *The Beggar's Opera* begins an astonishing revival of 1463 performances at the Lyric Hammersmith, directed by Nigel Playfair.	(July) *I'll Leave It to You* (Noël Coward)
	(Nov.) Walter Winchell writes his first Broadway gossip column for *Vaudeville News*.	(Nov.) *The Emperor Jones* (Eugene O'Neill)
	At London's Old Vic, Robert Atkins initiates an ambitious plan to present all thirty-six Shakespeare plays in the First Folio.	(Nov.) *Heartbreak House* (George Bernard Shaw) (Dec.) *Sally* (Music by Jerome Kern)
1921	(Jan.) *R.U.R. (Rossum's Universal Robots)* by Czech writer Karel Čapek introduces the term "robot."	(March) *The Circle* (Somerset Maugham)
	(Feb.) The Shuberts open the Ambassador Theatre.	(May) *Six Characters in Search of an Author* (Luigi Pirandello)
	(March) Gerald du Maurier opens a 430-performance run as detective Bulldog Drummond.	(Oct.) *A Bill of Divorcement* (Clemence Dane)
	(April) The Theatre Guild presents Ferenc Molnár's *Liliom*, on which Rodgers and Hammerstein's *Carousel* is based.	(Nov.) *Anna Christie* (Eugene O'Neill) (Nov.) *The Difficult Man* (Hugo von Hofmannsthal)
	(Jun.) Georges Feydeau dies.	
	(Jun.) *The Gas Heart*, by Tristan Tzara, is staged by the Paris Dadaists as part of a "Dada Salon" at the Galerie Montaigne.	
	(Jun.) The variety revue *The Co-Optimists* begins its first season at the Royalty Theatre, London.	
	(Aug.) Enrico Caruso dies.	
	(Sept.) Irving Berlin's first *Music Box Revue*.	
	(Nov.) John Gielgud makes his professional stage debut, playing the French Herald in *Henry V* at the Old Vic.	
	(Dec.) Sir John Hare dies.	

(Continued)

2. Other notable events in theatre, 1917–1933 (continued)

Year	Event	Premiere
1922	(Jan.) Paul Scofield born. (Feb.) Margaret Leighton born. (April) Laurence Olivier makes his first appearance in a "real" theatre, playing Katherina in a schoolboy production of *The Taming of the Shrew* at Stratford's Memorial Theatre. (May) Alfred Lunt and Lynn Fontanne marry. (Oct.) Marie Lloyd dies. (Nov.) John Barrymore opens as Hamlet at the Sam H. Harris Theatre on Broadway. (Nov.) Lord Cromer becomes Lord Chamberlain and bans *The Queen's Minister* because it depicts Queen Victoria and Lord Melbourne onstage.	(Feb.) *Henry IV* (Luigi Pirandello) (Feb.) *Back to Methuselah* (George Bernard Shaw) (March) *Loyalties* (John Galsworthy) (May) *Abie's Irish Rose* (Anne Nichols) (Jun.) *The Machine Wreckers* (Ernst Toller) (Sept.) *Drums in the Night* (Bertolt Brecht)
1923	(Jan.) The Moscow Art Theatre, under the direction of Konstantin Stanislavski, opens a triumphant first season on Broadway with *The Brothers Karamazoff.* (Feb.) Franco Zeffirelli born. (March) Sarah Bernhardt dies. (May) Alfred Lunt and Lynn Fontanne appear together onstage for the first time in Paul Kester's *Sweet Nell of Old Drury.*	(March) *The Adding Machine* (Elmer Rice) (April) *Aren't We All?* (Frederick Lonsdale) (April) *The Shadow of a Gunman* (Sean O'Casey) (Dec.) *Baal* (Bertolt Brecht) (Dec.) *Saint Joan* (George Bernard Shaw)
1924	(April) Eleanora Duse dies. (May) Paul Robeson appears in Eugene O'Neill's controversial play about miscegenation, *All God's Chillun Got Wings.* (May) John Gielgud and Gwen Ffrangcon-Davies star in *Romeo and Juliet* at the Regent Theatre, London. (Nov.) Laurence Olivier makes his professional London debut in Alice Law's *Byron* at the Century Theatre.	(March) *Juno and the Paycock* (Sean O'Casey) (March) *The Life of Edward II of England* (Bertolt Brecht) (Oct.) *In the Jungle of Cities* (Bertolt Brecht) (Nov.) *Desire Under the Elms* (Eugene O'Neill) (Nov.) *They Knew What They Wanted* (Sidney Howard) (Nov.) *The Vortex* (Noël Coward)

2. **Other notable events in theatre, 1917–1933** (continued)

Year	Event	Premiere
1925	(March) Peter Brook born. (July) First public performance in England of Bernard Shaw's *Mrs. Warren's Profession* (written in 1893 and banned by the Lord Chamberlain). (Nov.) Richard Burton born.	(March) *No, No, Nanette!* (Music by Vincent Youmans) (April) *Fallen Angels* (Noël Coward) (Jun.) *Hay Fever* (Noël Coward) (July) *The Prisoners of War* (J. R. Ackerley) (Sept.) *The Jazz Singer* (Samson Raphaelson) (Sept.) *The Last of Mrs. Cheney* (Frederick Lonsdale) (Dec.) *Easy Virtue* (Noël Coward)
1926	(Jan.) Gwen Verdon born. (Jan.) Patricia Neal born. (April) Sir Squire Bancroft dies. (April) Mae West's play *Sex* (written under the name Jane Mast) opens at Daly's 63rd Street Theatre, New York; a year later West is sentenced to ten days in prison and fined $500 for "corrupting the morals of youth." (May) Peter and Anthony Shaffer born. (May) Cornerstone of the Yiddish Art Theatre laid on Second Avenue in New York. (Sept.) Edith Evans opens as Rebecca West in Ibsen's *Rosmersholm* at the Kingsway Theatre, London. (Dec.) Vsevolod Meyerhold directs *The Government Inspector,* by Nikolai Gogol. *An Actor Prepares,* by Stanislavski, is published in the USSR.	(Feb.) *The Plough and the Stars* (Sean O'Casey) (May) *The Ringer* (Edgar Wallace) (Jun.) *Rookery Nook* (Ben Travers) (Sept.) *The Constant Nymph* (Margaret Kennedy and Basil Dean) (Sept.) *Gentlemen Prefer Blondes* (Anita Loos and John Emerson) (Oct.) *The Days of the Turbins* (Mikhail Bulgakov) (Nov.) *The Constant Wife* (Somerset Maugham) (Nov.) *Oh, Kay!* (score by George and Ira Gershwin)

(Continued)

2. Other notable events in theatre, 1917–1933 (continued)

Year	Event	Premiere
1927	(March) Sardi's Restaurant opens at its current location on West 44th Street, New York. (April) Kenneth Tynan born. (Jun.) Bob Fosse born. (Sept.) Isadora Duncan dies. (Oct.) *Porgy*, an adaptation of DuBose Heyward's novel, opens at the Guild Theatre on Broadway, directed by Rouben Mamoulian; it will be the basis of Gershwin's 1935 opera *Porgy and Bess*. (Nov.) Florence Mills dies. The first series of Harley Granville-Barker's *Prefaces to Shakespeare* is published.	(Jan.) *Strike Up the Band* (score by George and Ira Gershwin) (Nov.) *A Connecticut Yankee* (score by Richard Rodgers and Lorenz Hart) (Nov.) *Sirocco* (Noël Coward) (Dec.) *Show Boat* (score by Jerome Kern and Oscar Hammerstein II) (Dec.) *The Royal Family* (George S. Kaufman and Edna Ferber)
1928	(March) Edward Albee born. (May) The all-black cast of the musical revue *Blackbirds of 1928* includes Bill "Bojangles" Robinson. (July) Ellen Terry dies. (Oct.) The Dublin Gate Theatre Studio (later the Gate Theatre) opens with a production of Ibsen's *Peer Gynt* at the Abbey's small experimental Peacock Theatre. (Nov.) Edward Gordon Craig designs his first American production, *Macbeth*, directed by George C. Tyler, at the Knickerbocker Theatre in New York.	(Jan.) *Strange Interlude* (Eugene O'Neill) (March) *This Year of Grace* (Noël Coward) (Aug.) *The Front Page* (Ben Hecht and Charles MacArthur) (Aug.) *The Threepenny Opera* (Bertolt Brecht; music by Kurt Weill) (Sept.) *Machinal* (Sophie Treadwell) (Dec.) *Journey's End* (R. C. Sherriff)
1929	(Feb.) Lillie Langtry dies. (Aug.) Sergei Diaghilev dies. (Aug.) The first Malvern Drama Festival opens and includes the English premiere of *The Apple Cart*, by Bernard Shaw. (Sept.) Laurence Olivier makes his Broadway debut in Frank Vosper's *Murder on the Second Floor* at the Eltinge Theatre.	(Jan.) *Street Scene* (Elmer Rice) (Feb.) *The Bedbug* (Vladimir Mayakovsky) (March) *Rope* (Patrick Hamilton)

2. Other notable events in theatre, 1917–1933 (continued)

Year	Event	Premiere
	(Oct.) Joan Plowright born. (Dec.) British Actors' Equity is founded. (Dec.) John Osborne born. Spring: all of Mikhail Bulgakov's plays are banned in the USSR.	(March) *Pioneers in Ingolstadt* (Marieluise Fleisser) (March) *Wake Up and Dream* (score by Cole Porter) (July) *The Old Lady Says "No!"* (Denis Johnston) (Oct.) *June Moon* (George S. Kaufman and Ring Lardner) (Nov.) *Amphitryon 38* (Jean Giraudoux) (Nov.) *Fifty Million Frenchmen* (score by Cole Porter)
1930	(March) D. H. Lawrence dies. (March) Jessica Tandy makes her Broadway debut in *The Matriarch*, by G. B. Stern, Longacre Theatre. (March) At London's Savoy Theatre, Paul Robeson is the first black actor in a century to play Othello; his Desdemona is Peggy Ashcroft. (March) Stephen Sondheim born. (May) John Gielgud gives his first *Hamlet* at the Old Vic. (Oct.) Harold Pinter born. (Nov.) Peter Hall born. While a freshman at the university of Missouri in Columbia, Tennessee Williams writes his first play, the one-act *Beauty Is the Word*, and enters it in the annual Dramatic Arts Club contest.	(March) *Rise and Fall of the City of Mahagonny* (Bertolt Brecht; music by Kurt Weill) (Aug.) *Private Lives* (Noël Coward) (Aug.) *The Barrets of Wimpole Street* (Rudolf Besier) (Sept.) *Once in a Lifetime* (Moss Hart and George S. Kaufman) (Oct.) *Girl Crazy* (score by George and Ira Gershwin) (Dec.) *The Measures Taken* (Bertolt Brecht; music by Hanns Eisler)

(*Continued*)

2. Other notable events in theatre, 1917–1933 (continued)

Year	Event	Premiere
1931	(Jan.) Lilian Baylis reopens Sadler's Wells Theatre; the Vic-Wells Ballet, led by Ninette de Valois, becomes its first resident ballet company.	(Oct.) *Cavalcade* (Noël Coward)
	(Jan.) Anna Pavlova dies.	(Oct.) *Mourning Becomes Electra* (Eugene O'Neill)
	(Jan.) *Green Grow the Lilacs,* by Lynn Riggs, opens on Broadway; it will be the basis of the libretto of Rodgers and Hammerstein's *Oklahoma!* in 1943.	(Dec.) *Of Thee I Sing* (Score by George and Ira Gershwin)
	(Feb.) Dame Nellie Melba dies.	
	(July) The last edition of the *Ziegfeld Follies* produced in Ziegfeld's lifetime.	
	(Sept.) The Group Theatre, a New York city theatre collective founded by Harold Clurman, Cheryl Crawford, and Lee Strasberg, opens its inaugural season on Broadway with *The House of Connelly* by Paul Green.	
	(Sept.) Charles Laughton makes his Broadway debut in *Payment Deferred,* Lyceum Theatre.	
	(Oct.) The first public performance in England of Oscar Wilde's *Salomé* (written in 1891) at London's Savoy Theatre.	
	(Oct.) Orson Welles makes his stage debut in *Jew Suss* at Dublin's Gate Theatre.	
	(Oct.) Arthur Schnitzler dies.	

2. **Other notable events in theatre, 1917–1933 (continued)**

Year	Event	Premiere
1932	(Feb.) John Gielgud makes his directorial debut with a production of *Romeo and Juliet* for the Oxford University Dramatic Society, designed by Motley; Terence Rattigan, then an undergraduate, has a one-line part in the production. (April) The new Shakespeare Memorial Theatre, designed by Elisabeth Scott, opens in Stratford-upon-Avon. (May) Arnold Wesker born. (May) Ray Cooney born. (Jun.) Athol Fugard born. (July) Florenz Ziegfeld dies. (Nov.) Bulgakov's adaptation of *Dead Souls*, by Gogol, opens at the Moscow Art Theatre, directed by Stanislavski. *The Stage* Relief Fund is founded in America by Rachel Crothers and John Golden.	(Jan.) *The Mother* (Bertolt Brecht) (Feb.) *Richard of Bordeaux* (Gordon Daviot) (April) *Too True to Be Good* (George Bernard Shaw (May) *Dangerous Corner* (J. B. Priestley) (Sept.) *Words and Music* (Noël Coward) (Sept.) *Strange Orchestra* (Rodney Ackland) (Oct.) *Dinner at Eight* (George S. Kaufman and Edna Ferber) (Nov.) *Music in the Air* (Score by Jerome Kern and Oscar Hammerstein II) (Dec.) *Twentieth Century* (Ben Hecht and Charles MacArthur)
1933	(Jan.) Joe Orton born. (Jan.) John Galsworthy dies. (Feb.) In the wake of the Reichstag fire, Bertolt Brecht and his family flee Germany and settle in Denmark. (Sept.) Michael Frayn born. Tyrone Guthrie's first season as director of the Old Vic.	(Jan.) *Design for Living* (Noël Coward) (March) *Blood Wedding* (Federico Garcia Lorca) (Sept.) *Sheppey* (Somerset Maugham) (Oct.) *Ah, Wilderness!* (Eugene O'Neill) (Dec.) *Tobacco Road* (Jack Kirkland) (Dec.) *Escape Me Never!* (Margaret Kennedy)

NOTES

Preface

1. Hall (2004), 68.
2. On Fred Astaire's corporeal eloquence and its relationship to the art of ancient pantomime, see Riley (2010).

Introduction

1. Pollack (2006), 326 and 331.
2. *New York Times*, 14 June 1931.
3. The film in which Adele was to make her comeback was *Break the News*, directed by René Clair and costarring Jack Buchanan and Maurice Chevalier. Adele withdrew from the production after just two days of shooting at Pinewood Studios in England. She was disappointed with the preliminary results, believing she was ill suited to the role of "a female menace, no singing, comedy, or dancing," and fearing her continued participation in the film would embarrass her brother.
4. Hall (2004), 68.
5. The original female lead, June Allyson (Mrs. Dick Powell), discovered during rehearsals that she was pregnant. She was replaced by Judy Garland, whose fluctuating health and erratic behavior meant that she too had eventually to be replaced. Jane Powell, the third and final choice, was fortuitously closer in personality to the real-life model on which her character was based, having the requisite exuberance and air of mischief.
6. The twenty-second clip can be seen in the PBS documentary *Fred Astaire: Puttin' on His Top Hat*, first broadcast on 9 March 1980 and narrated by Joanne Woodward.
7. Mabel McElliot, *Illustrated Daily News*, 9 October 1919.
8. *Illustrated Sporting and Dramatic News*, London, 11 August 1923.
9. HRC.
10. FA/MS.
11. Review of, newspaper unknown, Seattle, [1916?], clipping (AAC).
12. HRC.
13. FA/MS.
14. Quoted in Marian Rhea, "Honors Shrugged Away by Noted Star's Mother: Mrs. Fred Astaire Finds No Change in Children," unknown magazine, 9 February 1935, (AAC).
15. HRC.
16. FA/MS.

17. This a reference to Fred and Adele's close friends Mary Elizabeth and James Altemus, siblings from Philadelphia whom they first met while vacationing at Galen Hall in Wernersville, Pennsylvania, in the summer of 1919.
18. Croce (1972), 9.
19. *San Francisco Chronicle*, 3 October 1926.
20. "London Seeks Charleston Ban, Branding It 'Glorified Shimmy,'" *Herald Tribune* (London), 25 April 1926.
21. Quoted in Matthew Sweet, "Mighty as Blighty," *The Times*, 4 August 2005.
22. Quoted in Matthew Sweet, obituary of Renée Gadd, *Independent*, 31 July 2003.

1 Opening the Bill

1. For details of the nineteenth-century Austerlitz genealogy, I am grateful to Alessandra Garofalo and the research she compiled for her monograph (2009).
2. The term "anti-Semitism" was introduced into political vocabulary in 1879 by the Hamburg pamphleteer Wilhelm Marr, who founded the League of Antisemites.
3. Astaire (1959), 17.
4. HRC.
5. This one-act play was excerpted from Langtry's legitimate success of the 1880s in Sardou's play *A Wife's Peril*.
6. HRC.
7. HRC.
8. *Theatre*, March 1908.
9. "Two-a-day" became synonymous with big-time vaudeville. On the small-time circuits, performers could expect to give three, four, or even five shows a day.
10. Billman (1997), 3.
11. Astaire (1959), 17.
12. Knowles (2002), 2.
13. Wayburn (1925), 61.
14. Ibid., 216.
15. *Variety*, 17 October 1908.
16. "Young Toe Dancer," *St. Paul Dispatch*, 19 April 1909.
17. Astaire (1959), 48.
18. The films, both produced at Columbia, were *You'll Never Get Rich* (1941) and *You Were Never Lovelier* (1942).
19. Nathan (1915), 280.
20. Ned Wayburn to Ann Astaire, 8 June 1911, (AAC).
21. Ibid.
22. In 1870, actor Joseph Jefferson, in trying to arrange a funeral service for his friend and fellow actor George Holland, was rebuffed by the rector of a nearby church but was advised that there was a little church around the corner where "they do that sort of thing." Jefferson thereby exclaimed, "God bless the little church around the corner." The finale of the 1920 hit musical *Sally*, by Jerome Kern, Guy Bolton, and P. G. Wodehouse, included the lines "Oh dear little Church 'Round the Corner / Where so many lives have begun / Where folks without money / See nothing that's funny / In two living cheaper than one."
23. Astaire (1959), 28.

2 Over the Top

1. Astaire (1959), 40.
2. Ibid., 41.
3. HRC.
4. HRC.

5. *New York Times*, 14 June 1908.
6. Astaire (1959), 42.
7. Ibid.
8. "A Weird Dance Creation," *Evening Post*, Wellington, New Zealand, 5 April 1924.
9. Duke (1947), 105.
10. Tiomkin and Buranelli (1959), 135.
11. Hermes Pan, interview on "Curtain Up," episode 1 of *The Fred Astaire Story*, BBC Radio 2, 22 March 1975. The music Gershwin wrote especially for Astaire's walk was a delightful and jaunty chamber piece entitled "Walking the Dog," which was used in the 1937 film *Shall We Dance* to accompany two pantomimic routines for Astaire and Rogers. These routines involved no formal dancing but simply showed Astaire and Rogers walking back and forth along the promenade deck of a ship.
12. Quoted by Nichols (1927), 111.
13. Seldes (1924), 273–74.
14. AAC.
15. HRC.
16. On the predominantly white Keith-Albee circuit, the practice was to allow no more than one black act per bill and no black soloists.
17. Astaire (1959), 49.
18. Dally (2002), 80.
19. Bojangles of Harlem" is often referred to as Astaire's only "blackface" number, but what he achieves here is not blackface (though the "dummy" face that becomes the feet is blackface). Neither his makeup nor his style of dancing is intended to caricature African Americans. The routine is very different in essence, therefore, from the blackface performances of, for example, Al Jolson and Eddie Cantor.
20. John Bubbles teamed with Ford Lee "Buck" Washington in 1919 to form the successful vaudeville act Buck and Bubbles. Buck played stride piano and sang while Bubbles tapped. Bubbles claimed to have given Fred one tap lesson in 1920 for a fee of $400. This was never verified by Fred, though he did express his great admiration for Bubbles on a number of occasions, an admiration confirmed by Adele.
21. Johnstone eventually quit show business to become a laboratory worker at the New York College of Physicians and Surgeons.
22. *Detroit Free Press*, 22 April 1917.
23. See Astaire (1959) 65.
24. SHU.
25. SHU.

3 Dancing Comedians

1. HRC.
2. Astaire (1959) 73.
3. Lonsdale's illegitimate daughter, Angela Worthington, was the daughter who inspired Noël Coward's song "Don't Put Your Daughter on the Stage, Mrs. Worthington."
4. HRC.
5. Composer Jerome Kern was meant to accompany Frohman on the voyage but overslept and missed the scheduled sailing.
6. Marra (2006), 83.
7. Charles Darnton, *Evening World*, October 1919.
8. The New Stagecraft was a reaction against the excesses of late nineteenth-century stage naturalism and sought to bring to scenographic art simplicity, even spareness, and poetic symbolism; to suggest an atmosphere of reality rather than reality itself.
9. A large section of the original painted mural was rediscovered in November 2006 by a Manhattan antiques dealer.

10. Quoted in Lochner (1951), 397.
11. Kreisler's first postwar appearance on the American concert platform was at Carnegie Hall on 27 October 1919 in a benefit for the Vienna Children's Milk Relief.
12. "Swanee" was introduced in Ned Wayburn's revue *Demi-Tasse*, which opened in October 1919. It made no great impact, but when Jolson heard Gershwin play it at a party he included the song in his show *Sinbad* at the Winter Garden Theatre.
13. Astaire (1959), 79.
14. Ibid., 80.
15. Ibid., 84.
16. *Observer*, 21 December 1902.
17. Coward (1974), 165.
18. In his autobiography, Coward wrote of his visits to Laurette Taylor and family: "On Sunday evenings we had cold supper and played games, often rather acrimonious games, owing to Laurette's abrupt disapproval of any guest (whether invited by Hartley, Marguerite, Dwight or herself) who turned out to be self-conscious, nervous, or unable to act an adverb or an historical personage with proper abandon. There were also, very often, shrill arguments concerning rules. These were waged entirely among the family, and frequently ended in all four of them leaving the room and retiring upstairs, where, later on, they might be discovered by any guest bold enough to go in search of them, amicably drinking tea in the kitchen. It was inevitable that someone should eventually utilise portions of this eccentricity in a play." Coward (1974), 157.
19. *Oh, Boy!*, with music by Jerome Kern and lyrics and book by Guy Bolton and P. G. Wodehouse, opened at the Princess Theatre on 20 February 1917 and enjoyed a Broadway run of 463 performances. It is considered to have modernized and Americanized musical comedy.
20. Among the musicals Alfred E. Aarons produced and wrote scores for were *Mam'selle 'Awkins* and *The Military Maid*, both in 1900. He later managed some of New York's most important theatres: the New Amsterdam, the Broadhurst, the Vanderbilt, and the National.
21. Astaire (1959), 89.
22. HRC.
23. *New York Times*, 7 October 1919.
24. *The Sunday Times*, 5 November 1933.
25. Ernst (1956), 164.
26. *Life*, February 1922.
27. Croce (1972), 9.
28. Mabel McElliot, *Illustrated Daily News*, 9 October 1919.
29. George Stevens directed *Swing Time*, and Landers Stevens played the part of Judge Watson, the father of Lucky's (Astaire's) fiancée, Margaret.
30. Mencken to Sara Haardt, 10 July 1923 (H. L. Mencken and Sara Haardt Mencken Collection, Goucher College Special Collections and Archives).
31. Mencken and Joshi (2010), 111–12.
32. *Judge*, [March?] 1922.
33. HRC.
34. "Dancing Drama," *Judge*, December 1922.
35. Lillian Gish quoted in Affron (2001), 202.
36. Quoted in Astaire (1959) 95.
37. AAC.

4 Nightingales in Berkeley Square

1. 3 June 1923.
2. July 1923.
3. AAC.

4. John Gielgud, interview on "Curtain Up," episode 1 of *The Fred Astaire Story*, BBC Radio 2, 22 March 1975.
5. Platt (2004), 144.
6. Ibid.
7. Morley (1987), 49.
8. Quoted in Green (1979) 24.
9. HRC.
10. Wodehouse and Bolton (1953), 198.
11. HRC.
12. AAC.
13. AAC.
14. *Hugh Selwyn Mauberley* (1920), 5.
15. Quoted in "Broadway's First Lady" (obituary of Adele Astaire), *Guardian*, 27 January 1981.
16. *Radio Times*, June 1924.
17. By "modernism" I refer to the distinct cultural movement that took place in Europe and the United States between 1890 and 1940. By "High modernism" I refer specifically to the inter-war period.
18. *Ein Brief*, written in 1902, is a fictional letter from Lord Chandos to Francis Bacon, in which Chandos confesses a crisis of language ("Sprachkrise")—symptomatic, Hofmannsthal believes, of "das Gleitende," a slipping away of cultural and social institutions hitherto taken for granted. Eliot depicts a similar phenomenon in *Four Quartets* ("Burnt Norton", 5): "Words strain, / Crack and sometimes break, under the burden, / Under the tension, slip, slide, perish, / Will not stay still."
19. Stern (1936), 105.
20. "The Swimmers," *Saturday Evening Post*, 19 October 1929: "France was a land, England was a people, but America, having about it still that quality of the idea, was harder to utter—it was the graves at Shiloh and the tired, drawn, nervous faces of its great men, and the country boys dying in the Argonne for a phrase that was empty before their bodies withered. It was a willingness of the heart."
21. 16 December 1924. The play was first performed at the Everyman Theatre, Hampstead, on 25 November 1924.
22. The premiere, on 8 May 1956, of John Osborne's *Look Back in Anger*, produced by the English Stage Company at the Royal Court Theatre in London, supposedly began a revolution in British stage drama, ushering in an era of plays of "kitchen-sink" realism and with working-class protagonists. For a more nuanced appreciation of this "revolution" and its origins, see Rebellato (1999).
23. Green (1979), 19.
24. "The deuce" is used here as an emphatic exclamation; it is equivalent to saying "interested as the devil" or "as the dickens."
25. It should be stressed that Astaire's use of the term "nigger" in this context was not intended to cause offense. It is indicative of a less sensitive and less enlightened era race issues. Similarly, Fred and Adele's correspondence does occasionally contain terminology that would nowadays be deemed politically incorrect or indeed offensive.
26. Quoted in Harry J. Robinson, "Fred and Adele Astaire—The Brilliant Dancing Comedians," *Ball Room*, May 1924.
27. Quoted in William Pollock, "The Astaires; An Interview with the Dancers Who Have Captivated London," *London Magazine* 52, 1923, 289.
28. Francis Birrell, Review of *Stop Flirting* (the Nation and Athenaeum was a literary magazine). *Nation and Athenaeum*, 16 June 1923.
29. "Dance Sprite: The Magic of Adele Astaire, Bizarre Delight," clipping, n.d., periodical unknown, (AAC).
30. 16 June 1923.
31. "What is an Actor's Greatest Quality?," clipping, n.d., periodical unknown, (AAC).

32. 23 December 1923.
33. 19 January 1924.

5 Fascinating Rhythms

1. Creighton Peet, "The Movies," *Outlook and Independent*, 14 May 1930, 72: "Mr. Whiteman took his orchestra into the sacred precincts of Aeolian Hall in an attempt to make an honest woman out of Jazz, at that time a cheap and notorious wench."
2. Quoted in Goldberg (1931), 139.
3. Astaire (1959), 128.
4. *New York World*, 23 November 1927.
5. You're weaving love into a mad jazz pattern, / Ruled by Pantaloon, / Poor little rich girl, don't drop a stitch too soon" (Noël Coward, "Poor Little Rich Girl").
6. Pollack (2006), 330.
7. Saroyan (1963), 17–19.
8. Mitchell (1956), 374–75.
9. In an address made on behalf of the Brooklyn Little Theatre movement, quoted in Matz (1963), 226.
10. Interviewed on "Lady Be Good," episode 3 of *The Fred Astaire Story*, BBC Radio 2, 5 April 1975.
11. Ibid.
12. The speech was made on 13 December 1928 and is quoted in Jablonski (1988).
13. Noguchi et al. (1994), 23.
14. Astaire (1959), 129.
15. George Gershwin, interview, 1926. Cited in Rosenberg (1991) 83.
16. Quoted in *The Fred Astaire Story: His Life, His Films, His Friends*, souvenir guide to *The Fred Astaire Story*, BBC Radio 2, 1975.
17. Obituary of Texas Guinan, *New York Times*, 6 November 1933.
18. Astaire (1959), 125.
19. Ibid., 127.
20. Ibid.
21. Cullen (2004), 207.
22. "The Astaires and Mathematics and Music," *New York Times*, 28 December 1924.
23. Pollack (2006), 330.
24. Astaire (1959), 134–35.
25. *New York Herald-Tribune*, 17 September 1925.
26. *New York World*, 18 September 1925.
27. AAC.
28. AAC.
29. Jimmy Altemus and Jock Whitney provided the lyrics for a song Fred composed, "Tappin' the Time." The number was used in the 1927 London revue *Shake Your Feet*.
30. Rodgers (1988) 41.
31. Astaire (1959), 153.
32. Victor Moore appeared with Fred as Pop Cardetti in the 1936 film *Swing Time*.
33. *New York Times*, 23 November 1927.
34. Astaire (1959), 154.
35. Robert Benchley, *Life*, 22 December 1927.
36. This accords with a comment by Al Hirschfeld: "George was so in love with work that he seemed asexual to me. Like [Frank] Crowninshield and [Alexander] Woollcott. Neither was homosexual or interested in women; their passions were all tied up in their work." Woollcott, in fact, had been rendered impotent after contracting the mumps.
37. AAC.
38. "There is no mistaking the fact that London is about to enjoy another outbreak of 'Astairia' this winter", *Morning Post*, 9 November 1928.

39. Behrman, 'People in a Diary (Part 2) ...' *New Yorker*, 27 May 1972.
40. Astaire (1959), 159.

6 The Golden Calf

1. Astaire (1959), 162.
2. Ibid., 160.
3. Ibid., 161.
4. Cullen (2004), 760.
5. Fred and Larry Adler, who were both more or less self-taught, became rival pianists at rehearsal. Fred believed Adler had harmony but no rhythm, while Adler thought Fred was all rhythm.
6. In "How Fred Astaire Helped Ann Sothern Find Happiness" (*Movie Mirror,* February 1937), Sothern recounts her fleeting experience in *Smiles* and says Fred "helped me keep my perspective and remember that there were many reasons why numbers were taken away from people and that many of them had nothing to do with the performer's ability at all."
7. This story is recounted by Larry Adler in an interview on 'After You, Who?', episode 4 of *The Fred Astaire Story*, BBC Radio 2, 12 April 1975.
8. *Boston Evening Transcript*, 29 October 1930.
9. See Astaire (1959) 164.
10. Astaire (1959), 163.
11. Ibid., 162.
12. *New York Times*, 19 November 1930.
13. *New Yorker*, 29 November 1930.
14. Quoted in Astaire (1959) 163.
15. Miller died at the age of thirty-seven from a toxic condition following surgery on her nasal passages.
16. Proving that *Smiles* at least did not inflict lasting damage on people's career prospects, Virginia Bruce was among "A Group of Glorified Girls" and Bob Hope one of the "Boys." Claire Dodd, who doubled as Clara and a society reporter, turned up as the spoilt Sophie Teale in the Astaire-Rogers film *Roberta* (1935).
17. *The Town Crier* aired from 1929 to 1942. It used to begin with a bell ringing out and the announcer Paul Douglas crying, "Hear ye! Hear ye! Hear ye!" This was followed by the host's quietly measured "This is Woollcott speaking."
18. Adler (1984), 44.
19. Ibid.
20. In his autobiography, Fred states that Aarons called him about a month after the premiere of *Smiles*. However, *Girl Crazy* opened at the Alvin Theatre on 14 October 1930, two weeks before *Smiles* had its first tryout in Boston.
21. *East Is West* was to be a musical adaptation of the 1918 hit stage play by Samuel Shipman and John B. Hymer and an approximation of the Madame Butterfly story. John Harkrider's costume designs for the abandoned project were used for the Chinese costume ball in *Smiles*. At one point Ziegfeld announced in the *New York Times* that Vincent Youmans had agreed to write the score for *East Is West*, even though the Gershwins had already, under contract, written several songs for it—a provocative piece of double-dealing that would not have endeared the producer to either Youmans or the Gershwins.
22. In the chorus of *Top Speed* was a young dancer named Hermes Pan, who was to become the resident choreographer for the Astaire-Rogers series at RKO and Fred's most frequent and trusted collaborator. The score for the show was written by Kalmar and Ruby, the songwriting team portrayed by Fred and Red Skelton in the MGM musical biography *Three Little Words* (1950).
23. Rogers (1991), 111.
24. Nochimson (2002), 315.

25. "Wedding Forecast," *New York Journal*, 6 February 1931.
26. AAC.
27. Oscar Hammerstein II, Richard Rodgers, and Lorenz Hart were also students at Columbia.

7 Frater, Ave atque Vale

1. Tony Hunter's next line is "Noël Coward and Gertie were over here in *Private Lives* at the Selwyn." *Private Lives* was indeed contemporaneous with *The Band Wagon,* but it was presented at the Times Square Theatre, built by the Selwyn brothers.
2. Jack Burton, *Billboard*, 4 November 1950, 43.
3. The first experiments in front-of-house lighting in American theatre were made by David Belasco in *The Passion Play* at the San Francisco Grand Opera in 1879, using an old bull's-eye lantern from a locomotive. With his electrician, Louis Hartmann, Belasco eventually developed the first incandescent spotlight, and in 1914 at the Belasco Theatre in New York he discarded the footlights and installed front lighting on the audience side of the proscenium arch. In Britain, William Poel's production of *The Two Gentlemen of Verona* at His Majesty's Theatre in 1910 used lighting from the front of the balcony, and Harley Granville-Barker, in his three Shakespearean productions at the Savoy Theatre between 1912 and 1914, replaced the footlights with a batten of "torpedo" lamps mounted in view of the audience across the front of the dress circle.
4. HRC.
5. Mordden (2005), 32.
6. Ibid., 29.
7. *New York Times*, 4 June 1931.
8. *I Love Louisa* was the working title for the 1953 film that eventually became *The Band Wagon*. The number does feature in the film, but it is sung and danced by the company in the confines of a hotel bedroom and not on a merry-go-round.
9. Alice Hughes, "Whole Town Costuming for '32 Eve," *New York World-Telegram*, 20 December 1931.
10. See the article about Spear's "excitement eaters": Theodocia Walton, "New Girl in Latest Phase," *New York Times*, 18 June 1922.
11. *New York Times*, 4 June 1931.
12. Taper (1984), 184.
13. Mordden (2005), 29.
14. Brooks Atkinson, *New York Times*, 14 June 1931.
15. Later that year, Rasch also staged a dream ballet for *The Cat and the Fiddle*, produced by Max Gordon at the Globe Theatre. So her efforts in this regard certainly predate those of Balanchine and De Mille.
16. Richard Watts Jr., *Herald Tribune*, 16 August 1931.
17. June 1931.
18. Richard Watts Jr., *Herald Tribune*, 16 August 1931.
19. *New Yorker,* 13 June 1931.
20. Reinhardt was invited to stage *A Midsummer Night's Dream* for the Southern California Chamber of Commerce at the Hollywood Bowl in 1934. None of his original "wish list" of stars (including Chaplin as Bottom and Garbo as Titania) appeared in the production or in the Warner Bros film of the following year. Helen Hayes tried to get Astaire to play Puck in a stage version one year, but he was unavailable.
21. The play was *Miss Brown of Worcester*, directed by Ernst Lubitsch and broadcast on CBS on 15 January 1939. Fred's character was known as "The Rhythm Romeo." His costars were Loretta Young and Herbert Marshall.
22. *Herald Tribune*, 16 August 1931.
23. *Chicago Herald-Examiner*, 28 February 1931.
24. The first 33⅓ LP recording was Beethoven's Fifth Symphony, performed by the Philadelphia Symphony under Leopold Stokowski.

25. Britain was ahead of the United States in making cast recordings and original London cast recordings of shows that had already opened on Broadway. Hence there existed a 1928 recording of the London cast of *Show Boat* (released in England on 78 rpm records) but no 1927 Broadway cast album.

26. Written by Ray Noble, Jimmy Campbell, and Reg Connelly. In Britain the song was made famous by Al Bowlly.

27. Astaire (1959), 173.

28. *Chicago Herald-Examiner*, 28 February 1931.

29. AAC.

30. Astaire (1959), 171.

31. Ibid.

32. In Astaire biographies, it is often incorrectly stated that Phyllis's father founded the Free Hospital for Women. The hospital was established in 1875, six years before he was born; its founder was in fact his father, Dr. William Henry Baker (1845–1914), who became professor of gynecology at Harvard.

33. Astaire (1959), 172.

34. HRC.

35. HRC.

36. HRC.

37. HRC.

38. HRC.

39. FA/MS.

40. HRC.

41. Guthrie McClintic to Fred Astaire in Chicago, Western Union cable, 10 March 1932 (AAC). What this play was and whether it came to pass without Fred I am not certain. When he approached Fred with the offer, McClintic would have been rehearsing a revival of A. A. Milne's play *The Truth about Bladys*, which closed in May. His next play at the Belasco was Edgar Wallace's *Criminal at Large* (the British title was *The Case of the Frightened Lady*), which opened on 10 October. So it appears there was no new play at the Belasco in August.

42. *Under Glass* was eventually produced by William B. Friedlander at the Ambassador Theatre, New York. It opened on 30 October 1933 and lasted a mere eight performances. Ross Alexander played the part of Tony Pell.

43. This revival of *Show Boat*, which opened at the Casino Theatre on 19 May 1932, was Ziegfeld's last production. He died in Hollywood on 22 July that year, while the show was still running. Helen Broderick, incidentally, was not part of the cast.

8 By Myself

1. The Production Code, the set of industry censorship guidelines governing the production of American motion pictures adopted in March 1930, included no provisions for effective enforcement. An amendment implemented in June 1934 established the Production Code Administration and required all films released after 1 July 1934 to obtain a certificate of approval before being released. *The Gay Divorcée* was released in October that year. In practice, the code was enforced through a system of self-regulation adhered to by the motion picture studios.

2. "No Evening of Unalloyed Satisfactions", 8 November 1932.

3. *New York Times*, 30 November 1932.

4. 30 November 1932.

5. Quoted in Lucius Beebe, "Fred Astaire Dances without Adele," *New York Herald Tribune*, 1 December 1932.

6. Robert Garland, *New York World-Telegram*, 30 November 1932.

7. *Daily Mirror*, 1 December 1932.

8. Astaire (1959), 179.

9. "The Private Life of Fred Astaire", *Photoplay*, January 1936, 34.
10. Frank Craven (1881–1945) was a homely character actor of stage and screen, with a worried smile, who often portrayed wry, small-town figures. He was the Stage Manager in Thornton Wilder's *Our Town* and was described by Brooks Atkinson as "the best pipe and pants-pocket actor in the business" (*New York Times*, 5 February 1938).
11. Mueller (1985) 6.
12. The live ostrich inevitably caused problems, not least of which was the hazard of its droppings on the stage. Before opening night it moulted and had to have feathers glued onto it. On another occasion it failed to stop when it got onstage and continued out into West Forty-First Street, still carrying Luce.
13. Astaire (1959), 176.
14. Mordden (2005), 65.
15. This particular recording remained number 1 in the Hit Parade for ten consecutive weeks.
16. "An Up-to-date Puck: Fred Astaire," *Illustrated London News*, 25 November 1933.
17. Interviewed on "After You, Who?," episode 4 of *The Fred Astaire Story*, BBC Radio 2, 12 April 1975. This was not the only crisis Luce faced. She was then married to the playboy millionaire and aviator Clifford Warren Smith, whose first wife sued him unsuccessfully for bigamy, arguing they had never been properly divorced. In late 1933, while Luce was appearing in *Gay Divorce* in London, Smith worked out a separation in which he agreed to pay Luce $25, 000 a year for life. The next year he divorced Luce, charging her with "cruelty, desertion, and infidelity."
18. *American*, 26 February 1933.
19. HRC.
20. AAC.
21. Fred Astaire to Adele Astaire, n.d. (preserved only in part and undated, with postscript indicating late winter/early spring 1933), AAC. Fred tells his sister: "Noël's show is a big hit—I liked it—very dirty but amusing in the Coward way. Some people take offence but it's one of those things to see." The show referred to is Coward's *Design for Living*, which opened at the Ethel Barrymore on 24 January 1933.
22. AAC.
23. AAC.
24. HRC.
25. In her autobiography, *Debbie: My Life* (1988, p.60), Debbie Reynolds "outed" the studio official as Burt Grady. I remain unconvinced of the authenticity of this assessment.
26. John Street was officially renamed Chesterfield Hill in January 1940.
27. Astaire (1959), 192–93.
28. HRC.
29. HRC.
30. "Lun Tertius", *Adeventurer*, No. 3, Tuesday, 14 November, 1752, p.16.
31. AAC.
32. 3 November 1933.
33. *The Stage*, 9 November 1933. The offending lines of the song were "Now men who once knew Missus Fitch / Refer to her as a bitch. / While the girls who once loved Mister Fitch / Say he always was a son of a bitch."
34. 10 January 1934.
35. "An Up-to-date Puck: Fred Astaire," *Illustrated London News*, 25 November 1933.
36. *Observer*, 5 November 1933.
37. 18 November 1933.
38. J. B. Yeats to W. B. Yeats, 1908, in Hone (1944), 116.
39. Burns Mantle, *Daily News*, 4 December 1932.
40. J. T. Grein, "An Up-to-date Puck: Fred Astaire," *Illustrated London News*, 25 November 1933.
41. *The Times*, 3 November 1933.

42. *The Sunday Times*, 5 November 1933.
43. Mordden (2005), 32.
44. Platt (2004), 145.

9 After the Dance

1. Wodehouse and Bolton (1953), 208.
2. RKO/UCLA.
3. RKO/UCLA.
4. RKO/UCLA.
5. Quoted in Eustis (1937), 379.
6. AAC.
7. The letter is reproduced in Wrench (1955) 339.
8. AAC.
9. AAC.
10. HRC.
11. AAC.
12. HRC.
13. Astaire (1959), 325.
14. McKenzie (1998), 310.
15. Quoted in Billman (1997) 290.

BIBLIOGRAPHY

Adler, Larry. (1984). *It Ain't Necessarily So*. London.

Affron, Charles. (2001). *Lillian Gish: Her Legend, Her Life*. Berkeley and Los Angeles.

Astaire, Fred. (1959). *Steps in Time*. New York.

Billman, Larry. (1997). *Fred Astaire: A Bio-bibliography*. Westport, Conn., and London.

Coward, Noël. (1974). *Present Indicative*. London. (First published 1937)

Croce, Arlene. (1972). *The Fred Astaire and Ginger Rogers Book*. New York.

Cullen, Frank. (2004). *Vaudeville, Old and New: An Encyclopedia of Variety Performers in America*. Vol.1. New York and London.

Dally, Lynn. (2002). "No Maps on My Taps: An Appreciation." In Mitoma (2002), 78–80.

Duke, Vernon. (1947). "Gershwin, Schillinger, and Dukelsky: Some Reminiscences." *Musical Quarterly* 33, 1: 102–15.

Ernst, Earle. (1956). *The Kabuki Theatre*. New York.

Eustis, Morton. (1937). "Fred Astaire: The Actor-Dancer Attacks His Part." *Theatre Arts Monthly* 21, 5: 371–86.

Garofalo, Alessandra. (2009). *"Austerlitz Sounded Too Much Like a Battle": The Roots of Fred Astaire's Family in Europe*. Trento.

Green, Benny. (1979). *Fred Astaire*. London and New York.

Hall, Edith. (2004). "Towards a Theory of Performance Reception." *Arion* 12: 51-89.

Hone, Joseph, ed. (1944). *J. B. Yeats: Letters to His Son, W. B. Yeats and Others, 1869–1922*. London.

Jablonski, Edward. (1988). *Gershwin*. London.

Knowles, Mark. (2002). *Tap Roots: The Early History of Tap Dancing*. Jefferson, N.C.

Lochner, Louis Paul. (1951). *Fritz Kreisler*. New York.

Macintosh, Fiona, ed. (2010). *The Ancient Dancer in the Modern World: Responses to Greek and Roman Dance*. Oxford.

Marra, Kim. (2006). *Strange Duets: Impresarios and Actresses in the American Theatre, 1865–1914*. Iowa City.

Matz, Mary Jane. (1963). *The Many Lives of Otto Kahn*. New York and London.

McKenzie, Richard. (1998). *Turn Left at the Black Cow: One Family's Journey from Beverly Hills to Ireland*. Boulder, Colo., and Dublin.

Mencken, H. L., and S. T. Joshi, eds. (2010) *Mencken on Mencken: A New Collection of Autobiographical Writings*. Baton Rouge, La.

Mitchell, Donald. (1956). "Concerts and Opera." *Musical Times* 97: 374–75.

Mitoma, Judy, et al., eds. (2002). *Envisioning Dance on Film and Video*. New York and London.

Mordden, Ethan. (2005). *Sing for Your Supper: The Broadway Musical in the 1930s.* Basingstoke, Hants and New York.

Morley, Sheridan. (1987). *Spread a Little Happiness: The First Hundred Years of the British Musical.* London.

Mueller, John. (1985). *Astaire Dancing: The Musical Films.* New York.

Nathan, George Jean. (1915). *Another Book on the Theatre.* New York.

Nichols, Beverly. (1927). *Are They the Same at Home? Being a Series of Bouquets Diffidently Distributed.* London.

Nochimson, Martha P. (2002). *Screen Couple Chemistry: The Power of 2.* Austin, Tex.

Noguchi, Isamu, Diane Apostolos-Cappadona, and Bruce Alshuler, eds. (1994). *Isamu Noguchi: Essays and Conversations.* New York.

Platt, Len. (2004). *Musical Comedy on the West End Stage, 1890–1939.* Basingstoke, Hants and New York.

Pollack, Howard. (2006). *George Gershwin: His Life and Work.* Berkeley and London.

Rebellato, Dan. (1999). *1956 and All That: The Making of Modern British Drama.* New York and London.

Riley, Kathleen. (2010). "A Pylades for the Twentieth Century: Fred Astaire and the Aesthetic of Bodily Eloquence." In Macintosh (2010): 99–119.

Rodgers, Richard. Ed. by William W. Appleton. 1988. *Letters to Dorothy, 1926–1937.* New York.

Rogers, Ginger. (1991). *Ginger: My Story.* London.

Rosenberg, Deena. (1991). *Fascinating Rhythm: The Collaboration of George and Ira Gershwin.* Ann Arbor.

Saroyan, William. (1963). "Paris in an American." *Country Beautiful* 17–19.

Seldes, Gilbert. (1924). *The Seven Lively Arts.* New York and London.

Stern, G. B. (1936). *Monogram.* London.

Taper, Bernard. (1984). *Balanchine: A Biography.* New York.

Tiomkin, Dimitri, and Prosper Buranelli. (1959) *Please Don't Hate Me.* Garden City, N.Y.

Wayburn, Ned. (1925). *The Art of Stage Dancing.* New York.

Wodehouse, P. G., and Guy Bolton. (1953). *Bring on the Girls! The Improbable Story of Our Life in Musical Comedy, with Pictures to Prove It.* New York.

Wrench, Evelyn. (1955). *Geoffrey Dawson and Our Times.* London.

INDEX

Adele and Fred in Ireland, 1960s.